The Intimidation Factor

The Intimidation Factor

How Scare Tactics Smother American Evangelicalism

CHARLES REDFERN

RESOURCE *Publications* • Eugene, Oregon

THE INTIMIDATION FACTOR
How Scare Tactics Smother American Evangelicalism

Copyright © 2020 Charles Redfern. All rights reserved. Except for brief quotations in critical publications or reviews, no part of this book may be reproduced in any manner without prior written permission from the publisher. Write: Permissions, Wipf and Stock Publishers, 199 W. 8th Ave., Suite 3, Eugene, OR 97401.

All Scripture quotations, unless otherwise indicated, are taken from the HOLY BIBLE: NEW INTERNATIONAL VERSION®; NIV®. Copyright ©1973, 1978, 1984 by International Bible Society. Used by permission of Zondervan Publishing House. All rights reserved.

Resource Publications
An Imprint of Wipf and Stock Publishers
199 W. 8th Ave., Suite 3
Eugene, OR 97401

www.wipfandstock.com

PAPERBACK ISBN: 978-1-7252-6582-0
HARDCOVER ISBN: 978-1-7252-6583-7
EBOOK ISBN: 978-1-7252-6584-4

Manufactured in the U.S.A.   07/06/20

For Andrea, my beloved and godly wife,
and Caleb, our son

Contents

Acknowledgments ix
Introduction: Surveying The Rubble xi
1 From Evangelicalism's Height to its Depths: One Man's Journey 1

PART ONE
TIPS OF THE ICEBERG: CASE STUDIES IN INTIMIDATION

2 Climate Change and a Heretic Hunt 17
3 Apostles, Prophets, & Protestant Popes 29
4 The Faustian Pact 44

PART II
PRESTIGIOUS HARASSERS: HOW EVANGELICAL INTIMIDATION BECAME RESPECTABLE

5 Cracks in the Foundation 59
6 A Battle Between Allies 70
7 The Beat Goes On 87
8 Moderate Complicity 97

PART III
BEACONS OF HOPE

9 Introducing the Real Jesus People 115
10 Gotham's Good Calvinist 120

11	Rescuing God's Creation	133
12	The Whole Gospel in the Midwest	148
Conclusion: Rowing at the Confluence		164
Bibliography		167

Acknowledgments

THIS IS DANGEROUS. I'M about to thank people, which means I'll invariably forget key individuals without whom I never would have survived. So I do this in fear and trembling.

I begin with Gil Salk, a great buddy who served as copy editor. He encouraged me (he said he found the book intriguing, which surprised him: he's isn't familiar with the evangelical world) and, more important, he rescued me from my blindness to my own errors. His requests for clarifications rendered this more understandable to non-religious readers. Gil is one of those non-Christians who prompt sentences like, "If more Christians were like Gil..."

I think back in time. I think of my parents, who raised me and my only sister and sibling in that rare find called "a healthy home." There was laughter; there were hugs; there was the Episcopal Church and its liturgy. I now realize that my parents' religion spawned a prenatal faith that prepared me for my spiritual birth at the age of 16. I think I disappointed my late father when I didn't seek ordination in his beloved Episcopal church, but he didn't object.

I think back to the beginning of my Christian life and the loving people of Wintonbury Church of Bloomfield, CT. There's Andrew Gerns, my best high school pal who eventually became an Episcopalian priest; there's Peter Mason, who became a Conservative Baptist pastor; there's his sister, Priscilla; there's Scott Davis, Steve Whiting, Mark and Gail Brewer, Billy and Doug Truit, and so many others—including Rich and Cathy Ainsworth, the pastoral couple who guided that local body for decades. Wintonbury—even today—defies the evangelical caricature and still weds love, grace, and biblical integrity. I always remembered its example as I navigated my way through the hostile world.

I think of my spiritual exhaustion in the wake of my spent journalism career and my rejuvenation in the mid-1980s (I learned that Ed Gorham, my best friend since college, was praying for me as I walked through my Dark Night of the Soul). God nurtured me through my professors at Gordon Conwell Theological Seminary. There was the gracious Garth Rosell, whom I still consider a friend, and the late Nigel Kerr of the church history department. There was David Wells, John Jefferson Davis, and Richard Lints in the theology department—and Stephen Charles Mott, a United Methodist who opened my eyes to the Gospel's social implications. I also fondly remember Greg Beale, a staunch Calvinist and genuinely caring New Testament professor. Many of my former professors would probably frown on this book—especially its characterization of Calvinism. To that I can only respond: "If only more Calvinists were like you."

I think of my spiritual journey shortly after seminary and someone I never met: John Wimber, the late founder of the Vineyard Christian Fellowship. Wimber led many down the path toward genuine kingdom living: Life in the Holy Spirit is not merely meant for the sweet bye-and-bye. It can be real now, and we needn't adopt an idiosyncratic theology. I thank him and the Vineyard as a whole.

I think of my denomination, The American Baptists, USA, and Judy Albee, Connecticut's executive director (now retired). I thank them for their warm welcome and collegiality.

I reserve my most important thanks for last. I married a godly woman named Andrea LaCelle Redfern in the winter of 1987 when I didn't know if I'd survive my first cancer bout. In 1993, she gave birth to our only child, Caleb, who has paid a price for his father's peculiar calling. We have navigated a sometimes precarious path together, and I am deeply grateful for their faith in Christ, their love, and their integrity. This book is dedicated to them.

Introduction

Surveying The Rubble

WHAT DO I DO when the river that swept me into the life of Christ now empties into a toxic swamp, rimmed with snarling attack dogs sniffing for political and doctrinal heretics? Is there hope or only despair?

I ponder those questions as the not-so-secret secret unravels: White American Evangelical Christianity has plunged into a theological, spiritual, and moral abyss. Many claiming the evangelical label laud an obviously decadent president while jettisoning the movement's time-honored convictions: Lifeway Research found that majorities believe the Holy Spirit is an impersonal force, that Jesus was a created being, and that family worship is an acceptable swap for regular church attendance.[1] Meanwhile, new doctrines have been traded for the old. Anyone affirming human-induced climate change, for example, is suspect—even though no traditional creeds or biblical passages are at stake.

So much for that ol' time religion.

Two questions hover over discussions among the movement's thinkers and academics: What went wrong and what's the remedy? An inevitable third question flows from the second: Should we fight to preserve the evangelical tag (for which Richard Mouw compellingly argues in *Restless Faith: Holding Evangelical Beliefs in a World of Contested Labels*), or must we abandon it as too sullied?

It's now difficult to remember what "evangelical" once conveyed. The term signaled a more ecumenical, gracious, and intellectually viable species

---

1. Block, "Evangelicals, Heresy, and Scripture Alone," *First Things*, 10/4/2016; Arakaki, "Evangelicalism Falling to Pieces?" *Orthodox Reformed Bridge*, 10/20/2016; *The State of American Theology Study, 2016,* commissioned by Ligonier Ministries and Lifeway Research.

of back-to-the-Bible Christian, more generous than "fundamentalist." Evangelicalism encompassed Anglicans, Methodists, Baptists, Presbyterians, Congregationalists, Pentecostals, Wesleyans, Calvinists, Lutherans, and others. They agreed to disagree on non-essentials and could even lean to the political left. In fact, scholars such as Timothy Smith, Donald Dayton, and David Moberg found that Wesleyan-oriented nineteenth-century evangelicals pushed for reform. Many advocated abolitionism; others intentionally dwelled in slums and befriended the poor; they were the first to ordain women.

Now? Not so much.

Again, what happened?

Various writers have diagnosed the disease and prescribed their remedies. Some Calvinists have lamented the movement's supposed drift from those halcyon days of the 16th and 17th centuries, when John Calvin reigned in Geneva and English Puritans wrote the Westminster Confession. They fear infiltrating theological liberalism, which left much of the Bible on the cutting room floor in its 19th-century heyday. They'd sanctify linear thinking, jettison almost all emotion, and relegate charismatics and Pentecostals to suspect status. I fear they've misdiagnosed the disease and now patrol a fortress-like doctrinal perimeter, often mistaking potential allies as opponents. They've nurtured intimidation.

Others—from Brian McLaren to Rob Bell to the late Rachel Held Evans to John Pavlovich to Frank Schaeffer—have decreed the opposite verdict. They've thrown out the label *and* the back-to-the-Bible theology it once described. They were often reared in fundamentalism, mistook it for evangelicalism, and now gather in social media flocks of embittered ex-evangelicals. I understand the resentment. I've felt it. I got mauled myself. But hear my plea: Please remember that hackneyed but truthful phrase, "Hurting people hurt people," often in the name of open-mindedness and dialogue.

Still others have struck closer to the mark. So-called progressive evangelicals have rightly criticized the movement's disastrous marriage to the political right. I applaud them and their alliance with the marginalized and the poor. I've gladly brandished the progressive evangelical badge and continue to write against that unholy alliance, which I distinguish from honest and compassionate political conservatism. But I've recently grown concerned: Sympathy for the marginalized—and, perhaps, a quest for left-wing validation—drives some to abandon the biblical view of marriage (a lifelong heterosexual union and the exclusive province for sex). Like them, I've befriended many gays and lesbians, including relatives. Like them, I find their stories compelling. Like them, I realize that many of our bromides fail to help. But, after all is said and done, we cannot cite the Bible as authoritative on social justice and dismiss it on marriage. We must beware "package-deal ethics," a trap discovered by British ethicist James Mumford: political loyalties subvert moral decision-making.[2]

I've come to see a more insidious malady lurking beneath the surface, of which political partisanship is a serious symptom. I see it as threats replace genuine debate and as innocents are branded heretical. Fact is, an ugly culture of intimidation has overthrown grace. I only discovered it after I was hurt and after I walked through my consequent anger. I then looked back on my own story and saw how evangelicalism devolved.

I mull over the takeover in three parts after I describe my saga (I came to Christ in the early '70's through a loving church but, eventually, got bruised). In Part One, I probe the anatomy of intimidation in three arenas. There's climate change, where deniers level heresy charges at anyone embracing the scientific consensus—even though no historic creed is at stake. There's the New Apostolic Reformation among Pentecostals and charismatic Christians, an evangelical subset: Self-proclaimed "apostles" and "prophets" issue purported divinely-inspired fiats, rendering disagreement impossible lest we risk God's wrath. And there's white American evangelicalism's 2016 Trump alliance.

A consistent theme emerges: Threats replace genuine discussion and debate, with conflict-adverse moderate evangelicals yielding all the way.

But why did intimidation take hold? That's where Part Two comes in. I trace bullying's seeds back to the mid-twentieth-century evangelical resurgence, when leaders such as Harold Ockenga, Carl Henry, and Billy Graham shelved the "fundamentalist" brand and called themselves neo-evangelicals (the "neo" was soon dropped). They were intelligent, gracious, and admirable. They encouraged cultural engagement and promoted the life of the mind. But, unfortunately, they never fully divorced themselves from fundamentalism and they embraced the 19th-century Princeton theologians, who led just one of evangelicalism's clans. The Princetonians encouraged creedal and biblical faithfulness along with intellectual rigor, and they sought to be fair to those with whom they disagreed. We can commend them and learn from them, but we must also beware their flaws: They sifted all teaching through a peculiarly dry, cerebral Calvinistic sieve that didn't do justice to Reformed theology's breadth (John Calvin is a monumental contributor to the Reformed school, but not the only one). An especially scowling brand of Calvinism lodged in Westminster Theological Seminary's Cornelius Van Til (1895–1987), who often misunderstood his perceived opponents and tarred their reputations. Many later evangelical academics sat in his classroom and

---

2. Mumford, "Package-Deal Ethics," *The Hedgehog Review*, Fall, 2017.

melted before his confidence and decisiveness, which set the stage for a neo-fundamentalist come-back in the late '70's. Even respected scholars blow down straw men and misrepresent those they deem opponents, who are really allies with minor disagreements. It's a grim story, soaked in power's allure.

Yet another chapter on moderate evangelicals brings more gloom: Their conflict avoidance—in the guise of "peacemaking"—enabled the bullies.

But there's hope, the theme of Part Three. Tim Keller flourishes a kinder, richer brand of Calvinism for his clan and from which others can learn; Ed Brown campaigns for the environment as he leads a world-wide network of Creation Care advocates; the Vineyard Church of Evanston, Illinois, exemplifies the Association of Vineyard Churches' quest for multi-ethnicity and holistic Christianity. A chapter describes each ministry.

To steal and remold a phrase from Bill Clinton's first inaugural address: "There's nothing wrong with evangelical Christianity that cannot be cured with what is right with evangelical Christianity." Perhaps the word "evangelical" should be shelved for the time being, but a remnant is preserving the tradition's compelling thought.

Thus this critical book ends in buoyancy as it pinpoints a solution: Evangelicalism's dilemma does not lie with grumbling ex-evangelicals or trendy new theologies—which are not that new—but in returning to the Scriptures its intellects once promulgated. The back-to-the-Bible people can run back to the Bible as they rediscover intimacy with God and fellowship with like-minded Christians. Counter-cultural action will flow.

The usual neo-fundamentalist reply to any criticism is ad-hominem attack, often questioning the writer's doctrine. My response: Here is my personal statement of faith. I'm a Bible-thumping holy roller.

Of God and the Holy Trinity

> I believe that there is one living and true God, infinite and perfect, the eternal ruler and sustainer of the universe. God is the fountain of all existence and is unchangeable, perfect in holiness, wisdom, goodness, justice, power and love. God has all life, glory, goodness and blessedness in and of Himself, and is all-sufficient in and of Himself, not needing any of the creatures He has made. God exists from all eternity as one being in three persons of one substance, the Father, the Son, and the Holy Spirit, equal in power and glory.

I believe that God's kingdom lasts forever. God is omnipresent (He is everywhere) and omniscient (He knows everything). Nevertheless, God is distinct from His own creation. He upholds and governs all that exists, including Heaven, the angels, and the material universe. God made everything good.

Of Satan and his kingdom

I believe that a mighty angel who eventually became known as Satan rallied a rebellion in Heaven in an attempt to usurp God. God cast Satan and his angels (whom we call demons) onto the Earth, where they established an evil counterfeit kingdom, where intimidation, duplicity, hatred, malice, selfish ambition, discord and rage are the norm. While Satan and his minions are powerful, their strength pales when compared with God's. Their doomed kingdom is being dispatched as Christ's kingdom spreads, and will be destroyed when Christ comes again.

Of humanity

I believe that God created humanity male and female in his own image, to glorify God, to enjoy God in a loving, eternal relationship, and to serve as God's delegate in stewarding the Earth. Humanity is the zenith of God's creation. Satan successfully tempted our first parents and they rebelled against God, bringing sin, sickness and the judgment of death onto the Earth. All of creation now suffers the consequences of this original sin: Instead of being born in a state of innocence prone to good and destined for eternal life, human beings are now born in a state of sin, prone to evil and destined for death; instead of living in the freedom of God's grace, we are now captive to Satan's kingdom.

Salvation history

I believe that God, in His infinite mercy and kindness, did not neglect his rule over the Earth. Instead, he continued to uphold the Earth while He began a process that would bring creation back into a proper relationship with himself. In order to bring redemption, God established covenants that revealed his grace. God established a covenant with Abraham, who, through his son Isaac and his grandson Jacob, would be the forefather of the people of Israel. This nation became enslaved in Egypt but was then freed by God through a covenant with Moses. God gave Moses His law. That law convicts human beings of their sin and shows God's righteousness. It shows how we can come to Christ for our salvation.

God wanted to rule Israel directly. The nation was not meant to have a king. However, God did establish a monarchy upon the nation's request. The first king was known as Saul, but he disobeyed God and the rule of Israel was not passed through his line. Instead, David became king and God covenanted with him, promising that his descendant would restore God's reign as the Messiah.

I believe that God sent His only Son, Jesus, conceived of the Holy Spirit and born of the Virgin Mary, fully God and fully human in one person, into the world as the fulfillment of His own covenants with Israel. Jesus was God's Messiah, or anointed one, empowered by the Holy Spirit, to launch God's kingdom reign on the Earth. He overpowered Satan by resisting temptation, casting out demons, healing the sick, raising the dead, teaching the good news of the kingdom's arrival, and bringing compassion and salvation to the lost. He formed a community that would become known as The Church, which would serve as the instrument of God's kingdom.

Jesus paid the penalty for our sins by dying on the cross, meeting the justice required by the law so that his followers would experience God's mercy. He rose again on the third day in victory over death. Christ disarmed Satan, fulfilled God's covenants with Israel's forefathers, and now stands as the eternal king, bringing about salvation throughout the Earth, culminating in his return.

After Jesus ascended into heaven, God poured out the Holy Spirit onto his church, baptizing its people and releasing his gifts for the purpose of ministry. The Spirit sanctifies us as we yield to him; brings us into intimacy with God; functions as a deposit guaranteeing our salvation; brings about a life leading to love, joy, peace, patience, kindness, goodness, faithfulness, humility, and self control; and grants us his varied gifts for serving others. I believe in the present-day ministry of the Holy Spirit and the exercise of all the gifts as they are described in the Bible.

The Spirit indwells every believer and functions as our abiding helper, teacher, guide, and advocate.

The Bible

I believe that the sixty-six books of the Old and New Testaments were written by human authors and inspired by the Holy Spirit. I affirm their truthfulness, accuracy, sufficiency, and authority. They are the only infallible and inerrant rule of faith and of practice.

The Church

I believe in the one holy, universal Church, which is known as both the Body and Bride of Christ, headed by Christ Himself. The Holy Spirit regenerates all who repent of their sins and confess Jesus as their lord and savior. The Church functions as the agent of God's invading kingdom, bringing people to Christ through the preaching of the Gospel, the performance of his deeds, and the display of his compassion and love. The Church is meant to reach out to and advocate the cause of the desperate and needy and promulgates the sound stewardship of God's Earth. Furthermore, the Church is God's agent in bringing people into deeper, more profound intimacy with Him.

The Church has celebrated two ordinances, sometimes described as sacraments, throughout its history. The sacrament of baptism signifies our death to our former life and our resurrection in Christ. Communion, also known as the Lord's Supper, recalls the all-important day when Christ shed his blood on the cross. The eating of the bread and the drinking of the fruit of the vine illuminates our union with his death to sin. All believers are welcome to participate in both ceremonies.

The End Times

I believe that God's kingdom reign was inaugurated in the ministry of Christ and that it continues in the current-day ministry of the Holy Spirit through God's body and bride, the Church. This reign will be consummated in the physical, visible, and victorious return of Christ, when he will establish his kingdom rule forever. There will be a general resurrection of the dead, both the saved and the lost. Those that are saved will be resurrected into life and those that are lost will be resurrected into eternal alienation from God. There will be a new Heaven and a new Earth, in which God's love and righteousness dwells forever. God will "wipe away every tear from their eyes. There will be no more death or mourning or crying or pain, for the old order of things has passed away" (Revelation 21:4).

1

From Evangelicalism's Height to its Depths

One Man's Journey

I BLAME MY PARENTS—AND the church that wooed me to Christ. Neither prepared me for the bully onslaught. Maybe Mom devastated me once with an ill-timed frown and my opera-buff father played his music too loud; but, otherwise, our home was filled with hugs and laughter. The church, which I discovered in my teens, was the epitome of love and integrity. How was I to know that the big bad world was filled with stress-suckling tyrants? And who knew that evangelicals would morph into a tribe of partisan pit bulls?

I was reared in the Sunday morning religion of the '50's and '60's: Dress up the kids until they itch and hush them during dirge-like hymns and the ten-minute sermon. It was, in H. Richard Niebuhr's words, a religion in which "a God without wrath brought men [and women] without sin into a Kingdom without judgment through the ministrations of a Christ without a Cross." Imagine my shock when I met the Christ of the New Testament: God lived a human life, died for our sin, reigned victorious over death at his resurrection, and shares that victory with his followers in a sheer act of grace.

I discovered the real Christ in high school after my family's final move (I was born in Minnesota in 1956, moved to California in 1960, then to New Jersey in 1969 and to Connecticut in 1972). I joined a group of teens who prayed before first-period classes and huddled in Tuesday evening Bible studies at the parsonage of a local Baptist church. My new friends were delightfully weird. They never swore or bad-mouthed each other or told dirty jokes—and they were hilarious, a veritable fit. True, they were fundamentalists (they strode great strides to disprove evolution), but they didn't condemn everyone. We were all emulating our mentor, Rich Ainsworth, a 25-year-old graduate of Dallas Theological Seminary, the hub for Dispensationalism—a theology popularized by John Nelson Darby (1800–1882) and Cyrus I. Scofield (1843–1921) and which segments history into distinct phases culminating in a climactic "Rapture," when the faithful will be snatched up before a Great Tribulation and Christ's Second Coming. The *Left Behind* series dramatizes Dispensationalism's angle. Rich did not fit the Dispensationalist rap of grim preachers condemning an apostate church. Nor did he denounce tongue-speaking Pentecostals, who embraced the contemporary movement of the Holy Spirit and the application of God's gifts. He disagreed with them (most Dispensationalists are cessationists: they believe the gifts died with the apostles), but he did not berate them from the pulpit or deny their Christian validity.

I leaned to the political left, but we did that in the early '70's without fear. Two of the most popular evangelical politicians were Republican Senator Mark Hatfield of Oregon, a moderate-to-liberal, and Democratic Senator Harold Hughes of Iowa. Born-again Christians rallied to Democrat Jimmy Carter in 1976, which Newsweek declared "The Year of the Evangelical." Almost all my friends saw that politics dwells in the gray area of a necessarily secular society, so we could agree to disagree between Bible studies.

I can't deny it. We '70's Jesus freaks were flaky. Dispensationalism seemed prone to that. There was Dallas graduate Hal Lindsey and his best-seller, *The Late Great Planet Earth*, which saw the oncoming rapture behind every headline. And the six days of Genesis One were literal, 24-hour periods—never mind that the sun and moon weren't created until the third day. Women could not teach men or lead a church, which made for awkward moments when they were Sunday-morning speakers. They weren't preaching, of course. They were *sharing*.

I want to be fair, so I'll defend my church's integrity even though I now disagree with its stance on women: Some biblical passages seemingly prohibit women from leadership—and I actually saw more esteem for women there than in a world plagued with sexual harassment. Women's opinions were respected; men kept their hands to themselves; and the lewdest comment might be, "Betty looks pretty today." Outright chauvinism does reign in many churches, but here—and elsewhere—believers were merely trying to obey the Scriptures. Many women were adamantly opposed to their own sex filling slots on the elder board.

And that's the way it was through my college years (I attended Drew University from 1975–1979, with my junior year in Oxford, England) and first career as a newspaper reporter (initally for a Connecticut weekly and then a small Delaware daily): Bible-thumping born-again Jesus Freaks were gracious and fun. Most were suspicious of Jerry Falwell even if they voted for Ronald Reagan. My agnostic and atheist friends snubbed them as hypocrites, then mauled each other in stomach-knotting office politics in go-for-the-jugular careers while playing musical beds.

No thanks.

I was happy to dump journalism after a year-long soul search in which I found that I was worshiping my career. I prayed a prayer of repentance on my bed in the summer of 1984 and something like electricity invaded my head and ran through my body. I felt cleansed. God was God again and I felt born-again again—and, despite myself, I was convinced that God was calling me into the ordained ministry. Friends confirmed it (one said he'd enlisted several people to pray for me so I'd finally get it). Five months later, I was unpacking my bags at Gordon Conwell Theological Seminary near Massachusetts' Cape Anne Peninsula.

Gordon-Conwell is one of several seminaries spawned by the evangelical resurgence, which began in the early 1940's and was led by Harold Ockenga, Carl Henry, and (most famously) Billy Graham, among several others. Each was reared in fundamentalism, which initially heaved intellectual heft in its summons back to basic doctrines, but quickly slid into a separatist, legalistic, anti-intellectual cacophony—especially after the infamous "monkey trial" of 1925: Darwinist Clarence Darrow humiliated creationist William Jennings Bryan on a witness stand in Tennessee. Fundamentalists retreated into a fortress of "no's": no drinking; no smoking (not a bad no, really); no card-playing; no mixing with those apostate, Modernist-Liberal-Progressive mainliners adoring Harry Emerson Fosdick (1878–1969), pastor of New York City's Riverside Church. Most were Dispensationalists.

Ockenga began calling himself a "neo-evangelical" or "new evangelical" to distinguish himself from hotheaded fundamentalists. Henry, who emerged as evangelicalism's informal academic dean, challenged back-to-the-Bible believers to abandon their cultural citadels in his 1947 landmark book, *The Uneasy Conscience of Modern Fundamentalism*. Graham ruffled feathers when he reached out to leaders in mainline and Catholic churches. Ockenga served as the founding president of the National Association of Evangelicals in 1942 and, in 1947, the troika joined radio evangelist Charles Fuller in establishing Fuller Theological Seminary in Pasadena, California. The school remains post-conservative evangelicalism's intellectual Mecca. Again, Ockenga served as the seminary's first president—and he graciously manned its board even after the school veered away from strict biblical inerrancy (more on this later; Fuller now describes the Bible as "infallible," a slightly looser word). So did Graham.

But Ockenga also fixed his eyes on the east coast and launching a Fuller-like institution there. He helped merge Gordon Divinity School and Conwell School of Theology in 1969 and took its helm in 1970. The seminary clung to inerrancy while employing more sophisticated exegesis than fundamentalists (inerrancy is often mistaken for wooden literalism, which is not necessarily the case). He led Boston's prestigious Park Street Church in his spare time.

Graham, of course, traveled the world and led mammoth revival meetings, founded a relief organization, and spurred the publication of *Christianity Today*, over which Henry presided as its first editor. Meanwhile, neo-evangelicalism's influence spread to Trinity Evangelical Divinity School in Illinois. Weslyan-flavored Asbury in Kentucky also played a key role, and The Evangelical Theological Society was launched in 1949 in an effort to deepen sound scholarship. The organization's publication, the *Journal of the Evangelical Theological Society*, or JETS, does not fly at supersonic speed and is no thrill ride, but it's learned.

The term, "evangelical," opened new vistas and panoramas for me. I could study the Bible from different angles without falling off orthodoxy's edge—and I needn't be anti-Catholic, anti-science, anti-women, anti-democrat, and anti-education. My professors relished the life of the mind (many did their graduate studies at Cambridge, Oxford, Harvard, Yale, and Princeton). They took a dim view of Pat Robertson and Jerry Falwell and dismissed the Moral Majority and Christian Coalition as passing fads.

Would that they had been right.

Most were Reformed, or Calvinist. I never came around to their view. I substantially agreed with Dutch theologian Jacob Arminias (1560–1609), who probed the Bible and found more latitude for free choice. John Wesley, Methodism's founder, popularized the Arminian view in 18th-century Britain. But I'm thankful for these Calvinists. They rid me of fundamentalism. The now-late Old Testament Professor Meredith Kline, for example, showed how Genesis One could be read as a prose poem, with its days interpreted symbolically. Others showed how the biblical genealogies are intentionally incomplete, which meant they couldn't be used to determine the Earth's age. And they opened my eyes to an entirely different approach to eschatology (the study of the end times) courtesy the writings of the late George Eldon Ladd (1911–1982). Ladd and others explored a slew of biblical texts and found that the blessings of the eschatological age began in the ministry of Jesus; they'll become complete at the second coming. We live between the *already* and *not yet*. Believers are meant to be tokens of the end times, a people of the future dwelling in the present. We're the future's harbingers, a people of "realized eschatology," to use a phrase coined by British scholar C.H. Dodd (1883–1973). Miracles, such as healings, point to a future of absolute health and blessing. Tokens of love underscore a future of absolute love. Holy lives point to a future of total holiness. Social and environmental justice prefigure an era of total harmony.[1]

The future is now. Eschatology invades through us—and, incidentally, there's no "there" there on the so-called Rapture. All the biblical proof texts supporting it can easily refer to the Second Coming itself. Perhaps that's why no Christian thinker mentioned the event before the rise of Dispensationalism. It's not in the Bible, so let's leave the *Left Behind* series behind.

My professors also showed me the biblical tension involving women in ministry. True, some passages seemingly prohibit it, but there's also Deborah, a judge over all Israel about 1100 years before Christ, and Huldah the prophetess (2 Kings 22:14–20; 2 Chronicles 34:22–28) and Phoebe in Romans 16:1 and Junias in verse seven of that same chapter. Most of my teachers supported ordaining women. I gladly followed them.

I was fascinated by the history of revivals, first with the 18th-century Great Awakening, led by Jonathan Edwards and George Whitefield in the American colonies and Methodist founder John Wesley in Britain. Converts wept and swooned and displayed other signs and manifestations of the Holy Spirit's power. Church attendance plummeted in the later 18th century but sky-rocketed after an enormous camp meeting in Cane Ridge, Kentucky, in 1801. Again, there were those manifestations: Swooning and weeping, even barking and roaring. Some historians dubbed the 19th century "The Methodist Century," which gave the era an Arminian hue. Many of its leaders helped spearhead abolitionism and moved into slums.[2]

Calvinism, of course, did not die. Some followers joined the Wesleyan fun and mingled with Methodists while remaining Reformed; a more cerebral branch lauded the scholasticism of Geneva theologian Francis Turretin (1623–1687) and found a home at Princeton Theological Seminary. The Old Princeton theologians—successively Archibald Alexander (1772–1851), Charles Hodge (1797–1878), AA Hodge (1823–1886), and Benjamin B. Warfield (1851–1921)—lobbed critical shells into the revivalist camp. They frowned on altar calls, the manifestations, and all the exhilaration. To their

---

1. Ladd wrote his analysis in the scholarly *The Presence of the Future* and the more approachable *The Gospel of the Kingdom*.

2. See Smith, *Revivalism and Social Concern*.

credit, they were intellectually rigorous and personally charitable, especially the elder Hodge, but they demanded stifling tidiness.

Thanks for the brain power, Old Princetonians, but do yourselves and everyone else a favor: loosen up; chill out; join the party. And Warfield: Could you walk beside the Pentecostals instead of disparaging them?

Sadly, the union of high spirituality and movement for societal reform dissolved in the later 19th and early twentieth centuries. Advocates of the Social Gospel, like Walter Rauschenbusch (1861–1918), embraced Liberal Christianity, and Evangelicalism devolved into anti-cultural and anti-intellectual Fundamentalism, with Modernist leaders like Fosdick predicting its demise.

Fosdick did not foresee the influence of Henry, Ockenga, and Graham.

The threesome and their cohorts were not flawless. First, Henry and Ockenga extolled the Old Princetonians even while they shook hands with Pentecostals and admired Wesley (his portrait hung on Ockenga's office wall). Pentecostal and Wesleyan churches joined the Reformed faithful in the National Association of Evangelicals, which would have prompted Warfield's glare, but Hodge and Warfield emerged as the new ideal. Old Princeton no longer scowled on a predominantly Wesleyan-Arminian universe. An unspoken covenant brooded: Everyone's a guest in Hodges' manse. Second, historian George Marsden observes that most leading new evangelicals supported Republican Ohio Senator Robert A. Taft, the guru of the GOP right in the 1940's and '50's[3] (it should be said: Billy Graham was a registered Democrat and pushed for civil rights and social action).[4] They did not baptize the Republican Party in Jesus' name, but perhaps their political unanimity rendered them near-sighted to the 1980 emergency. They failed to see the invasion of a gurgling partisan idol.

Third, and perhaps the most shameful, the mid-century neo-evangelicals initially stood on the wrong side in one of America's great moral struggles. Donald Dayton writes that *Christianity Today* panned the civil rights movement in the early1960's. Its editors defended "voluntary segregation," leveled socialism charges against Martin Luther King, Jr.'s call for integration, condemned demonstrations and civil disobedience, and labeled the 1963 March on Washington a "mob spectacle." They also scorned interracial marriage and hailed Mississippi when the state's leaders blocked James Meredith from attending its university. The magazine changed its

---

3. Marsden, *Reforming Fundamentalism*, 62.

4. Griswold, "Billy Graham's Striking Gospel of Social Action," *The New Yorker*, 2/23/2018.

stance by 1965; but, very unwittingly, the genteel new evangelicals left the door open for subsequent intimidators.[5]

I would see that later. For now, I was lapping it all up and tagging myself with the evangelical label. It was a liberating insignia. I breathed in the whole Gospel.

I also met my future wife at seminary (the former Andrea LaCelle) and, in a strange twist, I contracted tongue cancer just before our wedding. I submitted to twice-a-day radiation therapy at Massachusetts General Hospital. I stood before the altar in the winter of 1987, pledged the until-death-do-us-part oath, and wondered if I'd render my beloved a widow in a year. The cancer wouldn't return for another 27 years.

So I was ready and eager to pastor churches under the emancipating evangelical banner. I didn't know Billy Graham's gentlemanly image, which emblemized the movement for decades, was reshaping into a bruised religious boxer's. My career gave me and my family a ring-side seat at the slug fest.

INTIMIDATION: AN EYEWITNESS ACCOUNT

I signed on with the American Baptists (a smaller mainline denomination housing the full range of theological convictions) and took a church in Boston's Allston-Brighton section, about a mile and a world away from Cambridge's Harvard Square. The church itself was a lovable archetype of shrinking white urban congregations. Veterans fondly remembered its glory days while newbies brought in contemporary urban life: abuse, crumbled marriages, drug addiction, alcoholism and teen pregnancy—all wrapped in a Boston accent accompanying the city's up-thrusted middle finger (The Hub cultivates audacity, as seen in its drivers). Our car was stolen on August 26, 1993, the day after our only child, Caleb, was born.

Welcome to the big bad city.

But the people could be uproarious and they tolerated my rookie mistakes. Tempers often flared, but there was little intentional intimidation. I saw bullying on the larger scene after I discovered the refreshing teachings of John Wimber and the Vineyard Christian Fellowship, then headquartered in Anaheim, California. The Vineyard drew me into deeper intimacy with God.

Wimber had been a cessationist Quaker pastor after he shelved his musical career when he came to Christ in the early 1960's. He quit that church in the wake of burnout, signed on with the Fuller Institute of Church Growth,

---

5. Dayton & Strong, *Rediscovering an Evangelical Heritage*, 49–51.

heard Ladd's teaching on the present-day in-breaking of God's kingdom and agreed with it. He saw the prevalence of healing and other miracles in the Gospels and viewed them through that already-but-not-yet lens. By now, he was shepherding a church again. He and other leaders prayed for the sick in earnest and flopped for ten months. Healings finally came and, on a fateful 1980 Mother's Day, about two thirds of the church fell as the guest speaker cried, "Come, Holy Spirit!"[6] Ministers baptized about 700 that summer.

Anaheim emerged as a center for signs and wonders and Vineyard churches sprang up across America and throughout the world. An informal network formed a wider Vineyard penumbra, so conferences were often populated with Presbyterians, Baptists, Episcopalians, and even some Catholics. They didn't mandate tongues, repeatedly said not all were healed, and stressed holiness, social justice, and love for the poor. There was no naming and claiming or promises of health-and-wealth. The Vineyard staked its claim in the "radical middle," encouraging a holy life and sound exegesis.[7] Rick Nathan, a Vineyard pastor in Columbus, Ohio, described his colleagues as "empowered evangelicals" rather than charismatics.

I tried the Vineyard's method for healing prayer: Remain calm; ask questions; don't rush; let God be God. Shock of shocks, it worked. Several were healed. One woman gasped when jaw pain fled after she had visited a dentist with bad aim. Who would-a thunk it? Christianity's fun. The thrill ride rolled on as I drove to Canada in 1995, witnessed the so-called Toronto Blessing, and returned with glowing reports (a Vineyard church, which later separated from the association, displayed various "manifestations" reminiscent of the great revivals; thousands flocked from over the world).

Then I saw the slug fest.

Many evangelicals embraced the Vineyard. Some responded with reasonable concerns, but others followed the irascible John MacArthur, pastor of Grace Community Church in Sun Valley, California, who pastes the heretic label on good Christians everywhere. Both he and Bible-Answer-Man Hank Hanegraaff tossed unfounded charges like confetti: Vineyard and Toronto leaders supposedly mandated healing, favored experience over the Bible, and made manifestations compulsory. Some Reformed scholars—including the respected D.A.Carson—didn't check their facts and leaped into the bully fray.

Of course the Vineyard made mistakes—and the alliance stemming from the Toronto church would eventually turn inward and mire itself in

---

6. See Wimber, "A Hunger for God," in Springer, ed., *Power Encounters Among Christians in the Western World*, 3–14.

7. This "radical middle" terminology is used in Jackson, *The Quest for the Radical Middle: A History of the Vineyard*.

the teachings of the 1950's Latter Rain Movement, a quirky Pentecostal offshoot granting inordinate authority to supposed prophets and apostles. But that was not inevitable at the time, and many faultfinders still fail to acknowledge Wimber's separation from Toronto.

Okay, so some evangelicals weren't so nice. But surely intimidation was confined to MacArthur's narrow band . . .

How precious.

We left the Boston church on good terms in 1996 (I'm still in touch with many members; some still refer to me as "my pastor") and moved to southern New Hampshire. An alliance of church plants within a Pentecostal denomination was implementing a Vineyard-like vision and allowing Toronto-like manifestations. One of the plants caved-in on its own unique array of dysfunctions (turmoil and feuds left it with only twelve shocked adults and a few kids), and the denomination asked Andrea and me to resurrect it. Any pastor with a shepherd's heart would have pronounced the patient dead and guided those families to a more nurturing body, but I had lost that heart somewhere between Boston and New Hampshire. I was Mr. Visionary, the go-get-'em church planter. I threw away five years of my family's life in an attempt to resurrect a church that God was closing.

It finally did, which was an act of mercy.

I didn't realize I was sitting in that ring-side seat to evangelical intimidation yet again—this time in its Pentecostal wing. I was witnessing the dawn of what the late C. Peter Wagner would hail as the greatest thing since Protestantism's advent. He'd call it the New Apostolic Reformation. So-called prophets and apostles breezed through beleaguered New England and promised revival—as long as we saluted them as God's end-times representatives. The potential for abuse, authoritarianism, and intimidation was obvious.

My next church—an intentional interim pastorate nearer to New Hampshire's coast—was a veritable delight. An *intentional* interim actively brings healing and resolution to conflicted congregations, but these people healed me. They were hilarious—and they fawned over our son, loved my wife's cello, and tolerated my long sermons.

I seemed fated to serve Hatfield-McCoy churches, so I learned all about toxic organizations and conflict management. I signed up for workshops and seminars everywhere. My favorite organization was Peacemaker Ministries, founded in 1982 by Ken Sande, a Montana lawyer saddened by all the internecine church in-fighting. Sande imported the insights of Alternative Dispute Resolution, which offers more consensual mediation and arbitration methods, while bonding himself to God's Word. He wrote it all up in a book called *The Peacemaker*, which I recommended with enthusiasm and used as a basis for preaching.

I still recommend Peacemaker Ministries—with a huge caution: Conflict resolution must be seen as one stage in conflict *transformation*, where conflict is seen as an active agent in surfacing simmering diseases. Otherwise, bullies manipulate the ADR methods. Resolution becomes a euphemism for avoidance and feeds the beast. More on that in a later chapter.

Many were begging us to stay, but I felt it was best to stick to my word: Intentional interims promise not to apply for the settled pastor's job, so it was on to Connecticut and a seemingly thriving church. True, it had a history of brawls and two splits—sure-fire danger signs—but one leader was implementing Sande's approach while another advocated Vineyard-like ministry. Could this be the church of my dreams?

No. It wasn't. We were tossed from the ring-side seat into the ring itself.

A SLUG FEST

I'm not thrilled with criticizing a church I tried to serve. I really do love its individuals and I know I made many mistakes. They'd (correctly) say I was forever off-beat. I didn't connect and didn't fit. I can imagine their slackened jaws as they read my unflattering descriptions—especially since they welcomed me with open arms when I subsequently visited and many now pray for me. But there's no way around it: I met *evangelical* intimidation here, in all its inglorious splendor.

The church was actually ailing. Many reeled at the loss of my mild-mannered and beloved predecessor, who rescued them from one of those splits and loved them back to life. Most were actually wary of the spiritual gifts and few knew about Ken Sande. Conflict resolution was the ministry of one influential and (deservedly) respected leader, who was wounded after attempting to resolve past controversies. He's a good man, but he swung into full peacemaker mode at the first sign of disagreement, throttling friendly debates and the creative solutions they spawn—because, after all, debates spark conflict and conflict is always wrong.

And I seemed to stir controversy with every move. My wry humor fell flat.

So I was on precarious footing as current events piqued my dormant political interests. A PBS special on climate change forced me to look at my son and say aloud, "Oh . . . my . . . God." He faced a possible future of droughts and rising seas and widening deserts. My a-politicism wasn't helping him. Then there was Barak Obama's 2008 presidential run. I was impressed. He spoke to American voters as adults. And I didn't help myself in my quick, ad-hoc comment before a sermon: "The Earth is heating up." One influential member blasted me after the service for my "liberal" environmentalism and another berated the scientific consensus during a devotional at a general board meeting. I soon realized I was serving a congregation of climate-change deniers, with the consensus deemed left wing and, therefore, anti-Christian.

Then there was a member's eye-opening e-mail: Obama, apparently, was a Muslim terrorist. All the replies from church leaders were grist from the right-wing propaganda mill. No one commented on the unsubstantiated, implicitly racist charge.

One of my favorite members wondered if any liberal could land in heaven; others coupled Obama with the anti-Christ; one member, a leader in the local Republican Party, often stood in the foyer on Sunday mornings and loudly proclaimed his liberals-are-evil, science-denial views.

So much for inviting progressive friends to services in a blue state.

More startling, pastoral colleagues at a once-a-month breakfast meeting seemed to agree. Some froze when I challenged their assumptions. It was as if I breathed ice on their scrambled eggs—although a few pulled me aside later and muttered, "Thanks for speaking up. I'm a Democrat too."

Keep it hush-hush. Monty Python might smash in and holler something about the Spanish Inquisition.

No one seemed to be aware of the late David Kuo's 2006 book, *Tempting Faith*. The former Director of the Office of Faith Based Missions wrote of officials in the George W. Bush administration and their actual contempt for evangelicals. Kuo also opened a window into the power-hungry world of court evangelicals (the ones flocking to Washington) and confessed his own hypocrisy: He assailed President Clinton's moral failings while his own marriage crashed.

I'd never endorse a given candidate from the pulpit, but I felt duty-bound to remind all that our advocacy must glorify Christ. Beware Proverbs 12:18 ("the words of the reckless pierce like swords, but the tongue of the wise brings healing"); and James 1:19 ("My dear brothers and sisters, take note of this: Everyone should be quick to listen, slow to speak and slow to become angry"). And we needn't fear liberals.

Complaints rolled in as rumors spread that I wasn't a Republican: I wasn't preaching from the Bible; my sermons were too intellectual and too shallow. My popularity plummeted even as long-dormant dreams came alive. We moved out of the building and into a school to finish a construction project; we rallied church-wide home group studies on conflict resolution, accompanied by a sermon series; we returned to a new, expanded building. Nothing worked. Families left. Giving dropped—and I didn't help my cause when I unknowingly quoted an off-color comment from the pulpit (Honest. The phraseology sounded innocent.). Two influencers told me I was not a godly man and the rumor mill spun tales of Obama endorsements from the pulpit.

God's Word gave me no help in my quest for popularity. I now suspected Ken Sande was missing something, so I began reading the Gospel According to Mark with an eye for Jesus' conflict-resolution methods. It became clear: Christ *intentionally* sparked grumbling when he healed on the Sabbath and challenged the religious leaders. I closed Mark after the third chapter and chose a different path: I took the criticism seriously—especially the one stipulating I didn't preach from the Bible. I preached veritably verse-by-verse in a series on Psalms 120–134, the so-called "Songs of Ascents." It didn't work. One of the most prominent leaders pulled me into a side room and said he saw no sermon improvement.

I sat down after he left. It was obvious. Soon, the he-doesn't-fits would ripen into we-gotta-fire-hims, with a shredded congregation as a result even if I survived. I had no choice but to gamble and submit my resignation—in mid-September of 2009, when the unemployment rate hovered at 9.8 percent and foreclosures thundered across the land. I'd give the church a three-month notice in which I'd confess my wrongs ("I should have taken more time to get to know the congregation during my first year; I should have been more patient and devoted more time to listening; I should have paid more attention to body language that was being conveyed to me"). The idea: I'd model grace under fire during my lame-duck months. Perhaps such modeling would pull the church out of its irascibility and—just maybe—I could rescind the resignation.

I conferred with Andrea and she agreed (Her comment: "Our life is surreal") and, after notifying the general board, I read my confessional resignation aloud the following Sunday.

The board met that week and said I should step down at the end of the month—with a guarantee that I'd be paid through November. That made things awkward. I was already slated to take the last Sunday off because of a family obligation, so next Sunday would be my ignoble last. There'd be no grace under fire, no exit with dignity, no time for closure. I was out.

I was asked to attend a meeting the following week—after I was no longer the pastor—and slammed with a job review filled with personal invective.

Welcome to bully Christianity, where not even a resignation in the Great Recession is enough.

I admit it. I was angry, and I found no solace in the broader evangelical scene. I visited other churches and met other evangelicals. One normally reasonable and well-respected colleague stoked those Obama-the-Anti-Christ fears in an e-mail. He was serious. I nearly spilled my coffee on my laptop. I visited one church in which qualms about the Affordable Care Act were delivered as a "prophetic word," which meant Obamacare's defenders sided with the devil. All seemed to march to tea party's drumbeat as they saluted Rush Limbaugh.

They needed a reply, so I swung partisan in the opposite direction as a balancing act. I joined my local Democratic Town Committee. I also joined my town's Green Energy Committee, signed on with the board of directors of the state-wide Interreligious Eco-Justice Network, and volunteered for the steering committee for the Connecticut Roundtable on Climate and Jobs (a labor-environmentalist-clergy alliance advocating sound ecological policies). I wrote for an on-line religious journal in Connecticut before becoming a *HuffPost* contributor in 2011 (one friend described my columns as "rants"), then fanned out to other publications. I was even a panelist at conferences on climate change, both in Connecticut and in Washington DC.

What a thrill. I always wanted to be a panelist.

Meanwhile, my family hacked through the Great Recession's brambles as I dropped job applications into the era's black hole. Not even temp agencies wanted me. The bank account dried up. We missed mortgage payments, filed for relief, and threaded the lender's maze: Bank representatives claimed they lost the paper work and asked us to re-file; collectors threatened foreclosure unless they received this month's check. Our mortgage company was later cited for abuse.

I asked myself the dreaded question as I muttered on my neighborhood walks: Am I being evicted from my spiritual home as well as my physical home? Am I really a bona fide evangelical? I fit nowhere: Not with Pentecostals (tried that), not with right-wing evangelicalism, not with so-called progressive Christianity (I visited some theologically liberal gatherings; they felt like spiritual dead zones). I loved the Vineyard, but the association hadn't planted any churches in the Hartford area.

Finally, I remembered the American Baptist Churches, the denomination that ordained me right out of seminary. They always treated me well. I scheduled a meeting with Connecticut's executive director. Could I come back if I wolfed down humble pie?

Yes. They'd welcome me back—with open arms, even, especially since my ordination was still active (miracle of miracles: someone forgot to file the paperwork). Soon, I was the salaried, intentional interim at a church in a mid-Connecticut city. We caught up on our mortgage payments and silenced the bill collectors. The people of that church lauded me in job reviews while giving me helpful critiques and took no offense at my politics. I could even make those trips to Washington DC and hobnob with leaders in the evangelical environmental movement. I no longer walked in fear of bullies. The same was true at another intentional interim pastorate at a church near New London.

I eventually saw the weaknesses of today's condescending Democratic Party (all pro-lifers and supporters of traditional marriage were "extremists") and distanced myself from overt partisanship.

Then calamity struck: My cancer revived with a vengeance. Surgeons sliced out a huge chunk of my tongue in August of 2015 and rebuilt it with skin from my left arm. The disease struck my entire mouth in January 2016. We beat it back with rugged chemotherapy, complimented by radiation, but then it spread to an area near my sternum and returned to my tongue. Radiation burned it away from my sternum and more chemotherapy jailed it on my tongue, but I was told my cancer was incurable. I now speak with a severe speech impediment and can only eat soft food.

So much for preaching, speaking, and trips to Washington. I resigned from all the boards and helplessly watched events through chemotherapy's haze. The unthinkable unfolded. In 2016, many evangelical leaders endorsed a philandering, thrice-married, misogynistic, science-denying, anti-Mexican casino owner and reality television star, and surveys indicated that 81 percent of self-identified white evangelicals voted for him. That figure has since been questioned, but Trump remains popular among self-identified white evangelicals even as he plunges deeper into mendacity and obscenity. White evangelicals have slipped into an ethical vortex: In 2011, just 30 percent said a personally immoral politician can behave virtuously in a public role. In 2016, that figure leaped to 72 percent.[8]

I saw it now. The back-to-the-Bible people have drifted from the Scriptures, enticed by the allure of earthly power. But earthly power demands earthly weaponry. To put it in the Apostle Paul's language, we participate in the "acts of the flesh," among which are "hatred, discord, jealousy, fits of rage, selfish ambition, dissensions, factions, and envy" (Galatians 5:20–20). We emulate bullies instead of peacemakers and employ intimidation instead of sound argument and grace. We abandon Jesus's operating motif, found in Matthew 20:28: "The Son of Man did not come to be served, but to serve." We forget the insight of 2 Corinthians 12:9: God's power is "made perfect in weakness."

We'll see how far evangelicals have drifted in the following chapters.

---

8. Pulliam Bailey, "The Trump Effect?," *Washington Post* web site, 10/19/2016; Jones & Cox. "Clinton maintains double-digit lead (51% vs. 36%) over Trump." *PRRI.* 2016.

PART ONE

Tips of the Iceberg

Case Studies in Intimidation

2

Climate Change and a Heretic Hunt

Few arenas display Evangelicalism's bully takeover more than climate change, where the coal mine's canary has been hacking, spitting, and turning blue.

Deniers of the scientific consensus, often trained in political advocacy and marketing techniques, yell at the bird. They question its motives, tell it the fumes are imaginary, and drop hints that it's wheezing a heretical wheeze. Consensus-driven evangelical moderates rallied to the cause at first, then muted their voices when the fists slammed the tables. The sad result: The deniers hogged the microphone for far too long, needlessly embarrassing biblically-centered Christianity and harming the Gospel's advocacy.

The Board of Directors for the National Association of Evangelicals finally displayed moral courage in its resolution of October, 2015. The key sentence: "A changing climate threatens the lives and livelihoods of the world's poorest citizens."[1] Unfortunately but predictably, news outlets barely mentioned the statement, and American evangelical Christianity still houses the headquarters for anti-scientific denialism.

I deeply respect the NAE, which represents forty member denominations and a plethora of groups and individuals. I admire its recently-retired president, Leith Anderson. He wisely shepherded the organization through

---

1. "Caring For God's Creation: A Call To Action," https://www.nae.net/caring-for-gods-creation/.

pain and controversy when he took the helm in 2006. I have no wish to sully its reputation. But the NAE's slow response, however understandable, makes for a case study in bully evangelicalism's dynamics: Intimidators foment fear while conflict-adverse moderates silence themselves in the name of unity.

THE REALITIES

Cold reality prompts the canary's cough. Fact: The world's glaciers are shrinking. Fact: The polar ice caps are melting. Another fact: Peter Doran and Maggie Kendall Zimmerman discovered that 97% of all active climatologists are agreed—human activity spurs the Earth's rising temperatures, weird weather, glacial melting, and the ocean's acidification.[2] Then there are the reports: A federal advisory draft released in January, 2013, predicted catastrophe unless policies change,[3] as did a World Bank warning in November, 2012.[4] A UN study revealed that this century's first decade was the hottest in 160 years.[5] The 2018 reports grew even more ominous: The Intergovernmental Panel on Climate Change warned that average global temperatures may cross the crucial 1.5-degree Celsius threshold as early as 2030.[6] A Congressionally-mandated National Climate Assessment came the following month. It described climate change in the present tense and warned of rapidly rising sea levels.[7]

These facts and reports—as well as wild fires, droughts and super storms—resemble that poor canary in the coal mine, whose death signaled dangerous methane levels and the need for action.

Surely evangelical Christians can emulate their Catholic and Eastern Orthodox brothers and sisters and explore this dilemma without fear. No historic creed is at stake and Scripture advocates creation care: We're the

---

2. Doran & Zimmerman, "Examining the Scientific Consensus on Climate Change," *Eos*, Volume 90, 21–22.

3. Gillis, "An Alarm in the Offing on Climate Change," *New York Times Green: A Blog About Energy and the* Environment, January 14, 2013.

4. Potsdam Institute for Climate Impact Research and Climate Analytics, *Turn Down The Heat*, November, 2012; cf., Schneider, "World Bank warns of '4-degree' threshold of global temperature increase," *The Washington Post*, November 19, 2012. Also see Eilperin, "World on track for nearly 11-degree temperature rise, energy expert says," *Washington Post*, November 28, 2011.

5. UN News Center, "New UN report cites 'unprecedented climate extremes' over past decade," July 3, 2013.

6. The report can be found here: https://www.ipcc.ch/sr15/.

7. Found here: https://nca2018.globalchange.gov/.

Lord's designated stewards (Genesis 1:27–30). We were called to *guard* God's sanctuary (a more literal rendering of the wording in Genesis 2:15). Our Earthly rule fits Walter Kaiser's description: "The gift of 'dominion' over nature was not intended to be a license to use or abuse selfishly the created order in any way men and women saw fit. In no sense were humans to be bullies and laws to themselves."[8] Kaiser is right: God's leadership motif is "help" (Psalm 121:1–2), and service (Matthew 20:28). Psalms 19 and 104 testify to God's glory in creation and Romans 8:18–22 looks forward to its redemption. Kudos to Francis of Assisi, who cherished the animals and plants. And just to make sure everything's on the up-and-up, we've had our inside people: Sir John Houghton, a British evangelical, co-chaired the IPCC for many years.[9] Katharine Hayhoe, a Billy Graham fan, pastor's wife, and Texas Tech university professor, has served as a reviewer for the IPCC.[10]

The evidence, the Bible, and historic Christianity motivated 280 leaders to sign the petition, "Climate Change, An Evangelical Call to Action" in 2006.[11] The names read like an evangelical VIP litany: Andy Crouch, then *Christianity Today*'s executive editor; Jack Hayford of the International Church of the Foursquare Gospel; Gordon P. Hugenberger of Parkstreet Church in Boston; Duane Litfin, president of Wheaton College; Gordon MacDonald, editor-at-large for Leadership Magazine; David Neff, also of *Christianity Today*; Tri Robinson, pastor of the Boise Vineyard; Berten Waggoner, then the National Director of the Vineyard USA; and Rick Warren, senior pastor of Saddleback. To name a few. What's more, 44 Southern Baptist leaders, including the convention's president and two past presidents, signed the initiative, "A Southern Baptist Declaration on the Environment and Climate Change."

A WRENCH IS THROWN

But something was amiss. In some circles, calling attention to the hacking canary was both unpatriotic and unorthodox. Many were swayed. I've already mentioned my experience as a pastor: I was blasted as a "liberal" (perish the thought) because I agreed with these two assertions:

---

8. Kaiser, Davids, Bruce, Brauch, *Hard Sayings of the Bible*, 89.

9. See Houghton's presentation to the National Association of Evangelicals: "Climate Change: A Christian Challenge and Opportunity," March 2005.

10. See Hayhoe & Farley, *A Climate for Change*.

11. Goodstein, "Evangelical Leaders Join Global Warming Initiative," *The New York Times*, February 8, 2006.

- *"There is now a broad consensus in this country, and indeed in the world, that global warming is happening, that it is a serious problem, and that humans are causing it."*[12]
- *"we agree that climate change is real and threatens our economy and national security."*[13]

The late Republican Senator John McCain of Arizona wrote the first quote in 2007, along with Senator Joe Lieberman. Republican Senator Lindsay Graham wrote the second in 2009 along with Democrat John Kerry. The senators, along with retired generals and admirals alarmed about climate change's potential security concerns,[14] implicitly invited us to embrace an opportunity: We can shelve annoying labels. Let's brew enough caffeine to spike our blood pressure, roll in the whiteboards, and brainstorm while pacing back and forth with our Type A personalities on full display . . .

No. We're "liberal." We've failed a vague orthodoxy test, which means we're worse than erroneous: We're suspect. Forget evidence, the biblical mandate for stewarding creation, precedent, and recognized authorities. According to a 2007 CNN article, Tony Perkins of the Family Research Institute speculated that climate change is part of a leftist agenda threatening evangelical unity.[15] The late Jerry Falwell proclaimed this from his pulpit on February 25 of that year: "I am today raising a flag of opposition to this alarmism about global warming and urging all believers to refuse to be duped by these 'earthism' worshipers."[16] Calvin Beisner, head of the *Cornwall Alliance for the Stewardship of Creation*, suggested the worries are "an insult to God."[17] He also insinuated that diminishing our oil dependence aligns us with the unfaithful steward of Matthew 25:14–30.[18] After all, the oil is there: God gave it to us. We should use it (the same logic would render us fickle if we failed to smoke marijuana as well; after all, it's there for the asking). His organization veered close to rendering anthropogenic climate

12. McCain & Liebermann, "The Turning Point on Global Warming," *The Boston Globe*, February 13, 2007

13. Kerry & Graham, "Yes We Can (Pass Climate Change Legislation)," *New York Times*, October 10, 2009

14. Eleven retired generals and admirals, "National Security and the Threat of Climate Change," 2007.

15. CNN, "Global Warming Gap Among Evangelicals Widens," March 14, 2007,.

16. Banks, "Dobson, Others Seek Ouster of NAE Vice President," *Religion News Service*, March 2, 2007.

17. Beisner, Calvin, "Believing in Climate Change is an Insult to God," *Right Wing Watch*, November 19, 2012.

18. Fisher & Beisner, "Using Fossil Fuels Is An Insult to God," Right Wing Watch, November 20, 2012.

change a theological impossibility in its *Evangelical Declaration on Global Warming*: "We believe Earth and its ecosystems—created by God's intelligent design and infinite power and sustained by His faithful providence —are robust, resilient, self-regulating, and self-correcting, admirably suited for human flourishing, and displaying His glory. Earth's climate system is no exception. Recent global warming is one of many natural cycles of warming and cooling in geologic history."[19]

That's naïve. Our species is not immune to world-wide calamity. Remember the fourteenth century, when nature and human activity wed in a ghoulish marriage. Commerce flowed over new trade routes between East and West and conveyed flea-bearing rats. The fleas leaped onto humans and infected them with the Black Death. Roughly half of all Europe died.

I long to ask: Who defines unity? Is assessing evidence and asking questions inherently disruptive? Is it wrong to seek solutions to a potentially grave problem—especially since there are virtually no doctrinal risks (Beisner notwithstanding)? Apparently, yes. We're pagan "earthism" worshipers. We're divisive conspirators in a leftist plot—never mind that Perkins was flourishing a rhetorical ploy with a one-two punch: levy a nebulous charge no one can disprove; then, as the opponent reels, accuse him of divisiveness. Any challenge fulfills the charge. Few can stay calm and ask: Who is calling whom names? Who flings the accusations and mows down the straw men? Who is really divisive?

But none of those questions stems the accusatory tide. Deniers of climate change grab any real or imagined flaw. I've been warned, over coffee and doughnuts, that I'm falling prey to Al Gore, who, apparently, is evil incarnate and wields hypnotic power. The ice caps will recover if he vanishes—just like the Vietnam War would have evaporated if a tiger ate Dan Rather. I try to tell people I've never seen *An Inconvenient Truth*, but no one believes me.

GOTCHA . . . MAYBE NOT

For a brief moment in 2009, it looked like the deniers were onto something. Computer hackers stole more than 1,000 e-mails from a research unit at Great Britain's University of East Anglia. The e-mails, dating back some 13 years, held reams of information, "everything from the mundanities of climate-data collection to comments on international scientific politics to strongly worded criticisms by climate-change doubters," to quote Bryan

---

19. See the full statement at, https://cornwallalliance.org/2009/05/evangelical-declaration-on-global-warming/

Walsh of *Time*.[20] There seemed to be references to oppressing opposition, withholding information, pressuring editorial boards of academic journals, and skewing research.

Besides, the e-mails weren't nice.

The unit's head, Phil Jones, took a leave of absence pending an investigation.

Nothing came of it. Parliamentary and university reports exonerated Jones. Perhaps he could have been more forthcoming and more couth, but, in the words of the parliamentary committee: "In the context of sharing data and methodologies, we consider Professor Jones's actions were in line with common practice in the climate science community."[21] References to performing research "tricks" were in-house slang for legitimate scientific procedures—and yes, Jones and his e-mail partners were a little rough in their private e-mails. They didn't anticipate their theft.

What a scandal.

THE MODERATE VOICE—OR LACK OF IT

At first, the moderates—epitomized by the gentlemanly NAE—vied for the lead on this issue. The NAE's 2004 framework for social engagement, entitled "For The Health of the Nation," delineated seven vital arenas: religious freedom, family life and children, the sanctity of life, caring for the poverty-stricken and helpless, human rights, peacemaking, and creation care. One eventual outcome: Dorothy Boorse's 56-page pamphlet, "Loving The Least of These: Addressing A Changing Environment." The Gordon College professor stressed that "environmental change" strikes the poor most severely. Richard Cizik, the organization's vice president of government affairs, spurred seismic shifts that would free the movement from reactionary captivity. Climate change was one of his top priorities.

Push-back arose, of course. James Dobson tried to get Cizik fired, but the NAE president at the time, Ted Haggard, was unimpressed: "The last time I checked," he told Dobson, "you weren't in charge of the NAE."[22] A more muted approach came early in 2006 from the so-called "Interfaith Stewardship Alliance," the Cornwall Alliance's predecessor. The signatories—among whom were the distinguished Charles Colson along with a who's-who in the Religious Right, including James Dobson (again), John Hagee, the late

---

20. Walsh, "Has 'Climategate' Been Overblown?" *Time Magazine*, December 7, 2009.

21. Romm, "House of Commons exonerates Phil Jones," *ThinkProgress: Climate Progress*, March 30, 2010.

22. Sullivan, *The Party Faithful*, 191

James Kennedy, and Richard Land—said they "appreciated the bold stance that the (NAE) has taken on controversial issues like embracing a culture of life, protecting traditional marriage and family, promoting abstinence as AIDS prevention, and many others," but they requested it lay off climate change: it was "not a consensus issue." An "official stance" should be filtered through official channels, and "individual NAE members or staff should not give the impression that they are speaking on behalf of the entire membership, so as not to usurp the credibility and good reputation of the NAE." Then came the twist: "We respectfully ask that the NAE carefully consider all policy issues in which it might engage in the light of promoting unity among the Christian community and glory to God."[23]

To underscore: NAE officials were "bold" when advocating the signatories' positions but potentially divisive (". . . in the light of promoting unity . . .") on climate change. Invoking "unity" often knocks the debate off the merits. Suddenly, a thousand eggshells rattle across the floor, freezing us in our tracks lest we break our delicate bonds. Don't even dare ask: What about *your* position's potential divisiveness? Have you pondered our possible disunity with Christianity's other legitimate branches, such as Catholicism, Eastern Orthodoxy, and traditional Protestantism? They've endorsed the scientific consensus.

It worked. The NAE blinked. Haggard answered in late January by defending the organization's pro-environment stance but demurring on climate change. His executive committee directed NAE staffers "to stand by and not exceed in any fashion our approved and adopted statements concerning the environment contained within the Evangelical Call to Civic Responsibility." Catch a glimpse of American evangelicalism's blind spot toward the end. Haggard said: "I believe there are pro-environment, pro-free market, pro-business answers to the environmental questions facing our community."

Do the Scriptures rally to free enterprise? Cultural standards were now mixed into a back-to-the-Bible organization, a charge evangelicals often levy against theological liberals. And pro-creation statements ring hollow without identifying its destructive agents. Imagine federal authorities banning the mention of cigarettes while promoting cancer-free living.

The year, 2006, proved pivotal. In February, 86 evangelical leaders—including pastors, 39 Christian college presidents, and not a few current NAE board members—signed the "Evangelical Climate Initiative," which asserted the reality of human-induced global warming and said it imperiled

---

23. The letter can be found here: http://www.cornwallalliance.org/docs/appeal-letter-to-the-national-association-of-evangelicals-on-the-issue-of-global-warming.pdf.

national security and the poverty-stricken: "Love of God, love of neighbor, and the demands of stewardship are more than enough reason for evangelical Christians to respond to the climate change problem with moral passion and concrete action. Christians must care about climate change because we are called to love our neighbors." In May, one of the last creditable denial hold-outs, Gregg Easterbrook, cried uncle: "Based on the data I'm now switching sides on global warming, from skeptic to convert."[24]

But then calamity struck. In November, Haggard resigned in the wake of a sexual scandal. Anderson, who served as president before, was recalled and brought his steady hand. The evangelical world breathed a sigh of relief. "There's an enormous trust that people have with (Anderson), and that allows him to lead," said Jo Anne Lyon, general superintendent of the Wesleyan church.[25] The Minnesota megachurch pastor brought administrative efficiency and showed he was no right-wing poster boy: He opposed the death penalty, supported immigration reform, and signed the Evangelical Climate Initiative. A Religion News Service profile said he "continues to press the issue of justice for the poor in the developing world, working hard behind the scenes to craft an official NAE statement on climate change."[26] Anderson's pastoral style seemed the right prescription for a stunned organization laboring under a recent leadership humiliation—and it fit with the NAE's gentlemanly and lady-like ethos.

Calamity struck again in 2008. National Public Radio's *Fresh Air* host, Terry Gross, asked Cizik a question in an on-air interview: "A couple of years ago when you were on our show, I asked you if you were changing your mind on that. And two years ago, you said you were still opposed to gay marriage. But now as you identify more with younger voters, would you say you have changed on gay marriage?" Cizik waffled: "I'm shifting, I have to admit. In other words, I would willingly say that I believe in civil unions. I don't officially support redefining marriage from its traditional definition, I don't think."

This went too far those who believe we should insist on the Church's traditional teaching on sex (I'm among them). Cizik apologized for his comment and re-affirmed the NAE's official stance, but it was too late. He stepped down from the NAE.

Christianity Today interviewed Anderson immediately after Cizik's resignation. He said NAE officials should speak for the association, not for

24. Easterbrook, *The New York Times*, June 24. 2006.

25. Macdonald, "Pawlenty's pastor stays politically neutral," *USATODAY.com*, June 21, 2011.

26. Macdonald, "Pawlenty's pastor stays politically neutral," *USATODAY.com*, June 21, 2011.

themselves. When asked about Cizik's climate change advocacy, he replied: "'For the Health of the Nation' does state that creation care is one of our priorities. It does not state in that document that we have a specific position, because we don't, on global warming or emissions. So he (Cizik) has spoken as an individual on that. However, to most of our constituents, marriage and related moral issues and of greater importance and significance than specific stances on the climate."[27]

The question hovers: "But is it right?" Does the Bible prioritize family moralities over others? Did you, Anderson, not sign a statement underscoring the moral imperative entwined in climate change? Post-interview quarterbacking is easy (and let's shout "take two" on Cizik's NPR conversation), but we're left with that vague "opportunity lost" feeling. Reel back the tape. Say this: "The NAE has no formal position on climate change, but Richard was educating us and I'm on record as agreeing with him. I hope the education process can go on." No doubt some would have screamed for Anderson's professional head so they could line it up on Cizik's platter, but aren't mega-church pastors writing books on courageous leadership? Did NAE heroes like Luther, Calvin, and Wesley—or founding President Harold Ockenga—poll their constituents? Haven't evangelicals always claimed that truth trumps popularity? Otherwise, Ockenga would have fawned before Henry Emmerson Fosdick and Carl Henry would never have written *The Uneasy Conscience of Modern Fundamentalism*.

Perhaps the NAE ailed with the same malady once infecting me: Conflict avoidance in the guise of resolution. Many in its institutions and churches offer courses in communication and negotiation in an attempt to quell their internecine battles. Such efforts are laudable, but they can lead to unintended consequences: Argument (the process of defending a viewpoint by marshaling facts in a quest for the truth) is deemed intrinsically bad. Suddenly, we're nomads in the labyrinth of passive aggressiveness, choked by stilted "I statements" and confined by the tyranny of the sensitive. And, for the sake of "unity," absurdities gain the respect of actualities. Imagine representatives from the Flat Earth Society and the American Astronomical Society sitting at the same table while Luther withdraws his 95 Theses because he did not validate the bishop's feelings. Meanwhile, bullies see concessions as weaknesses: The Flat Earthers pound the table, yield nothing, display offense when the astronomers show photographs of a round planet, and demand a wider audience. The sad fact is that enemy-centered, antagonistic parties do not play for win-win resolutions.

27. Pulliam, "Interview: NAE President Leith Anderson on Richard Cizik's Resignation," *Christianity Today*, December 11, 2008.

More on that dynamic later. Suffice it to say that such has been the scene in the debates over climate change and creation care: The deniers kept at it while the moderates demurred, darkening discussions over national policy.

FOR INSTANCE . . .

A few samples of denial in Christ's name illuminate the underlying dynamic.

Sample One: In 2009, Republican US Rep. John Shimkus of Illinois read from Genesis 8:21–22 in a hearing of the Energy and Commerce Committee: "Never again will I curse the ground because of man, even though all inclinations of his heart are evil from childhood and never again will I destroy all living creatures as I have done. As long as the earth endures, seed time and harvest, cold and heat, summer and winter, day and night, will never cease." Then a passage from Matthew 24: "And he will send his angels with a loud trumpet call, and they will gather his elect from the four winds, from one end of the heavens to the other." The Congressman interpreted: "The earth will end only when God declares it's time to be over. Man will not destroy this earth. This earth will not be destroyed by a flood . . . I do believe that God's word is infallible. Unchanging. Perfect."

I applaud Shimkus' reverence for God's Word. I'll also point out that most credible scientists are not predicting the earth's destruction or humanity's extinction. They are, however, forecasting droughts, weird weather, and rising sea levels—all of which expand the possibilities of calamity.

Shimkus also said this: "Today we have about 388 parts per million [of carbon dioxide] in the atmosphere. I think in the age of the dinosaurs, when we had most flora and fauna, were probably at 4,000 parts per million. There is a theological debate that this is a carbon-starved planet, not too much carbon."[28]

Sea levels in the dinosaur era were 550 feet higher than today's. Much of the modern United States was under water.

Sample Two: Shimkus was at it again in 2012, when Mitch Hescox, President and CEO of the Evangelical Climate Network, testified before the House Energy and Power Subcommittee on the merits of Environmental Protection Agency regulations aimed at reducing mercury pollution from coal-fired plants (research indicates that one in six children are born with threatening mercury levels). Hescox stood on a solid consistent life foundation, which places the protection of the unborn within a broader pro-life

---

28. Quoted in Parkes, "The Politics of Global Warming," in *Environmental Philosophy*, 88

context: All human life is sacred, from conception to the grave—which means curbing mercury levels is a pro-life issue. "Let's not endanger our children with a substance we can control," said Hescox. "We must protect the weakest in our society, the unborn, from mercury poisoning."

Shimkus responded by reading a statement from the Cornwall Alliance web site: "The life in pro-life denotes not quality of life but life itself" and only refers to "opposition to a procedure that intentionally results in dead babies."[29] Senator James Inhofe (R-Oklahoma) employed the guilt-by-association tactic: "I find it extremely ironic that Rev. Michell Hescox and the Evangelical Environmental Network think that the pro-life agenda is best aligned with a movement that believes there are too many people in the world, actively promotes population control, and sees humans principally as polluters."[30]

Apparently, Senator Inhofe was unaware that the US Conference of Catholic Bishops also supported the regulations.

Sample Three: The Family Research Council had already impugned Hescox and the EEN when it claimed the organization "has received funding from such liberal groups as the Rockefeller Foundation, and specific signatories are beneficiaries of the largesse of far-Leftists like George Soros and Ted Turner" (Hescox denied that charge). An FRC e-mail issued a dire caution: "Since the beginning, factious people and religious cults have tried to infiltrate, divide, deceive and delude us (Ephesians 6:10–13)." So EEN is suspect.

I cry to the FRC: Why are you so sure *you* have not been seduced, deceived, and deluded?

Sample Four comes from Mark Tooley, president of the Institute on Religion and Democracy. While dazed Philippine survivors picked through debris of Typhoon Haiyan, he inaccurately blogged on November 13, 2013: "Much of the worst hysteria about apocalyptic Global Warming has cooled, especially after more than 15 years of no global temperature increases, evincing at least that climate computer models are less than infallible." He then skipped past warnings from President Reagan's Secretary of State, George

---

29. Quoted here: https://creationcare2015.wordpress.com/author/evangelicalenvironmentalnetwork/page/12/.

30. Imhof's press release is quoted here: https://www.epw.senate.gov/public/index.cfm/press-releases-republican?ID=5E700C58-802A-23AD-478D-7FEF03416208; I commented on his statement: Redfern, "The Far Right Embarrasses The Pro-Life Movement—Again," *Huffpost*, April 16, 2012.

Schultz,[31] The World Bank, the US commander of the Pacific Fleet,[32] a dozen retired admirals and generals,[33] two hundred evangelical scientists,[34] the Christian Reformed Church (an NAE member),[35] and the many leaders who signed Evangelical Climate Initiative, and declared: "Some of the most committed believers in the theory that human activity is uniquely fueling a disastrous increase in temperature are on the Religious Left." He singled-out former Chicago Theological Seminary President Susan Brooks Thistlethwaite, "who's ordained in the ultra-liberal United Church of Christ" and who "faulted Global Warming skeptics for the murderous typhoon in the Philippines." She allegedly displays "unwavering faith in apocalyptic global warming" and "strict adherence to climate fundamentalism." His last line evokes Greek mythology's earth goddess: "But zealots like Thistlethwaite will not likely forsake the solace of Gaia's temple, from which they'll continue to issue thunderbolts against the heretics who dare to doubt."[36]

I could supply other samples, but that will do for now.

Many US evangelicals are in danger of sealing themselves in a clannish cul-de-sac, perhaps isolating themselves from their own international tribe. Their brothers and sisters throughout the world embrace the imperative of addressing human-induced climate change. Yet the deniers have monopolized the US debate, invoking "unity" to silence their perceived enemies while growing shriller themselves. This is not sound argument. This is classic intimidation.

Unfortunately, climate change is a symptom of an overall ethos. We'll probe another symptom in the next chapter.

---

31. Bielo, "A Republican Secretary of State Urges Action on Climate Change," *Scientific American*, July 24, 2013.

32. Bender, "Chief of US Pacific forces calls climate biggest worry," *Boston Globe*, March 9, 2013.

33. Burns, "US Admirals, Generals, Link Climate Change To National Security," *Public News Service*, 7/11/2013.

34. Hayhoe & Ackerman, "Climate Change: Evangelical Scientists Say Limbaugh Wrong, Faith and Science Complement One Another," *The Christian Post*, 8/31/2013; see the evanagelical scientists' letter here:: https://www.eenews.net/assets/2013/07/15/document_cw_02.pdf.

35. Christian Reformed Church News, "Synod Recognizes Climate Change," 6/13/2012.

36. Tooley, "The Heresy of Doubting Apocalyptic Global Warming," *Juicy Ecumenism,*, 11/13/2013.

3

Apostles, Prophets, & Protestant Popes

HIGHLIGHT IN BRILLIANT YELLOW: I'm all enthusiasm for the so-called "charismatic gifts"—prophesy, healing, miracles, glossolalia (praying in unknown languages), among others—and I love those wacky Pentecostal-charismatics, who form an evangelical subset and trace their roots to a 1906–1915 prayer meeting on Los Angeles's Azusa Street. That meeting bred a host of denominations and alliances largely responsible for Christianity's post-World War 2 spread across the globe. I quibble over their two-tiered view of sanctification (some are "baptized in the Holy Spirit" and marked by speaking in unknown tongues; others are not), but I think they're more right than wrong and I've learned to bring earplugs to their uproarious gatherings.

It's just that another symptom of intimidation wells in this wing of evangelicalism. Many of my beloved brothers and sisters have leaped from their endearing eccentricity and plunged into a bizarre world in which "apostles" and "prophets" fawn over Donald Trump and predict God's wrath on anyone committing voting-booth heresy. Esoteric spirituality reigns. Sound exegesis and theology are dismissed as speculations from nefarious intellectuals. And, strangely, we're drawn inward and away from outreach even amid assurances of global revival.

Welcome to the exotic universe of what I call the apostolic-prophetic movement, a Pentecostal-Charismatic offshoot also christened the New

Apostolic Reformation by its late fan and most prestigious spokesman, C. Peter Wagner (1930–2016). It's really a loose network of like-minded ministries, with some proponents wearing Wagner's NAR tag and making extravagant claims of a new era. Read the on-line testimony of the International Coalition of Apostolic Leaders, which Wagner helped establish: "The Second Apostolic Age began roughly in 2001, heralding the most radical change in the way church is done since the Protestant Reformation. This New Apostolic Reformation embraces the largest segment of non-Catholic Christianity . . ."[1] The web site supplies no supporting statistics.

Others render humbler avowals and are merely friendly with the NAR. Some call themselves apostles; others say they're prophets; still others claim a hybrid: they're apostle-prophets or prophetic apostles or apostolic-prophetic intercessors. Most agree that the offices of the apostle and prophet, supposedly vacant since the first century, must be restored before God can launch his great end-times revival.

Everyone else's role, it seems, is to yield power to these purportedly benevolent commanders.

I saw this movement coalesce when I served that Pentecostal church from 1998–2003. I should emphasize: Many—such as Randy Clark of Global Awakening; John and Carol Arnott of Catch the Fire in Toronto, Canada; Bill Johnson of Bethel Church in Redding, California; and missionary Heidi Baker—are fine people. Baker is especially laudable. And Wagner—a church-growth expert who taught at Fuller Theological Seminary for decades—was kindly and gracious. He helped many climb out of stifling cessationism, which padlocks the Holy Spirit's gifts into the first century. Wagner befriended John Wimber and welcomed him into his classroom. They team-taught a popular and controversial course entitled, "Signs, Wonders, And Church Growth," featuring "clinics" in which students prayed for people. Many said they were healed.

Wagner famously theorized that the Holy Spirit's power swept through the Church in three waves during the twentieth century. There was Pentecostalism, originating at Azusa Street; there was the charismatic movement, which rolled in during the 1960's and '70's and brought Pentecostal theology and practice into mainline denominations; and there was the "Third Wave" of the 1980's and '90's, which embraced the charismata, or gifts, but rejected Pentecostalism's two-tiered theology.

I'm Third Wave.

But, unlike Wimber, Wagner was blinded by innocence and seemed impressed with every Pentecostal-charismatic fad—and he was easily awed

---

1. Cottle, "Definition and Description of an Apostle," 2015.

by assertive, triumphant leaders. He failed to see how influential apostolic-prophetic notables had unconsciously slipped into intimidation. Clear opinions are articulated as prophetic words. Consider a few comments from prominent figures: There's Alice Patterson in 2011, who said a "demonic structure" lay behind the Democratic Party.[2] There's Lou Engle, who frowned on the huge crowds gathered for the historic 2017 women's marches, held shortly after President Trump's inauguration. He called the multi-city protests "an unprecedented summons of witchcraft to curse President Trump, his Cabinet and all those aligned with a biblical worldview" and appealed for a three-day fast on the president's behalf.[3] There's Rick Joyner of North Carolina's Morning Star Ministries, who said the march in Washington DC "was one of the most blatant manifestations of the Jezebel spirit ever manifest in our country."[4]

Notice the implications. Democratic sympathizers not only endorse supposedly errant policies; they're aligned with demons. Marchers cannot simply be wrong; they're lured into witchcraft and reveal the "Jezebel spirit," a term frequently used to describe the rebellious and divisive. Mentioning this "spirit" often, but not always, is used to quench vocal women.

Those statements snuff out even-handed discussion, which might weigh the possibility of Hell's minions in *both* American political parties. Wagner's own response to Patterson, in this instance, showed wisdom: "I personally would not endorse each one of her statements and especially the statement about the Democratic Party being demonized, any more than the Republican Party is. I mean, I believe there's a lot of demonic control over Congress in general that needs to be dispersed."[5] More balance and nuance would grapple with the marchers' legitimate griefs (remember that *Access Hollywood* tape) along with genuine concerns (holistic pro-life organizations were excluded from speakers' platforms; in 2019, two leaders veered toward anti-Semitism).

The political statements hint at deeper alarms, which I'll tease out as I probe the movement's origin.

---

2. Gross, "A Leading Figure in the New Apostolic Reformation," *Fresh Air*, transcript of an interview with Peter Wagner, 10/3/2011.

3. Engle, "Lou Engle Sounds Urgent Call for 3-Day Esther Fast Over America," *Charisma*, 3/8/2017.

4. Joyner's statement was found on this Facebook page: https://www.facebook.com/RickJoyner.MorningStar/videos/1523335721032573/,; accessed, 7/11/18.

5. Gross, "A Leading Figure . . ."

KANSAS CITY AND THE LATTER RAIN

It seems the movement stems most directly from a church planted in 1982 and led by Mike Bickle, first known as the Kansas City Fellowship. Bickle promoted the "Kansas City Prophets:" Bob Jones, Larry Randolph, James Goll, John Paul Jackson, and, especially Paul Cain. The prophets often articulated impressive "words of knowledge," which made everyone wonder if they'd been flies on their living room walls the previous night. It was uncanny.

But Bickle's church stirred local controversy even as it drew national attention. In 1990, Pastor Ernie Gruen of the Full Faith of Love Church in Shawnee, Kansas, published a book-length broadside in which he complained of spiritual abuse, manipulation, doctrinal aberrance, and inaccurate prophesies. What's more, the prophets were encumbered by the quirky thinking of an earlier Pentecostal offshoot called the Latter Rain movement, which began in Saskatchewan in the late 1940's and trickled across North America. Cain had participated in it. Latter Rain followers emphasized the "five-fold" ministry of the Holy Spirit described in Ephesians 4:11: The offices of the apostle and prophet would be restored. They'd take charge of the other ministries mentioned in the verse (evangelists, pastors, and teachers) and catalyze a great end-times revival, complete with miracles and massive conversions. It was all so heady—especially when one of the celebrity apostle-prophets picked *you* out in a crowd and told everyone *you* were among the apostolic elite: a member of the "new breed," a soldier in "Joel's Army," one of the "manifest sons of God."[6]

In practice, such an ethos "kills evangelism and church planting," as Steve Nicholson of the Vineyard Church in Evanston, Illinois, observes.[7] The Latter Rain faithful refuse to evangelize because the super-star apostles are not fully in position. We're captured in a hyper-spiritual web. Scripture falls prey to the allegorical method, an interpretive approach seeking deep spiritual meanings behind every text, and participants veil themselves in intercession and prayer at the mere mention of outreach. Phrases such as "we don't want to get ahead of God" and "we need to pray more" and "we need to be more loving" smother action. Such generalities always bear some truth, so it's difficult to respond.

---

6. Ephesians 4:11 lists several offices, rendered apostles, prophets, evangelists, pastors and teachers in our English translations. The verse, of course, is interpreted differently among different readers. Many point out that "pastors and teachers" is actually one office in the Greek, so it's better to refer to this list as the "four-fold" ministry of the Holy Spirit. Many say the list is not meant to be exhaustive.

7. Nicholson, *Roots of the Vineyard, Part 3*.

Bickle and the prophets befriended Wimber, who tried his hand at moderating the Kansas City antagonists. Bob Jones, who confessed to moral failure, was disciplined; John Paul Jackson was brought to Anaheim for mentoring; the Kansas City Fellowship joined Wimber's association and changed its name to the Metro Vineyard, which supposedly rendered Bickle accountable.

But Wimber, who later admitted he lost his discernment, endorsed the prophets and gave them a platform. That meant the Latter Rain mentality seeped into the Vineyard and collided with its leader's everybody-gets-to-play model (we're in the presence of the future right now; all believers are ministers; solid exegesis and theology are valued; evangelism ranks high as a priority). Rifts yawned. Some churches, along with key leaders, left the Vineyard. By 1991, Wimber himself was no longer impressed. As Gruen had pointed out, many prophesies proved inaccurate—including Cain's prediction of an October, 1990 revival in England. Wimber traveled to Great Britain to witness the Holy Spirit's outpouring and Christianity's resurgence. He was disillusioned when it failed to come.

Vineyard leaders distanced themselves from the Kansas City Prophets.

Wimber apologized to Vineyard pastors in 1995 for allowing his association to drift off track. He reflected in 1997: "I turned my brain off for a couple of years. My son Sean went through years of alcohol and drug addiction. Some prophetic people came and said, 'God is offering you a grace package. If you'll do thus and so, God will retrieve your son.' This man prophesied when and how. And it came to pass exactly as he had said. Since then Sean has been free of any kind of addictive behavior. I was so grateful. He got married. He had his first baby during that era. I just was preoccupied. And my leadership model failed me. I was too directive. I didn't listen to my lieutenants."[8]

Bickle's church eventually withdrew from the Vineyard and he established Kansas City's International House of Prayer. Many are blessed, but idiosyncratic Latter Rain thinking prevails, along with an over-emphasis on the end times and an unhealthy form of Christian Zionism, which fails to see legitimate Palestinian needs.

The prophetic advocates then tacked toward Canada as the Toronto Blessing blossomed.

To refresh the memory: In 1994, crowds flocked to Toronto's Airport Vineyard Christian Fellowship, curious about claims that the Holy Spirit was pouring himself on a church of about 360 members near a runway's end

---

8. Stafford & Beverly, "Conversations: God's Wonder Worker," *Christianity Today*, 7/14/1997.

at Pearson International Airport. So-called manifestations were on display in nightly meetings, with "holy laughter" the most publicized. Participants were falling down, getting drunk in the spirit, roaring like lions, barking like dogs, and laughing up a storm. The church swelled, forcing it to move into a conference center on nearby Attwell Drive. Wild denunciations cascaded over Christian radio stations, led by "Bible Answer Man" Hank Hanegraaff (who, ironically, left Protestant Evangelicalism for Eastern Orthodoxy in 2017) and the ever-disparaging John MacArthur.

I found the Blessing exhilarating in my three visits. I saw Christianity's panorama: Baptists, Presbyterians, Catholic nuns and even old Mennonites all under one roof. There were Chinese, Norwegians, Germans, British, Asians, and Africans. And there was no mistaking God's presence. The air seemed charged; the atmosphere brimmed with joy and love. Of course there was immaturity, as in the 18th and 19th-century revivals and at Azusa Street, but I knew such outpourings were a mess. Besides, the barking was minimal and most of the laughter seemed genuine (it was not mimicked). Frankly, I felt a little tipsy myself. I even fell. I reasoned: Can't we experience the reality of a real God? Besides, Wimber was blessing it.

Then came the jolt. The Vineyard board withdrew its approval in 1996. The Toronto church left the association, pared its name to The Airport Christian Fellowship (it eventually changed again to "Catch The Fire"), and formed its own alliance, Partners In Harvest. Roughly a quarter of all Canadian Vineyard churches fled and many soured on Wimber.[9] Wimber said the manifestations were over-emphasized and called all to focus on "the main and plain things in Scripture."[10] Todd Hunter, Wimber's protégé and future successor, explained to his association's pastors: "There is a general agreement that the renewal over the course of the past two years has been from God, a blessing to many, and a wonderful work of God. However, there has also been a growing awareness of an increasing difference of direction and understanding concerning pastoral administration of the renewal, philosophy of ministry, and theological implications of the renewal."[11]

I was among many who felt betrayed. I knew nothing of the back-channel disagreements between Toronto and Anaheim and I took a risk in defending the Blessing at the church I served. MacArthur and Hanegraaff followers called a meeting and I was forced to defend my orthodoxy.

---

9. Loren, "The Legacy of a Humble Hero," *Charisma*, 10/31/2007.

10. Beverley, "Vineyard Severs Ties with 'Toronto Blessing' Church," *Christianity Today*, 1/8/1996.

11. Hunter, "Letter from Todd Hunter on the TAV/AVC Separation, on behalf of the John Wimber and the AVC Board," 12/13/1995.

Wimber died of a massive stroke the following year and it seemed like his association dropped off the face of the Earth. As Julia Loren wrote: "Many believed that the Vineyard movement would not survive after Wimber died in 1997 . . . Indeed, the group of churches have struggled against the ebb tide of Wimber's legacy."[12]

I now see the decision's wisdom. The Vineyard stayed in what its leaders call "the radical middle" while others veered off the rails. To their credit, Toronto's directors repeatedly downplayed the spectacular manifestations. I heard the assurances each time when I was there: No one need laugh or cry or fall or bark or chirp. But, like it or not, the bizarre behavior became spirituality's measuring rod in the wider Toronto penumbra. Something was amiss with anyone abandoned in spiritual sobriety, so you'd better shriek or whelp or weep or writhe or laugh lest you were slapped with that dread label, "Hard To Receive."

Meanwhile, that Latter-Rain psyche reared its whack-a-mole head again as the informal Apostolic-Prophetic movement gelled ("apostle" and "apostolic" replaced "prophet" and "prophetic" as the in-vogue gifts). Apostle-Prophets often breezed through a given region and predicted that great end-times revival, so let's retreat into our intercessory prayer closets until the coming of the "new breed," or the "forerunners." Evangelism, outreach, church planting, and social action are forever delayed as participants coil inward under the banners of intercession and intimacy—and we'll slip a wedding ring on the GOP as we unearth Democratic demons, witchcraft, and the "Jezebel Spirit."

A gulf now unglued the Vineyard from such unnecessary peculiarity and, I would later discover, the association thrived even as its popularity among charismatics faded. Those who called themselves "spirit filled" zeroed-in on the apostles and prophets.

The superstars shriveled in the limelight.

FOUR GLIMPSES OF UGLINESS

First, there were those never-fulfilled promises of revival, so enticing to those of us living in spiritually sterile New England. Predictions said the land of Jonathan Edwards would teem and lead North America in another Great Awakening. I admit I was thrilled—when I first heard the preachers (they really do possess a persuasive power that I can only describe as "spiritual"). But, eventually, I couldn't help but ask: Where's the revival? My doubts swelled when I traveled to a Canadian conference and saw a tape of

12. Loren, "The Legacy of a Humble Hero."

one of these celebrity prophets. Don't worry, she said, *Canada* would suddenly teem and lead North America into another Great Awakening. I felt like the proud owner of five vats of snake oil. The seers were proclaiming the same message wherever they traveled—and we were lapping it up and abandoning 2 Timothy 4:2 (we minister in season and out of season).

Second, the mask fell off Paul Cain, who was lifted high as the most insightful holy man. True, his sermons meandered between islands of incomplete sentences, but his words of knowledge probed deep. Even international leaders coveted his insights—and he was so devoted he opted for life-long celibacy. Or so we were told—until October of 2004. Rick Joyner, Jack Deere, and Mike Bickle released a statement with the following key sentences: "In February 2004, we were made aware that Paul had become an alcoholic. In April 2004, we confronted Paul with evidence that he had been recently involved in homosexual activity." And: "Paul admitted to these sinful practices and was placed under discipline, agreeing to a process of restoration which the three of us would oversee." But: "Paul has resisted this process and has continued in his sin. Therefore, after having exhausted the first two steps of Matthew 18:15–17, we now have a responsibility to bring this before the church. Our sincere hope remains to see Paul restored. We are deeply committed to Galatians 6:1, which states, 'Brethren, even if a man is caught in any trespass, you who are spiritual, restore such a one in a spirit of gentleness; each one looking to yourself, lest you too be tempted.'" A telling paragraph: "We apologize to the body of Christ for our lack of discernment in promoting Paul's ministry while he had these significant strongholds in his life. We failed to see them until this year."[13]

I appreciated the apology, but wondered: What else have these esteemed prophets missed? Joyner, especially, claims a vast prophetic domain. He supposedly sees God's calling on certain individuals; he's seen that elusive revival, complete with children laying hands on the sick and emptying hospitals; he denies human-induced climate change; he discerns the Jezebel Spirit. Yet he failed to detect Cain's serious character maladies (whatever our view of homosexual activity, it was clear that Cain lied even as he called us to deeper integrity). Dare we ask: "If you were blind to Cain, can you not be blind in other instances—like the impending awakening?"

Third, there was the lamentable 2008 Lakeland Revival.

A rising star, Todd Bentley of Canada, began a scheduled week-long visit to Ignited Church in Lakeland, Florida, in April of that year. Bentley,

---

13. Found at https://www.truthforfree.com/html/article_paulcainscandal.html. Joyner, Deere, and Bickle had written another version of their letter, which Joyner did some editing touch ups and published. The two versions say roughly the same thing; so, as a matter of courtesy, I'm quoting from the edited version.

the founder of Fresh Fire Ministries, stayed for over four months as thousands flocked from all over the world. Many more viewed internet broadcasts on GOD TV, a YouTube-like site for the charismatically-inclined. But something wasn't quite right. His prayer method was, to say the least, unusual. He shouted "Bam, Bam!" and allegedly pushed supplicants until they fell—supposedly under the Spirit's power. And he described visions of an angel named "Emma."

Emma?

Nevertheless, three apostolic leaders—Che Ahn of Pasadena, California; Bill Johnson of Redding, California; and John Arnott—teamed up publicly in Lakeland to declare Bentley's "apostolic alignment." Wagner, who participated in the ceremony, said the commissioning "represents a powerful transaction taking place in the invisible world." He gave us a glance into his spirituality, which holds that God grants his apostles edict-delivering power: "I take the apostolic authority that God has given me, and I decree to Todd Bentley your power will increase. Your authority will increase. Your favor will increase. Your influence will increase. Your revelation will increase. I also decree that a new supernatural strength will flow through this ministry."[14]

Everything crashed in August of that year. Bentley separated from his wife, resigned, and admitted to an inappropriate, unconsummated relationship with a female staff member. He eventually divorced and remarried. Ignited Church tried to sustain the revival until October, when it finally shut the effort down. In 2020, a panel of several prestigious charismatic leaders found no change in Bentley's morality and concluded: "We state our theological opinion and can say with one voice that, without a doubt, Todd is not qualified to serve in leadership or ministry today."[15]

Fourth, there were the disastrous 2008 election-year forecasts. In the summer, a prophet named Chuck Pierce alerted the world to the supposed insights of his friend Dutch Sheets, with whom he traveled on a 50-state tour and made pronouncements on God's destiny for each state. Sheets' web site says he heads "an apostolic, prophetic and teaching ministry throughout American (sic) and the world."

According to Pierce, his friend watched GOP presidential candidate John McCain introduce his newly-selected vice-presidential nominee, Alaska Governor Sarah Palin, to applauding Republican convention delegates. Sheets wept with joy "even though he knew nothing about her," then

---

14. Geivett & Pivet, *A New Apostolic Reformation?* Location 3971 in Kindle edition.

15. Brown, "Official Statement from the Leadership Panel on Todd Bentley," *ASK-DrBrown*, 1/20/2020.

"asked the Lord what the significance of this 44-year-old woman was." The clock read 4:44, which prompted him to look up Ezekiel 44:4. The New King James translation reads: "He brought me by way of the north gate to the front of the temple; so I looked, and behold, the glory of the LORD filled the house of the LORD, and I fell on my face.'"[16]

Ezekiel's "north gate" apparently represented Alaska, which Pierce and Sheets had previously proclaimed "the alpha and omega state." Things "begin and end" there because its islands straddle the International Date Line. It all added up: "Alaska is a gateway for the Ancient of Days to come into the nation." Sheets decreed that Palin would enter the White House—after all, the US had "come into a new level of alignment [with] the Lord and His purposes"—and he declared she'd be "the Margaret Thatcher of America" upon her presidential ascendance. McCain, it seems, would die in office.[17]

McCain was not elected, did not die in office, and Palin did not ascend.

Sheets' response: God will judge those in the Church "who aligned themselves with abortion forces" and Christian leaders "who refused to take a stand for fear of losing people, money, and tax-exempt status" and "those . . . who voted money over morality—a potential raise for better health insurance over the life of the baby." America could expect "more economic woes," more violence, disease, death, natural disasters, and war ("perhaps on our own soil"). The Supreme Court would be stacked against the sanctity of life. There'd be "more rejection of God's laws" and more theft of "our godly heritage," which would "perpetuate a cycle of even more judgment."[18]

Sheets was wrong on almost every count. The economy backed away from the precipice and recovered; violent crime has largely dropped (with a brief spike from 2014–2016);[19] the Supreme Court's balance remained the same; no war was fought on American soil (unless we include the "war on drugs" or another vague conflict), and the abortion rates continued to decline since their mid-1980s peak.[20] And please note that a Republican Supreme Court appointee wrote the majority opinion on the decision legalizing homosexual marriage.

---

16. Neaveill, "The Insane Theocracy of Conservative Christians," 9/10/2008.
17. Neaveill, "The Insane Theocracy of Conservative Christians," 9/10/2008.
18. Sheets, "Response to the 2008 Presidential Election," 12/21/2008.
19. Gramlich, "Five Facts About Crime in the US," *Pew Research Center*, 1/30/2018.

20. See the graphs in Kasprack's Factcheck article, "Abortion Rates Fall During Democratic Presidencies and Rise During Republican Ones," 11/11/2016. Kasprack debunks the myth that the rates fall during Democratic administrations and rise during Republican administrations, but there's been an overall downward trend over the decades.

Weather forecasters with such a track record would be laughed out of the room, but the apostolic-prophetic networks didn't even blink. They sojourned on to 2012 and predicted Mitt Romney's victory. Sheets finally chose the victor in 2016 and said this of Trump: "I personally believe he has changed. I also believe God has gripped his heart for the nation, and is in the process of further transforming Mr. Trump. God has certainly allowed him to be humbled. Of course, the statements made by Trump on the video released from 2005 were despicable. However, if we reject him because of the sins of his past, we would also have to reject Abraham, King David, Rahab, 'the woman at the well', Mary Magdalene—all adulterers in their unrighteous past. And don't forget murderers like the Apostle Paul. A lot of formerly despicable people will be in Heaven! And a lot of them, by the way, became great leaders and champions for God. Some changed the world."[21]

He spared Clinton and Obama of such charity and graciousness. And, incidentally, the Bible doesn't mention Mary Magdalene's alleged adultery.

A TIME TO THINK

Confusion and circular thinking broods over dialogues in the apostolic-prophetic movement. It's like we're talking through vapor in a cacophonous fog. Consider all those revival-around-the-next-bend assurances. Doubts inevitably meet the reply, "The prophets don't know the revival's timing." After all, the Old Testament writers didn't see the gaps between their pronouncements and the Messiah's arrival—and questioning the pope-like apostle-prophet is tantamount to a lack of faith. The incongruity: we've swapped faith in Jesus, which thrives in the darkest prison, for awe of a human leader. We've even idolized revival.

We inevitably feel sapped.

More confusion mounts when we express reservations about the apostle-prophet's insight. I experienced this. My growing skepticism met the reply: "You no longer believe in prophesy," which defied my point. I doubted this particular movement, not God's capacity to grant the gift. I've seen genuine prophets. They've read my mail, to use the lingo in these circles. Interestingly, those prophets—who really were gifted—prefaced their comments with phrases like, "Take this for what it's worth . . .," or, "weigh this . . ." or, "I may be wrong but . . ." They see themselves as humble brothers and sisters in the overall *Jesus* Movement—not a prophetic movement or apostolic movement or any other human-centered endeavor. They were

---

21. Sheets, "Election 2016: The Christian's Dilemma," *Elijah List*, 10/21/2016.

accountable to a multi-gifted body and focused on the great apostle and high priest whom we confess (see Hebrews 3:1).

The cloud thickens even more with elusive definitions: What, exactly, is a prophet? Or an apostle? The terms, "prophet" and "prophetic" are used in at least two distinct ways among modern-day American Christians. Many Mainline Protestants—United Methodists, Episcopalians, members of the Presbyterian Church USA, the United Church of Christ, and others—employ "prophetic" when they speak truth to power and advocate justice. The terminology can become code for left-wing political opinions. To Pentecostals and charismatics, a prophet is a seer who discerns God's will at a specific scene. In my opinion, both models are rooted in the Bible. Both can be abused. Perhaps we should remember this: A prophet is primarily a forth-teller, with foretelling an important subsidiary role. The Hebrew prophets reminded Israel of God's clear commandments, obedience's rewards, and disobedience's penalties.

The word "apostle" stirs even more bewilderment because the New Testament writers employed it in several ways, the most recognized of which referred to Jesus's twelve closest followers, often just called "the Twelve" (see Matthew 26:14, 20, 47; Mark 4:10; 6:7; 9:35; Luke 8:1; 9:1; 18:31; John 6:67; 20:24).[22] Interpreters across the theological spectrum agree that such apostles no longer exist. But other apostles are mentioned (see the Greek phraseology in 2 Corinthians 8:23; Philippians 2:25; and Romans 16:7). The word itself means "sent one" and referred to an envoy or representative or messenger or ambassador, so there isn't necessarily any authority latent in the term. Of course, words evolve and mean different things in different arenas, and that may have been the case in the first-century church: Apostles, it seems to me, were the foundation-laying entrepreneurs. They established ministries from the ground up, like today's church planters and missionaries.

Which means they've never left us. Think of Saints Patrick, Augustine, Francis, and Ignatius of Loyola—and Martin Luther, John Calvin, and John Wesley. Or John Wimber or Timothy Keller or Heidi Baker. Think of all the anonymous church planters and founders of urban soup kitchens. They're no longer called apostles because language changes and they couldn't care less about titles. They're there nevertheless.

But I'm afraid that sucks the wind out of the apostolic-prophetic movement and the New Apostolic Reformation. The offices can't be restored because it was never dissolved—and, to add insult to injury, they're

---

22. General Council of the Assemblies of God, position paper, "Apostles and Prophets," 2.

no more important than any other ministry. An apostle is not necessarily an almighty commander. The ancients used another term for that, "epískopos," which we translate as bishop. Many Catholic-phobic Protestants don't like that word, so they invoke "executive minister" or "district superintendent" or "area supervisor" just to keep the pontiff at bay.

Whatever.

So I give a bland reply when someone claims the apostolic title: "Great. Go to it and have fun." Calls for my submission meet a blank stare. Pastors are plagued with would-be bosses: church board members, area ministers, district superintendents, bishops, and major donors threatening pledge reductions. We don't need more chiefs.

The wind stills even more with an observation from an Assemblies of God position paper: "It is instructive," it says, "that nowhere in the New Testament after the replacement of Judas is any attention given to a so-called apostolic succession." Elders function as leaders along with apostles in Acts 11:30; 15:2; and 16:4. The Pastoral Epistles (1 and 2 Timothy and Titus) reveal concern over the appointment of qualified overseers and deacons (1 Timothy 3:1–12; Titus 1:3–9) but none for apostles. This doesn't render apostles extinct. Perhaps those very elders would commission entrepreneurial types for ministry to unevangelized communities, much like the Antioch church sent Barnabas and Saul (see Acts 13:1–3). But leadership hinged on the elder-epískopos-pastor (interchangeable titles in the middle of the first century; the episkopos would be lifted to a higher niche a few decades later).[23]

It seems the original apostles didn't exalt the apostolic office and saw no need for a New Apostolic Reformation.

SOFTENING THE BLOW

Obviously, I'm critical of what I call the apostolic-prophetic movement or the New Apostolic Reformation. I'm not alone. Thoughtful critics abound both inside and outside Pentecostal-charismatic Christianity.

But I must temper my disapproval as I remember the alliance's nebulous nature. Some evaluators, such as R. Douglas Geivete and Holly Pivec, lumped a cluster of ministries into a NAR monolith. Leaders of Kansas City's International House of Prayer expressed surprise and explained why on their web site: they're friendly to NAR advocates but do not embrace

---

23. General Council of the Assemblies of God, position paper, "Apostles and Prophets," 4–5.

all their views.[24] Roger Olson was more on the mark when he called it "an affinity." Secular faultfinders glanced at some of the political views and immediately blared warnings of a conspiratorial American Taliban, citing the "seven mountain mandate," which calls Christians to influence society in education, religion, family, business, government-military, arts-entertainment, and media. Most NAR leaders are not advocating a hostile, theocratic takeover of those spheres, and such paranoia only cements the faithful in their media-is-out-to-get-us convictions.[25]

And I think of the joyful and godly Heidi Baker. She's drawn censure for her association with apostolic-prophetic ministries, but she doesn't brandish an apostolic title, which is intriguing: She, along with her husband, Rolland, moved to Mozambique in 1995 and ministered to orphans and abandoned children. The ministry grew after she was healed of tuberculosis in Toronto. She radiates God's love and holiness. Often, she breaks into dance. Few would guess she has a Ph.D.

She and Rolland really are apostles in the sense I've discussed. There are many like her, and we critics must remember that in our unease.

BACK TO BASICS

Still, the unease is legitimate. The apostolic-prophetic movement can, potentially, drain Pentecostal-charismatic Christianity of its golden contribution: God avails his gifts to all. Remember William Seymour, the African American preacher who initiated the racially-integrated Azusa Street meetings. He was one of eight children of emancipated slaves, reared in Louisiana's poverty. He prayed with a shoe box over his head so no one would see him. He wanted everyone focusing on God.

Will these contemporary apostle-prophets remember that visual paradigm? Will they entertain the possibility that they're unwittingly drawing their followers into an intimidating, human-centered faith, a faith that implies we can only reach the Holy Spirit through ecclesiastical super-heroes?

These supposed seers would be dismissed in any other undertaking. Their forecasted revival has not materialized in North America or Europe; their decrees thudded on Lakeland's floor; their election predictions proved less accurate than standard opinion surveys; dire prophecies of God's post-November doom did not unfold; key leaders—such as Bob Jones and Paul

---

24. IHOP leaders addressed the issue on their web site: "What Is IHOPKC stance on the New Apostolic Reformation?"

25. Wagner tried to clarify the "Seven Mountains Mandate" in his *Fresh Air* interview.

Cain—committed immorality even while they summoned us to holy living. And the biblical foundation for their apostle-centered leadership model is precarious at best.

Which is a relief. Such monocracies inevitably foster domineering, coercive leaders who wield intimidation.

It's time we heed the warnings of the General Council of the Assembly of God. It condemned the Latter Rain movement in the 1940's and did not endorse the apostolic-prophetic movement. Let's follow the Vineyard. Let's get back on track, even if it means less glitz, glitter, and glamour.

4

The Faustian Pact

THE EARTHQUAKE FINALLY STRUCK in 2016. The walls tumbled and the intimidation factor was exposed. Polls said eighty-one percent of self-identified white evangelicals voted for a certified bully, with Donald Trump pouring contempt on Mexicans, Muslims, women, the handicapped, and anyone else deemed foreign. Those polls would be revealed as misleading (about 40 percent of self-identified white evangelicals didn't vote for president in 2016); but it remains true that a huge swath of evangelicals would embrace a president who flaunted his marriage vows, dumped his wives, tweeted churlish broadsides teeming with ignorance, and displayed little knowledge of the Bible or the US Constitution. Perhaps enthusiasm for Trump was not surprising, since many of those self-identified white evangelicals had drifted far from traditional Christian teaching.

The circle seemed complete. Classic evangelicalism, which established itself on traditional doctrine and a personal relationship with Christ, was fading into cultural evangelicalism, rooted in vague notions of a Christian America with its flag-draped Bible. It's as if an intimidation-infected movement was a moth to an intimidator's flame. The movement's participants were blind to the irony, but most others were not. Many biblically-centered Christians were hunting for a new name. Indeed, Beth Moore would tweet in December, 2019: "Evangelicalism as we knew it, as imperfect as it was because we are imperfect, passed away in 2016. History will plant its grave marker there. A disclaimer is always necessary these days so I'll add this: This, of course, is not to say conservative Christianity passed away."

An acknowledgment: The Democrats heroically strove to alienate the evangelical voter. They slid from President Bill Clinton's safe-legal-rare abortion terminology—along with his recognition that abortion is difficult issue upon which well-meaning individuals disagree—to their 2016 call to repeal the Hyde amendment, which bars federal abortion funding except when the mother's life is endangered. They also offered us a candidate who failed to inspire. But repealing the Hyde Amendment would have mandated Congressional approval, and evangelicals could have registered their protests by voting for third party candidates and revving up their political involvement.

Alas, such subtleties are lost in today's polarized storm.

A WARNING SHOT

The Trumpian takeover was all the more devastating because the pendulum actually swung to hope at times. Classic evangelicals—usually politically reticent—rose up and warned of the candidate's dangers.

The pendulum first swung to despair.

Troubling omens loomed before the campaign shifted into high gear. One surfaced on July 17, 2015, a day after Muhammad Youssef Abdulalazeez killed four US Marines and a Navy sailor in Chattanooga, Tennessee. A Marine recruiter and a police officer were also wounded before Abdulalazeez was shot dead in a fire fight. Franklin Graham, the CEO of the Billy Graham Evangelistic Association and Samaritan's Purse, replied with a Facebook paragraph anticipating Trump's worst rhetoric:

> . . . We are under attack by Muslims at home and abroad. We should stop all immigration of Muslims to the U.S. until this threat with Islam has been settled. Every Muslim that comes into this country has the potential to be radicalized—and they do their killing to honor their religion and Muhammad. During World War 2, we didn't allow Japanese to immigrate to America, nor did we allow Germans. Why are we allowing Muslims now? Do you agree? Let your Congressman know that we've got to put a stop to this and close the flood gates. Pray for the men and women who serve this nation in uniform, that God would protect them.

Jaws dropped across the land. The US government negotiates with countries, not with religions. It's legally obligated to protect its six million

Muslim residents, 77% of whom are citizens. And how do we break the news to Turkey, a NATO ally? Do we slip a note under its embassy door? And what about persecuted Sufis, whom militant Islamists view as heretics, and oppressed Burmese Muslims fleeing nationalistic Buddhists? What of Christian refugees escaping intimidation in Muslim countries? They look and talk like Turks and Palestinians and Syrians and Iraqis—because they are. Jenny Yang of World Relief said Graham's proposal would thwart resettlement efforts.[1] Perhaps we could admit those pledging their Christianity, but that would open the door to Islamic militants: They believe they can lie for God and would check "Christian" on the necessary forms. Perhaps most important, how did this proposal help Graham's first imperative, which is supposedly evangelism? How does this glorify Christ? Surely his gentlemanly father would have weighed the fall-out and declined to post it (sorry, Franklin, but you occupy your position because of your heritage; the comparison is inevitable).

The issue dwindled to a footnote until December of that year, when Trump called for banning all foreign Muslims. It was a scandalous suggestion, made all the more outrageous because an evangelical leader anticipated him.

Another omen appeared in 2014 and again in 2016. A study and a follow-up showed that self-identified evangelicals displayed little knowledge of traditional Christian teaching: 71% believed Jesus was a created being (as opposed to God incarnate); 56% thought the Holy Spirit was an impersonal force (as opposed to the third person of the Holy Trinity); and only 52% agreed that sex outside traditional marriage is a sin (Christianity has always advocated sexual abstinence for unmarried people).[2]

Evangelicalism's instability walked onto the stage with some high-profile Trump endorsements, led by Liberty University President Jerry Falwell, Junior, in January of 2016: "In my opinion, Donald Trump lives the life of loving and helping others as Jesus taught in the great commandment."[3] Pat Robertson told the real estate mogul in February: "You inspire us all."[4] Robert Jeffress, pastor of the First Baptist Church of Dallas, gave Trump this incredible review: "We need a strong leader and problem-solver, hence many

---

1. Morgan, "Franklin Graham's Call to End Muslim Immigration Could Backfire," *Christianity Today*, 7/24/2016.

2. See Block, "Evangelicals, Heresy, and Scripture Alone," *First Things*, 10/4/2016; Arakaki, "Evangelicalism Falling to Pieces?" *Orthodox Reformed Bridge*, 10/20/2016; Ligonier Ministries & Lifeway Research, *The State of American Theology Study, 2016*

3. Bruenig, "Jerry Falwell, Jr., Endorses Donald Trump for President," *New Republic: Minutes, News & Notes*, 12/5/2016.

4. Richter, "Pat Robertson to Trump: 'You Inspire Us All'" *Newsmax*, 2/24/2016.

Christians are open to a more secular candidate."[5] Opinion polls pointed to Trump's popularity among southern evangelicals during the primaries—even while authentic Christians were candidates. John Kasich was one.

OUT OF THE SILENCE

That's when classic evangelicals abandoned their usual a-politicism. The pendulum swung to hope.

Russell Moore, president of the Southern Baptist Ethics and Religious Liberty Commission, said in February of 2016 that he no longer described himself as an evangelical in everyday conversation because "the word itself is at the moment subverting the gospel of Jesus Christ." He marveled at a ballooning double standard: "I have watched as some of these who gave stem-winding speeches about 'character' in office during the Clinton administration now minimize the spewing of profanities in campaign speeches, race-baiting and courting white supremacists, boasting of adulterous affairs, debauching public morality and justice through the casino and pornography industries."[6] Editors of the largely conservative Christian Post, an on-line religious journal, urged their readers to "back away" from the candidate: "Trump is a misogynist and philanderer. He demeans women and minorities. His preferred forms of communication are insults, obscenities and untruths. While Christians have been guilty of all of these, we, unlike Trump, acknowledge our sins, ask for forgiveness and seek restitution with the aid of the Holy Spirit and our community of believers."[7] Max Lucado was appalled at Trump's lack of "decency"[8] and Peter Wehner warned that backing Trump is a "huge mistake."[9] Richard Land, Southern Evangelical Seminary's president and Moore's predecessor, wrote in *Charisma News* on March 3: ". . . it must be said, before it is too late, that whatever the problems may be, Donald Trump is not the answer. I fear that the millions of Americans who are putting their trust in Mr. Trump will be bitterly disillusioned if he were to obtain the nation's highest office."[10] James Dobson said he could support neither Trump nor Florida Senator Marco Rubio because they acquiesced to the US Supreme Court ruling legalizing gay marriage.

  5. Horton, "The Theology of Donald Trump," *Christianity Today*, 3/16/2016.
  6. Moore, "Why This Election Makes Me Hate The Word 'evangelical,'" *The Washington Post*, 2/29/2016.
  7. Christian Post Editors, "Donald Trump Is a Scam," 2/20/2016.
  8. Lucado, "Trump doesn't pass the decency test," *Washington Post*, 2/26/2016.
  9. Wehner, "What Wouldn't Jesus Do?," *The New York Times*, 3/1/2016.
  10. Land, "Donald Trump is a Scam," *Charisma News*, 3/3/2016.

Theologian Michael Horton chimed in. He traced Trump's meager spirituality to the feel-good theology of Norman Vincent Peale (1898–1993), author of *The Power of Positive Thinking* and pastor of New York City's Marble Collegiate Church for 52 years, which Trump's family attended. Peale drew criticism for thinning the Gospel with bromides and pop psychology. Horton cited Jeffress' approval of Trump and said: "Vague on doctrine, infiltrated by consumerism and a sentimental moralism intent on helping us all 'become a better you,' and sort of interested in 'family values' as long as they don't interfere with our own family breakdowns, many cultural evangelicals are tired of losing the culture wars. They want a winner—'a strong leader.' I'm hardly the first to point out that it's the stuff of which demagogues are made." He also saw the room's elephant: "Trump reveals, in short, that for many evangelicals, the word *evangelical* means something that many increasingly do not recognize as properly Christian, much less evangelical."[11]

Perhaps this would be the draw-the-line-in-the sand year, the year when classic evangelicals finally rose up and asserted themselves.

But the pendulum swung back. Trump was nominated and some evangelical leaders fell in line, especially after he wooed them by appointing a 24-member Evangelical Advisory Board. He declared: "I have such tremendous respect and admiration for this group and I look forward to continuing to talk about the issues important to Evangelicals, and all Americans, and the common-sense solutions I will implement when I am president."[12]

Land joined the board and eventually endorsed Trump as the lesser of two evils, employing apocalyptic terms in his portrayal of Hillary Clinton: " . . . the financial corruption of the Clintons is a truly lethal threat to American democratic government."[13] Dobson also enrolled on the board and flipped: "Mr. Trump has been unwavering in his commitment to issues that are important to evangelicals such as myself. In particular, I have been heartened by his pledge to appoint conservative Supreme Court justices, preserve religious liberty, rebuild the military, and defend the sanctity of human life. On the issue of abortion, I choose not to evaluate him based on his past position but rather on what he says are his current convictions. I believe God can change the hearts and minds of people and I celebrate when they support principles of righteousness."[14]

11. Horton, "The Theology of Donald Trump"

12. Peters & Woolley, "Press Release—Trump Campaign Announces Evangelical Executive Advisory Board," *The American Presidency Project*, 6/21/2016.

13. Eschliman, "Dr. Richard Land Makes Surprising Announcement About Donald Trump," *Charisma Caucus*, 8/24/2016.

14. Dobson, "Dr. James Dobson Encdorses Donald Trump For President of the United States," *Religion News Service*, 7/22/2016.

All of which was tediously predictable. Prying the supposedly pro-family Dobson from the Republican Party would be too much to ask, especially since he holds one of the patents on the anti-Clinton slime machine. The same is true of Land. Don't bother inquiring, "Would you support a philandering Democrat whom fact-checkers give a 78-percent falsehood rating?"[15]

But the real shocker was Wayne Grudem's July 28th essay, "Why Voting For Donald Trump is a Morally Good Choice."[16] Grudem is a professor of theology and biblical studies at Phoenix Seminary and author of the popular and helpful *Systematic Theology*, which actually describes theological issues in readable English. He made no qualms about his tea party leanings in another book, *Politics*, but he's usually thoughtful.

Not now. How "Trump" and "morally" can meet in the same sentence defies the imagination. Apparently, everything hinged on Supreme Court appointees: Grudem believed Trump would fulfill his pledge and appoint conservatives while Clinton would choose left-wingers. "The nation would no longer be ruled by the people and their elected representatives, but by unelected, unaccountable, activist judges who would dictate from the bench about whatever they were pleased to decree. And there would be nothing in our system of government that anyone could do to stop them. That is why this election is not just about Hillary Clinton. It is about defeating the far left liberal agenda that any Democratic nominee would champion."

Grudem seemed deaf to Trump's many anti-democracy statements and his serial lying. He made this incredible statement:

> (Trump) is egotistical, bombastic, and brash. He often lacks nuance in his statements. Sometimes he blurts out mistaken ideas (such as bombing the families of terrorists) that he later must abandon. He insults people. He can be vindictive when people attack him. He has been slow to disown and rebuke the wrongful words and actions of some angry fringe supporters. He has been married three times and claims to have been unfaithful in his marriages. These are certainly flaws, but I don't think they are disqualifying flaws in this election.[17]

A question: Would Grudem tolerate such "flaws" in a Democrat?

---

15. CiHizza, "A fact checker looked into 158 things Donald Trump said. 78 percent were false," *The Washington Post*, 7/1/2016.

16. Grudem, "Why Voting For Donald Trump Is A Morally Good Choice," *Townhall*, 7/28/2016.

17. Grudem, "Why Voting For Donald Trump Is A Morally Good Choice," *Townhall*, 7/28/2016.

But not all were swayed. Russell Moore remained critical, as did Lucado. Albert Mohler, the conservative president of Southern Baptist Seminary, also noticed the Clinton irony: "If I were to support, much less endorse, Donald Trump for president, I would actually have to go back and apologize to former President Bill Clinton. I would have to admit that my commentary on his scandals was wrong. I don't believe I was. I don't believe evangelicals who stood united that time were wrong."[18]

The denunciations came apace. Michael Gerson kept writing anti-Trump columns; Ronald Sider wrote in *Christian Ethics Today* under the banner, "The Most Important Election in My Lifetime," ". . . the (Republican) candidate . . . lies, nurtures racism, violates our history of religious freedom for all, supports torture and appeals to much of the worst in our society." He listed many other failings, then concluded: "I believe a Donald Trump presidency would seriously undermine much of what is best in American history, culture, and life. Christian voters, I hope, will help us avoid that tragedy."[19] The Christian Post listed several conservative evangelical thinkers who took aim at Grudem. Thomas J. Kidd and Erick Erickson criticized him in separate articles.

But perhaps the most touching was Amy Gannett's "Why Evangelicals Are Losing An Entire Generation." She wrote in behalf of her fellow millennials:

> Over the last several months, I have lost respect for the Republican party, and I honestly thought that would be the biggest tragedy of this election. But the disappointing truth is this: I'm losing faith in evangelicals. And this is frightening. I am an evangelical. I hold to evangelical theology. I have attended not one, but two evangelical schools. But I fear that we're going to lose an entire generation because of the actions, words, and teachings of some evangelicals. Including Wayne Grudem.

She said Grudem erected an arbitrary "hierarchy of morals" in which traditional family values outrank racism, justice, and poverty.[20]

I thought of myself after I read Grudem's essay. I thought of my spiritual birth in the 1970's and my renewal in the 1980's. I thought of Henry and Ockenga and all those powerful minds. I thought of John Wimber and the Vineyard and all the liberation I experienced under the evangelical brand. I was loath to abandon the term. But I was forced to admit it: By 2016,

---

18. Mohler, "Character In Leadership: Does It Still Matter?" *Albert Mohler*, 6/24/2016.

19. Sider, "The Most Important Election in My Lifetime," *Christian Ethics Today*, 4.

20. Gannett, "Why Evangelicals Are Losing An Entire Generation," *Word & Craft*, 7/29/2016.

the "evangelical" label had walked the path of "awful," which once meant "filled with awe" but is now synonymous with "terrible." The word no longer conveyed a more open-minded back-to-the-Bible Christian; it didn't even convey a happy but simple-minded believer. It now conjured images of a spiteful, racist intimidator.

I began to think Russell Moore was right: "the word itself is at the moment subverting the gospel of Jesus Christ." The pendulum now seemed jammed in despair.

But then it was freed. Evangelical women rose up after one of the creepiest weeks in US political history. Trump did not hide in shame after a ten-year-old *Access Hollywood* video surfaced in which he bragged about his license to be a total letch. Instead, he stalked his Democratic opponent in a live television debate and threatened to send her to jail if elected. It was unnerving. Bob Schieffer said it best: "This is the United States of America. People keep asking me if I've ever seen anything like this. I keep saying no and I hope to God I don't see another campaign like this one. America can do better than what we have seen tonight. This was just disgraceful."[21]

The gutter week dragged on as women came forward with allegations of groping while Trump claimed he was battling a world-wide conspiracy.

Many GOP Brahmans wavered. Some withdrew their announcements but later returned to the fold. Incredibly, Religious Right leaders still fired their Trumpian guns. Ralph Reed said this: "I've listened to the tape. My view is that people of faith are voting for president on issues like who will defend and protect unborn life, defund Planned Parenthood, grow the economy and create jobs, oppose the Iran nuclear deal. I think a 10-year-old tape of a private conversation with a TV talk show host ranks pretty low on their hierarchy of their concerns."[22] Jerry Falwell, Jr., James Dobson, Tony Perkins, and Pat Robertson also still cleaved to Trump. Grudem nobly rescinded his endorsement on October 9—but then emulated Republican politicians when he restored it on the 19th.

Which prompted the women's outcry. Beth Moore, an a-political and popular Houston-based Bible teacher, tweeted: "Try to absorb how acceptable the disesteem and objectifying of women has been when some Christian leaders don't think it's that big a deal." Another Beth Moore tweet: "I'm one among many women sexually abused, misused, stared down, heckled, talked naughty to. Like we liked it. We didn't. We're tired of it." Sarah Groves,

---

21. Bob Schieffer BLASTS Second Presidential Debate "Disgraceful" https://www.youtube.com/watch?v=tTvbLdBlUbI, accessed November 25, 2016.

22. Stetzer, "What Is Going On Inside Trump's Religious Advisory Panel," *Christianity Today, The Exchange*, 10/10/2016.

a Christian singer and Dove Award winner, commended Moore.[23] Katelyn Beaty and Jen Hatmaker added their declarations and Kay Warren threw in her twitter voice (to her credit, Hatmaker had blasted Trump early on).[24] The Moody Bible Network's Julie Roys wrote: "I honestly don't know what makes me more sick. Listening to Trump brag about groping women or listening to my fellow evangelicals defend him."[25]

These women were not alone. Andy Crouch editorialized in *Christianity Today*: "Enthusiasm for a candidate like Trump gives our neighbors ample reason to doubt that we believe Jesus is Lord. They see that some of us are so self-interested, and so self-protective, that we will ally ourselves with someone who violates all that is sacred to us—in hope, almost certainly a vain hope given his mendacity and record of betrayal, that his rule will save us."[26] And there were petitions: Over 20,000 signed *A Declaration by American Evangelicals Concerning Donald Trump* while some Liberty University students launched a protest drive against their president's Trumpian enthusiasm.

Breathe in the fresh air. The moderates had abandoned their usual quiescence and the Religious Right was forced to defend itself, leaving us with only one burning question: Would the moderates stay at the microphone after Hillary Clinton's inevitable victory?

But, of course, Clinton's victory evaporated despite her plurality of 2.9 million votes.

AFTERMATH

Much can be analyzed: The Democrats lost their former Rust Belt constituency in the blur of identification politics; Hillary Clinton fed a she's-untrustworthy narrative when she bobbed and weaved around e-mail allegations; the public lapped up fake news; Clinton's party was so enamored with spread sheets that it failed to feel America's pulse. And, of course, Vladimir Putin loomed over e-mail hacks and planted fake news.

All that's fodder for political pundits. I'm focusing on the stark reality: Trump's victory exposed the metastasis eating away at white American

---

23. DuBois, "Powerful Evangelical Women Split From Male Church Leaders To Slam Trump," *The Daily Beast*, 10/10/2016.

24. Beaty, "'No more': Evangelical women are done with Donald Trump and his misogyny," *The Washington Post*, 10/13/2016.

25. Roys, "Evangelical Trump Defenders Are Destroying The Church's Witness," *The Christian Post*, 10/11/2016.

26. Crouch, "Speak Truth To Trump," *Christianity Today*, 10/10/2016.

evangelicals. According to Robert Jones, the movement that bewailed President Clinton's moral character now dismissed Trump's as irrelevant. In 2011, only 30% of white evangelicals said candidates can erect barriers between their private and public lives. That figure sky-rocketed to 72% in 2016. "In a shocking reversal," he wrote, "white evangelicals have gone from being the *least* likely to the *most* likely group to agree that a candidate's personal immorality has no bearing on his performance in public office. Today, in fact, they are more likely than Americans who claim no religious affiliation at all to say such a moral bifurcation is possible."[27]

The "hypocrite" allegation now sticks. The politest response to Gary Bauer's assessment (Trump's triumph was a "victory for values voters") is awkward silence.[28] Bauer is like the well-meaning grandfather who makes embarrassing statements before passing the mashed potatoes. What morals, grandpa? And pop the bubble surrounding you. Don't you see the perils of a dangerous president? To white evangelicals dwelling in the same bubble: Are you blind to the *earned* contempt from the rest of America? The nation's skeptics no longer laugh at our supposed primitive piety and naivete. Witness Tess Rafferty's message: "You voted for Trump—I am tired of trying to see things your way while you sit in your holier-than-thou churches/white power meetups, refusing to see things mine. You voted for the same candidate as the KKK. You voted for the candidate endorsed by the KKK. For the rest of your life, you have to know that you voted the same way as the KKK. Does that feel good to you? Here's a hint—it really shouldn't, especially if you call yourself a Christian."[29]

Such are the reactions when we claim belief in Christ but vote for an intimidation-heaving billionaire.

None of this was lost on seventy global evangelical leaders in a post-election conference call. "There is massive disappointment within Christian communities in most of central and eastern Europe, [and] concern about the loss of credibility of Christian witness—especially the credibility of evangelicals," said Croatian scholar and Gordon Conwell professor Peter Kuzmic. Grace Matthews of the Lausanne Movement also saw harm in the Christian witness. Greg Thompson, a scholar at the University of Virginia's Institute of Advanced Studies in Culture, said: "This is an extraordinary

---

27. Jones, "Donald Trump and the Transformation of White Evangelicals," 11/19/2016.

28. Bauer, "You Won!," *Gary Bauer Today . . .* , 11/9/2016.

29. Velez, "Aftermath 2016: Tess Raffrty's hard-hitting statement on the election of Trump," *Daily Kos*, 11/17/2016.

moment when Americans—many, many conservative Christian Americans—have said, 'We don't really care about personal virtue that much.'"[30]

Tony Compollo and Shane Claiborne viewed evangelicalism's post-election landscape and concluded: A "Jesus-centered faith needs a new name. Christians have retired outdated labels before," such as fundamentalism. They advocated "Red Letter Christians," referencing the red quotes of Christ in some translations.[31] That doesn't sit well with me. There were no quotation marks in the original languages and, more important, all Scripture is God's Word. But their overall point rang true: "Evangelical" no longer brings us to the image of Jesus.

Katelyn Beaty, a former *Christianity Today* editor, expressed what many felt. She spoke of her post-election heartache: "Wednesday greeted me as it did half the voting population, with waves of grief. But since then, the grief has turned into a more complex emotion — something like soul abandonment. After an election in which 81 percent of my white coreligionists supported Trump, the faith that has been my home for 20 years seems foreign, even hostile." She remembered her spiritual birth at thirteen, her youth group involvement, her attendance at prayer rallies outside her high school. "Evangelicalism exposed me to authentic kindness, service and awe. It taught me that love of God and neighbor was a force in the world and, indeed, could heal its deep brokenness." She defended the evangelical label into her adulthood, noting how the faithful sheltered refugees and rescued sex trafficking victims. "To myself, I said that evangelical was about theology, not politics, and at Christianity Today, we always transcended political divides to root the gospel in a local church and not a voting bloc." She thought the Religious Right was a "relic of railing radio preachers and big-haired moral scandals." None of her evangelical friends were Trump enthusiasts. "Many of us were troubled by the other candidate, to be sure. But, as so many wise evangelical leaders had noted, electing Trump would seriously harm our already fragile democracy and undo the church's witness, and I believed the white evangelical community would take heed." The day after Trump's victory, "I woke up to an evangelical family I no longer resembled." She remembered that the word, evangelical, is rooted in the Greek word for "good news." No political candidate can embody such good news, but "when evangelical starts to sound like very bad news for very many Americans, it has drifted far from its roots. A prophetic consensus has emerged that U.S. evangelicalism is irreducibly linked with white privilege."

30. Shellnutt, "Global Evangelical Leaders: Trump's Win Will Harm the Church's Witness," *Christianity Today: Gleanings*, 11/15/2016.

31. Compolo and Claiborne, "The Evangelicalism of Old White Men Is Dead," *The New York Times*, 11/30/2016.

Her heart still beat with the faith birthed in her as a teenager, but "this time, this election, I can't defend my people. I barely recognize them." She thought of the embarrassing "off-beat uncle" who moans about threats to his freedom and pervasive political correctness. "You sympathize with him on many points. But when he starts in with racial slurs and sexist jokes and complaints about 'illegals,' at some point you have to get up and leave the table."[32]

Beaty spoke for me. I was stunned. My theology has not substantially changed. Now, more than ever, I affirm Christ's Lordship and the need for a personal relationship with him. I affirm the Bible's authority. I affirm the Trinity. I affirm the time-honored creeds. I affirm so-called "traditional family values" and the Bible's call to social and environmental justice. I affirm that God justifies us by faith and sanctifies us through the Holy Spirit. I affirm that the New Testament portrays the radical, counter-cultural, Christ-centered life. I'm wary of innovative theologies jettisoning time-tested doctrines.

Those affirmations once easily fell under the evangelical label, so it was a label I gladly bore. But it's been peeled off me and other classic evangelicals and pasted onto adherents of a spiteful civil religion. Such a religion fears the worst from Clinton, gives Trump the benefit of the doubt, forgives Republicans while holding Democrats to a high moral standard, and now caters to moral relativism and unorthodox doctrines. In short, today's cultural evangelicalism is now anti-evangelical. Like it or not, America now thinks of cultural evangelicals whenever the e-word is mentioned. Thus, the label is a grotesque caricature of its former self.

So what to do? My tentative solution: I'll keep calling myself an evangelical among the dwindling remnant who understands the term's historic meaning, but I'm trying on other labels for the general public—just to see how they fit. Maybe I'll follow Thomas Oden's lead and describe myself as a "Classic Christian," which invites us to the consensus of the faith's early theologians and creeds and offers links with Catholics and Eastern Orthodox Christians.

Meanwhile, I cannot help but mourn a tragic loss: A word that once conveyed spiritual vigor is now aligned with a politician who shamelessly nurtures and exploits intimidation.

---

32. Beaty, "I was an evangelical magazine editor, but now I can't defend my evangelical community," *Washington Post*, 11/14/2016.

PART II

Prestigious Harassers

How Evangelical Intimidation Became Respectable

5

Cracks in the Foundation

THE QUESTION OF THE hour: Who signed the bully permits so intimidators could grab power, canonize political opinions, and troll their opponents with unfounded accusations?

The answers, I'm sure, are complex and the stuff of Ph.D. dissertations, but two hidden keys open the door to the obvious. First, it must be said: Mainline church leaders are not innocent. Many laid the foundation for partisan religion when they uncritically tilted toward the fist-pumping left, peppering their meetings with so many cliches you'd swear the Gospels were written by Mohandas Gandhi, Robert F. Kennedy, Betty Friedan, and Edna St. Vincent Millay. And please rehearse all your sentences so they're shorn of political incorrectness.

Second, there were cracks in the foundation of the mid-century evangelical resurgence, in which leaders such as Carl Henry, Harold Ockenga, and Billy Graham invited fundamentalists out of their cultural and intellectual cocoons. The term "evangelical" signaled sophistication, elegance, even urbanity. Maybe some of the Presbyterians saw Broadway plays and sipped Chablis. But did they really free themselves from intimidating fundamentalism? I'm now not sure. In fact, I've grown more convinced that the seeds for "Fox Evangelicalism," as Amy Sullivan characterizes today's religious concoction,[1] were unwittingly planted at the movement's advent. Most mid-century leaders never fully wrenched themselves from fundamentalism's grip. They lionized the austere Old Princeton theologians of the previous century—Archibald Alexander, Charles Hodge, and BB Warfield—and the founders of Westminster Theological Seminary in Glenside, Pennsylvania, which pits John Calvin's 16th-century Geneva against 17th-century Puritan England as rivals for the Heavenly Land award. The school's influence spreads far beyond its campus. One of its founding professors, Cornelius Van Til (1895-1987), flaunted an especially ingenious brand of thick-headedness. It's as if his wagging finger still lives.

Just to throw in confusion: Many Westminster teachers are thoughtful even as they pay Van Til homage. They've infused evangelical academia with scholarly rigor.

CALVINISM'S HEIGHTS . . .

I've needled Calvinism, so I'll drop back and give it some deference.

To repeat, Calvinism deserves a hearing. Its thinkers legitimately trace their origins back to Augustine of Hippo (AD 353-430), arguably Western Christianity's most influential theologian after the Apostle Paul. His influence wends its way through Catholic Augustinian and Dominican orders and Protestantism's two most famous fathers, Martin Luther (1483-1546) of Wittenberg, Germany, and Calvin himself (1509-1564), who gave the theology systematic shape in his *Institutes of the Christian Religion*, one of the Reformation's paramount documents.

There's more to Calvinism than its deterministic reading on predestination, much of it commendable, but discussion usually freezes on that subject.

Geneva evolved into a Protestant Mecca under Calvin and his successor, Theodore Beza (1519-1605). Some British divines exported the theology to their native land and were tagged as Puritans. The label stuck. Richard Baxter, John Owen, and Richard Sibbs were among the many English notables—although Baxter, along with others, followed Moses Amyrald's subtly different teaching on election. John Knox spread the word in Scotland and the 17th-century New England settlers planted the theology in North America. Jonathan Edwards (1703-1758), arguably America's outstanding theologian and leading spokesman for a sweeping revival called the Great Awakening, was thoroughly Calvinist. He was also a Platonist and a mystic,

---

1. Sullivan, "America's New Religion: Fox Evangelicalism," *New York Times*, 12/15/2017.

and he saw nothing wrong with the Awakening's strange manifestations: groaning, crying, shaking, screaming, and falling down.

Full disclosure: Although I don't consider myself a Calvinist, I wouldn't feel slapped if anyone called me "Reformed," a broader theology to which Calvin is a foundational contributor. As I've said, I agree more with Jacob Arminius, the Latinized name of Dutch theologian Jacob Hermanzoon (1560–1609), who walked back from Calvin's determinism and tried to restore the teaching of most early church theologians.[2] John Wesley, Methodism's founder, popularized his theology in 18th-century Britain. Methodism spread like wildfire and Arminianism became America's predominant evangelical theology in the 19th century.

But I understand Calvinism's underpinnings, which hinge on humanity's depravity and God's sovereignty. The depravity comes into view with Adam and Eve's rebellion: The prototypical human couple was made in God's image, which meant both played the role of temple idols on the Earth and represented God in his rulership, holiness and love. They violated their essence and purpose upon their mutiny and devolved into anti-gods and anti-humans, much like my cells become anti-me when they mutate into cancer. We could even argue: The Sovereign Being who spans, rules, and sustains the universe not only has the right to kill off such a "spoiled species," as CS Lewis called us, he's obligated to do so—for the sake of the universe and the world's animals. After all, gardeners wipe out ants and aphids; I seek total annihilation of my malignant cells. Which means, say Calvinists, we can breathe a sigh of relief because, in a wild act of extravagant grace, God selected some of those demon-like beings for salvation and ultimate transformation. He even came to the Earth and died in an atonement limited to those he called. God jettisoned cold reason, which would have trashed us all, and chose the path of mercy.

Augustine, Calvin, and Luther give us keen insights: The universe's story is God's story, not ours. God is transcendent and rules the cosmos. He's an absolute, sovereign King, not a constitutional monarch and not bound to justify himself to us. They didn't blink when they followed the Apostle Paul and saw our aberrance. We're not now in our natural state. We'd look far more like gods and goddesses if we were.

The only question: Is the Augustinian conception of predestination correct? Arminians point to passages either implying or declaring human choice as well as Jesus' death for the "whole world" (some examples: John 1:29; 1 John 2:2; 1 John 4:14). Their solution: Humans are, indeed, just as depraved as the Augustinians said, but the Almighty is even more gracious

---

2. Oden, *The Transforming Power of Grace*, 139–159.

than they saw. God grants prevenient grace to everyone, giving each the ability to say yea or nay to Christ. Those who follow Him are justified if they "continue in (their) faith, established and firm, and do not move from the hope held out in the gospel" (Colossians 1:23). Passages invoking predestination usually refer to groups, not individuals.[3]

I say all that not to convert Calvinists (that involves a much longer argument packed with proof-texts and debate over what biblical predestination actually is, and it's usually a lost cause), but to make the all-important point: Arminians paddle with the Church as a whole, which has always retreated from determinism. In 529, conveners at the Second Council of Orange affirmed human depravity while rejecting the Augustinian outlook. Their words left little room for doubt: "We not only do not believe that any are foreordained to evil by the power of God, but even state with utter abhorrence that if there are those who want to believe so evil a thing, they are anathema." What's more, Philip Melanchthon (1497–1560), Luther's collaborator and Protestantism's first systematic theologian, guided Lutheranism away from his friend on this score. Calvinists often cite the dictums of the Synod of Dort (1618–1619), where Dutch Reformers spurned and imprisoned followers of Arminius, and the Puritan Westminster Confession of Faith (1646); but, again, the Church Universal has agreed to neither Dort nor Westminster. Anglicans as a whole never signed on and Catholic and Eastern Orthodox Christians barely involved themselves in the argument.

Perhaps anyone bucking the tide would adopt humility—especially when they spill gallons of ink proving universal human depravity, which would include themselves.

. . . AND DEPTHS

Many Reformed thinkers are, indeed, gracious. Retired pastor and author Tim Keller is one (I devote a chapter to him); Richard Mouw, president emeritus of Fuller Theological Seminary, is another—and I think of many of my seminary professors. But much of staunch Calvinism snarls with a mean streak and some of its thinkers now patrol like sentries, blowing down straw men right and left. They follow the precedent laid by their forbears, who often sprayed a bewildering array of accusations at Arminians: Arminians are works-righteous (they supposedly say we must earn our way to heaven), antinomian (they're lawless), closet Catholics, Pelagians (alleged followers of Augustine's adversary, Pelagius [cerca 360–418], who didn't believe in Original Sin), and anti-Trinitarian. The Calvinists pick out errant

---

3. Witherington, *The Problem with Evangelical Theology*, 53–80.

pseudo-Arminians as well as America's most famous 19th-century evangelist, the Pelagian-leaning Charles Finney, and hold them aloft as the norm. Old Princeton's academics were especially disparaging.

Arminians replied by labeling Calvinists the "frozen chosen."[4]

Princeton Theological Seminary eventually reorganized and opened up to theological modernism, whereupon old-schoolers led by John Gresham Machen (1881–1937) bolted and established Westminster Theological Seminary in 1929. Westminster possesses Old Princeton's strengths (academic rigor and intellectual scrupulousness) and weaknesses (a halo gleams over Calvin's head and the Westminster Confession is God-breathed). Some of the school's faculty, especially its founders, made a profession of attacking anything failing to measure up to their strict interpretation of Calvinism. Chief among them was Van Til. He articulated his basic assumption in an article blasting the monumental thinking of Swiss theologian Karl Barth (1886–1968): "Only Reformed theology, based upon the doctrine of a really sovereign God, creator of heaven and earth, whose decrees include 'whatsoever comes to pass,' can bring men to a real Entscheidung (decision). Against Barth, as against modern theology which he seeks to oppose, we must once more raise the banner of a sovereign God and of His complete revelation in Scripture."[5]

I long to ask: "Did you just say that?" *Only* Reformed theologians affirm a sovereign God created the universe and inspired the Scriptures? And just how does this strain of Reformed theology, which proclaims a brand of predestination never encoded in an ecumenical creed and rejected by most Christians, compel us "to a real decision"? Everything's foreordained. The Westminster Confession says so: "God from all eternity, did, by the most wise and holy counsel of His own will, freely, and unchangeably ordain whatsover comes to pass" (see III:1). Salvific decisions are above our pay grade.

But such was Van Til's launching pad, and all who disagreed were fair game to unfair, inaccurate, and unbridled attack.

His feud with Barth serves as a prime example. Barth guided Protestantism away from 19th-century Liberalism, which gutted Christianity of its inspired Scriptures, the miraculous, the Trinity, Original Sin, and the resurrection. Theological Liberals whittled Jesus to a mere exemplary human. The Bible, trimmed of miracles and unsavory brood-of-viper comments,

---

4. Olson surveys Calvinist mischaracterization of Arminian theology in *Arminian Theology, Myths and Realities*.
5. Van Til, "Karl Barth on Creation," *The Presbyterian Guardian*, 2/27/1937, 205.

contained profound teaching for generous souls craving the "fatherhood of God and the brotherhood of man."[6] We're not bad. We just need education.

But then came World War One's slaughter. Supposedly kindhearted, civilized Europeans lobbed poison gas, lit flame throwers, and braved machine-gun fire over lunar-like landscapes so they could bayonet each other. Optimistic theological liberalism lay on life support. Barth pulled the plug with his commentary on Romans, the first edition of which was published in 1918. He constantly urged in later writings: "back to Luther; back to Calvin" and insisted on an orthodox view of the Trinity (he didn't call the Father, Son, and Holy Spirit "persons" but, instead, described them as three co-existing, eternal, and self-aware "modes of being;" this was not heretical modalism, as his *Church Dogmatics* makes clear[7]). Barth would eventually be lumped with theologians such as Emil Brunner, Dietrich Bonhoeffer, and others and tagged "Neo-Orthodox."

Evangelicals faced a choice: Was Barth a friend or foe? True, his view on Scripture didn't align with theirs (Barth said the biblical authors were God's ordained "witnesses" to His Word) and he was fuzzy about universalism (as was Gregory of Nyssa, a revered fourth-century church father), but surely he veered the theological world in the right direction—and kudos for standing up to Hitler and the Nazified "German Christians" in 1934: He wrote the Barman Declaration while living in Germany and was exiled. Perhaps friendly dialogue and genuine debate might tilt him and others into unvarnished orthodoxy.

Van Til would have none of it. Barth was the enemy, a veritable wolf in sheep's clothing. He saw Barth through the prism of presuppositionalism, which says the (Reformed) Christian faith lays the only platform for rational thought. Thus, there was little room for reasoned debate with non-Reformed thinkers due to mutually exclusive assumptions. In practice, this meant Van Til wouldn't really argue. He'd second guess his opponent's hidden presuppositions—often unknown to the adversary himself—and attack them. He convinced himself that Barth's theology was dangerous because it was anchored in the pivotal but enigmatic philosophy of Immanuel Kant (1724–1894), who seemingly viewed organized religion skeptically; second, Barth supposedly believed that God's activity never intersected with history, which quashed the possibility of Christ's physical resurrection. Which is intriguing. Bernard Ramm (1916–1992) spent a year studying under Barth and explored all thirteen volumes of the great theologian's unfinished

---

6. This phrase sums up the thinking of German theologian A. Harnack, discussed in Dunn, *Christianity in the Making*, Volume 1, 38.

7. See Allen, *Karl Barth's Church Dogmatics: An Introduction and Reader*, 30–41.

Church Dogmatics. Says Ramm: "(Barth's) theology has its own twists and turns, but I found him defending the ancient Christology of the church fathers as well their doctrine of the trinity. His statement on the authority of Scripture would satisfy the most stringent orthodox theologian. He defends the virgin birth, the bodily resurrection, and the cosmic, visible return of Christ."[8] Ramm also comments: "Evangelicals are quick to identify Barth as a Kantian and so dismiss him as one who corrupts biblical faith with Kantian philosophy. This charge is surprising, for in the approximately forty times Barth cites Kant in the *Church Dogmatics*, he is uniformly criticizing Kant."[9]

Van Til summed up his views in the 1946 publication of *The New Modernism: An Appraisal of the Theology of Barth and Brunner*. The reviews have been pouring in ever since. T.F. Torrance, a British Barth sympathizer, said this: " . . . there is in fact no attempt made to form a fair judgment of the views which are so bitterly criticized from end to end of this volume. . ."[10] One normally cool-headed internet observer characterized the book as "comically grotesque."[11]

Yet Van Til stubbornly clung to his misreading despite all evidence, violating the fundamental rule shared by scholars and respectable journalists: Get your facts right. Lewes Smedes was once a Van Til student and admirer ("I was mesmerized for one semester by the boldness of Van Til's thinking"), but then saw his pig-headedness:

> Van Til was convinced that if anyone's assumptions about God are wrong, she cannot be trusted even when she says that she believes the gospel truth about Jesus. He wrote a book called *The New Modernism* in which he contended that the star theologian of the century, Karl Barth, was a modernist because, in Van Til's view, he denied that Jesus was God in human form and denied as well that he had risen from the dead. The hitch was that Barth had affirmed these things over and over and, in fact, was largely to be credited with bringing the gospel back into the churches of Europe. But Van Til said that even if Barth shouted from the tower of St. Peter's that Jesus was the Son of God, he could not believe what he was saying. His philosophical presuppositions would not let him.

---

8. Ramm, *After Fundamentalism*, 11–12.
9. Ramm, *After Fundamentalism*, 34.
10. Torrance, "Review of The New Modernism," 148..
11. Myers, "The Worst Book Ever Written on Karl Barth," *Faith and Theology*, 7/20/2005.

> Several years later, after I had finished my graduate studies in Amsterdam, I had occasion to put the question to Barth himself: "Sir, if you will permit me an absurd anachronism, let us suppose that a journalist carried a camera into Jesus' tomb about eight o'clock on Easter Sunday morning and took pictures of every inch of the tomb, what would have showed up on his film?" Barth sighed. This again? He had been asked questions like this by every skeptical evangelical who got within shouting distance of him. But he was patient: "He would have gotten nothing but pictures of an empty tomb. Jesus was not there. He had walked out of the tomb early that morning."
>
> I told Van Til about this conversation. His answer was, for me, a final exhibition of intellectual futility. "Smedes," he said, "you have studied philosophy, you should know that Barth *cannot* believe that Jesus rose from the dead." Cannot! Not merely does not, but *cannot* believe what he said he believed. Conversation finished.[12]

Van Til's straw-man arguments roared past intellectual honesty and veered into raw bullying. Eventually, Barth—no stranger to grouchy assertiveness himself—stopped replying to the constant bombardment from him and his followers, including Carl Henry. He wrote to Geoffrey Bromily: "Please excuse me and please try to understand that I cannot and will not answer the questions these people put." He explained:

> Such a discussion would have to rest on the primary presupposition that those who ask the questions have read, learned, and pondered the many things I have already said and written about these matters. They have obviously not done this, but have ignored the many hundreds of pages in the *Church Dogmatics* where they might at least have found out—not necessarily under the headings of history, universalism, etc. —where I really stand and do not stand. From that point they could have gone on to pose further questions.
>
> I sincerely respect the seriousness with which a man like [G.C.] Berkouwer studies me and then makes his criticisms. I can then answer him in detail. But I cannot respect the questions of these people from *Christianity Today*, for they do not focus on the reasons for my statements but on certain foolishly drawn deductions from them. Their questions are thus superficial.

---

12. . Smedes, *My God and I*, 68–69.

The decisive point, however, is this. The second presupposition of a fruitful discussion between them and me would have to be that we are able to talk on a common plane. But these people have already had their so-called orthodoxy for a long time. They are closed to anything else, they will cling to it at all costs, and they can adopt toward me only the role of prosecuting attorneys, trying to establish whether what I represent agrees or disagrees with their orthodoxy, in which I for my part have no interest! None of their questions leaves me with the impression that they want to seek with me the truth that is greater than us all. They take the stance of those who happily possess it already and who hope to enhance their happiness by succeeding in proving to themselves and the world that I do not share this happiness. Indeed they have long since decided and publicly proclaimed that I am a heretic, possibly (van Til) the worst heretic of all time. So be it! But they should not expect me to take the trouble to give them the satisfaction of offering explanations which they will simply use to confirm the judgment they have already passed on me.[13]

Van Til's failure to see nuance in his for-me-or-against-me world even rocked his staunchly Calvinist ghetto. He went after fellow presuppositionalist Gordon Clark (1902–1985), whom Henry hailed as "one of the profoundest evangelical Protestant philosophers of our time" and whom Ronald Nash praised as "one of the greatest thinkers of our century."[14]

Not according to Van Til, who rallied many of his Westminster colleagues in a move to defrock Clark in 1944 after the latter was ordained in their small denomination, The Orthodox Presbyterian Church. Clark's crime: He believed God's knowledge and humanity's knowledge are quantitatively but not qualitatively different. Since all truth is one truth, God's knowledge and humanity's knowledge coincide when each apprehends the same reality. We humans can never know anything exhaustively because we're not omniscient, so our grasp of truth will forever remain a mole hill compared with God's Everest—even unto eternity.

Van Til said Clark had it all wrong: There's an insurmountable wall between God's knowledge and our knowledge, rendering God quantitatively and qualitatively incomprehensible. We only know things as fallen

---

13. Barth, "Letter 3: To Geoffrey W. Bromiley, Pasadena, CA.," *Barth's Letters*, 342–343.

14. Robbins, "An Introduction to Gordon H. Clark," *The Trinity Review*, July-August, 1993, 1.

creatures; God knows things as a holy creator. We can only know God via Scriptural analogy and we can never understand as God understands.[15]

Most believers respond, "Yawn."

This debate is all very interesting (I guess), but hardly the stuff of heresy trials. I doubt Spanish Inquisitors would even mumble in their afternoon siestas. But Van Til and his Westminster colleagues went full-bore even after Clark's vindication. They drummed up charges against one of his defenders, so the wearied Clark faction left the denomination.

Van Til's bullying would remain a single enclave's historical curiosity but for one thing: Some of evangelicalism's most influential leaders sat in his classroom. Harold Ockenga graduated from Westminster in 1930; Edward John Carnell, Fuller Theological Seminary's second president, earned two Westminster degrees and once admired Van Til (although he would differ with him later); Francis Schaeffer attended Westminster before transferring to an even more conservative school and popularized Van Til's misinterpretation of Barth.

Again, there's the snag stymieing cartoonish caricature: Westminster's influence is far from thoroughly evil. The gracious Harvie Conn (1933–1999) taught there. Renowned historian George Marsden is an alumnus. Timothy Keller, the pastor of Manhattan's Redeemer Presbyterian Church, earned his Doctor of Ministry Degree under Conn's supervision and served on the seminary's faculty. Meredith Klein (1922–2007) split his time between Westminster's western campus (which eventually established its independence), Gordon-Conwell, and other seminaries. He wrote orthodox yet innovative interpretations of the Genesis creation narratives. Westminster graduates often earn doctorates and populate seminary faculties. Most, like Emeritus Gordon-Conwell Professor Richard Lovelace, follow Ockenga's lead and embrace a more irenic Reformed theology.

So there's a Jeckyl-and-Hyde Westminster, with the much-admired Van Til revealing Mr. Hyde.

Mr. Hyde dampens evangelical academia. An assumption—usually unspoken—hovers in the background: The old Princetonian Calvinists reign on a pedestal and keep an eye on those bratty Arminians. That's astonishing, since the 19th-century Princetonians rarely came out to play during the revivals. They remained the party's somber wall flowers. Fortunately, thinkers at Asbury Theological Seminary and Methodists like the late Thomas Oden hold the Calvinists at bay—and theologian Roger Olson needles them from his perch at Baylor University's George W. Truett Theological Seminary.

15. Van Till's anti-Clark complaint is found here: "The Text of a Complaint," *Notes on Gordon H. Clark*, http://notes-on-gordon-h-clark.blogspot.ca/2014/07/document-1944-text-of-complaint.html.

But more troubling is the normalization of Van Til's ignore-the-facts belligerence among influential evangelical intellects, which eventually fomented an atmosphere of fear and fostered aggressive neo-fundamentalism. The irenicism of Ockenga, Henry, and Graham would fade into the husky cantankerousness of Harold Lindsell, another leader in the mid-twentieth century evangelical resurgence. He'd write an incendiary book in the mid-1970's that launched a needless "battle for the Bible," pitting evangelicals against themselves.

We'll turn to that mostly forgotten but decisive chapter in American evangelical history.

6

A Battle Between Allies

THERE WAS SUCH PROMISE. Van Til's bulldog style could have faded into the ether. Perhaps historians would tag him and his clan "Reformed fundamentalists" or even tip their hats with the complimentary, "proto-evangelical." After all, they influenced the leaders of the mid-century evangelical resurgence.

Lamentably, the growling spirit didn't dissipate. It merely plowed underground and simmered until its 1976 public eruption in Harold Lindsell's combative *The Battle for the Bible*. Theologian Roger Olson says the book spun the evangelical world sharp right, "too conservative for its own good."[1] Gone were the days of thoughtful dialogue.

The tragic irony: Lindsell had hailed the birth of neo-evangelicalism and extolled Ockenga. But warnings lurked beneath polite critiques. Henry said his spirit was "too hurried."[2] in an otherwise complimentary job recommendation; George Marsden euphemistically described him as a "debater."[3]

Lindsell worried that some of his tribe's theologians and scholars slid down the slippery slope when they questioned the time-honored doctrine

---

1. Olson, "When did evangelicalism start to go wrong (right)?," *My Arminian Theological Musings*, 5/11/2001.

2. Henry, *Confessions of a Theologian*, 294.

3. Marsden, *Reforming Fundamentalism*, 280.

of biblical inerrancy. Most were cautious and held to the Bible's overall truthfulness, authority, and unity; they simply wondered if "inerrant" did justice to the holy book's literary expanse, which embraces narrative, poetry, apocalyptic writings, and generalized wisdom statements. Like it or not, inerrancy now conveyed wooden literalism, which blinds us to poetry's symbolism and binds us to literalistic interpretations of Genesis 1. More adventuresome scholars stirred the pot when they fixated on relatively small biblical variances and insisted on outright errancy. All doubters asked: Would different phraseology preserve reverence for the Bible's authority and truthfulness? Perhaps they could borrow from Wesleyan and pietist evangelicals, who either qualified the word or didn't use it all. Witness the Nazarenes: The "Old and New Testament Scriptures, given by plenary inspiration, contain all truth necessary to faith and Christian living." Or the Free Methodists: "The Bible is God's Written Word, uniquely inspired by the Holy Spirit. It bears unerring witness to Jesus Christ, the living Word. As attested by the early church and subsequent councils, it is the trustworthy record of God's revelation, completely truthful in all it affirms. It has been faithfully preserved and proves itself true in human experience." Or The Evangelical Covenant Church, which shies from creeds but "adheres to the affirmations of the Protestant Reformation regarding the Bible. It confesses that the Holy Scripture, the Old and the New Testament, is the Word of God and the only perfect rule for faith, doctrine, and conduct. It affirms the historic confessions of the Christian Church, particularly the Apostles' Creed and the Nicene Creed, while emphasizing the sovereignty of the Word of God over all creedal interpretations."

The debate motivated Fuller Theological Seminary to swap "infallibility" (no fallacy) for inerrancy (no mistakes) in 1970. Its statement of faith on Scripture once read: "The books which form the canon of the Old and New Testaments as originally given are plenarily inspired and free from all error in the whole and in the part. These books constitute the written word of God, the only infallible rule of faith and practice." It now read: "Scripture is an essential part and trustworthy record of [God's] self-disclosure. All the books of the Old and New Testaments, given by divine inspiration, are the written word of God, the only infallible rule of faith and practice. They are to be interpreted according to their context and purpose and in reverent obedience to the Lord who speaks through them in living power."

Was Fuller easing onto the path of Britain's more moderate evangelicals? Or was it marching into modernism's theological quicksand? The peril was obvious to Lindsell: "A great battle rages today around biblical infallibility among evangelicals. To ignore the battle is perilous. To come to grips with it is necessary. To fail to speak is more than cowardice; it is sinful."⁴ A book advertisement quoted his call to arms: "More and more evangelicals are propagating the view that the Bible has errors in it." It was time to "read it and act!"⁵

The gloves were off. Absolute inerrantists were pitted against flexible inerrantists and infallibilists. As Olson says, Lindsell "declared that no one can be authentically evangelical without affirming inerrancy. Few outside separatistic fundamentalist circles had said that before Lindsell."⁶ The smoke from this needless "battle for the Bible" still hangs in the air.

For the record, the statement of faith for one of my ordaining denominations affirms inerrancy and I have no trouble signing it. I know what the term means. It allows for rounded numbers and incomplete genealogies and hyperbole and differing interpretations. The word describes my approach to the Bible far more than not, but I also see much more agreement than disagreement between inerrantists and prudent, orthodox non-inerrantists. Of course there was room for caution and pointed debate in the 1970's, but a little perspective shows there was no reason for a fear-stoking "battle."

PERSPECTIVE

Inerrancy's critics often claim the concept is new. It is not. The late Donald Bloesch (1928–2010), no fan of the word's use today, cited references to *inerrabilis* in esteemed theologians such as Augustine, Thomas Aquinas and Duns Scotus. John Wycliffe, a fourteenth-century British Bible translator, used *infallibilis*.⁷ Lindsell is right on this score: infallibility was synonymous with inerrancy in that era.

But bear in mind: The plethora of evangelical statements on inerrancy apply to the Bible's so-called "original autographs." The scroll on which Paul's scribe wrote the Book of Romans was supposedly free of mistakes, as was the case with all other biblical books. Those scrolls eventually fed family hearths or were burned in fear of persecutors or rotted in the desert wind. They don't exist anymore. They were copied and re-copied through the centuries by hand, which meant some errors sneaked into the manuscripts. But we needn't panic. Textual critics have ferreted the vast majority of scribal additions and subtractions and brought us within a hair's breadth

---

4. Lindsell, *Battle For The Bible*, 26.

5. Dayton, "The Battle for the Bible: Renewing the Inerrancy Debate, *Christian Centiury*, 11/10/1976, 976.

6. Olson, "When did evangelicalism start to go wrong (right)?"

7. Bloesch, *Holy Scripture: Revelation, Inspiration, & Interpretation*, 34–35.

of the original writings. Wonder of wonders: Christianity's major doctrines survive and thrive. This means, however, that the entire inerrancy battle embroils us in a fight over non-existent documents. Our current Bible is infallible at best (it tells no lies).

Which should give us pause. If strict inerrancy—as opposed to overall accuracy, truthfulness, and authority—is so important to God, why didn't our Lord preserve some of the original inerrant manuscripts? We're left with mere accuracy, and that doesn't seem to bother God. Perhaps we have an intriguing glimpse into the Lord's mind: Maybe God isn't an obsessive neat freak or a detail-focused engineer. Maybe he's a holistic artist. Chains break at their weakest links; beautiful paintings remain masterpieces despite a corner's tiny smudge.

Perhaps all can back off from the vitriolic edge, especially since the doctrine was never encoded in a historic ecumenical creed.

We'll relax even more when we peer deeper into the minds of our venerated Protestant icons, who did not confuse inerrancy with scientific precision. Martin Luther drifted especially far even while he invoked error-free terminology. He suggested lopping off the books of Hebrews, James, Jude, and Revelation from the canon. His advice to worried strugglers over minor differences in Scriptural accounts of the same event: "Let this pass." He didn't lose sleep over whether the cock crowed once or twice at Peter's betrayal of Jesus (compare and contrast Matthew 26:34—along with Luke 22:34 and John 13:38—to Mark 14:30).

Protestantism's early thinkers dwelled in a world of corrupt Renaissance popes and off-with-your head kings, where all affirmed The Prince of Peace's death and resurrection while they burned each other at the stake. The ground of controversy gradually shifted over the centuries and, in the era of the 19th-century Princeton theologians, the backdrop was Newtonian science. Charles Hodge (1797–1878) took his cue from its disciplines. Precision and objectivity were all the rage: The Bible displays the raw facts, said Hodge; theologians sift through the facts like sample-culling researchers, labeling and classifying their way to data-informed theories.[8] We needn't laugh him off. He was articulating an analogy with an eye toward German theological modernists, who employed science's language as they sliced out the miracles from the Scriptures, leaving us with nothing more than high ethics. God dwindled to a professorial wraith on the Rhine. If Hodge lived today, he'd say those scholars dwelled in a world of alternative facts. Genuine scientists don't adjust the data to conform to their theories; likewise the theologian. The Bible informs theology, not vice versa.

---

8. Olson, *The Journey of Modern Theology*, 228–231.

It's not a bad analogy if we understand Hodge's context.

His son, Archibald Alexander, also taught at Princeton and teamed up with B.B. Warfield in a landmark 1881 essay. Key quotes seem to bring inerrancy more in line with scientific scrupulousness, making the younger Hodge and Warfield fundamentalist heroes and non-inerrantist villains. One quote: "The writers of this article are sincerely convinced of the perfect soundness of the great Catholic doctrine of Biblical Inspiration, i.e., that the Scriptures not only contain, but ARE THE WORD OF GOD, and hence that all their elements and all their affirmations are absolutely errorless, and binding the faith and obedience of men," (emphasis in the original text).[9] Another: ". . . the historical faith of the Church has always been, that all the affirmations of Scripture of all kinds, whether of spiritual doctrine or duty, or of physical or historical fact, or of psychological or of philosophical principle, are without any error, when the ipsissima verba of the original autographs are ascertained and interpreted in their natural and intended sense."[10]

Other quotes reveal subtlety: "It must be remembered that it is not claimed that the Scriptures any more than their authors are omniscient. They were not designed to teach philosophy, science, or human history as such. They were not designed to furnish an infallible system of speculative theology. The record itself furnishes evidence that the writers were in large measure dependent on sources and methods in themselves fallible; and that their personal knowledge and judgments were in many matters hesitating and defective, or even wrong."[11]

Warfield made allowances for evolution's possibility.

Civility remained even while the Princetonians honed inerrancy's parameters. For example, an 1873 meeting of the world-wide Evangelical Alliance featured a floor debate in which The Rev. James McCosh, President of the College of New Jersey (now Princeton), attempted to reconcile Darwinism with the Bible. Pointed objections arose, of course—especially from the venerable Charles Hodge—but few questioned McCosh's orthodoxy.[12] Even *The Fundamentals*, ninety essays published from 1910–1915, often cited as foundational to the fundamentalist movement, featured an offering from Scottish theologian James Orr. Orr was not an inerrantist.

The Fundamentals, incidentally, merely called Christians back to their basic doctrines and actually heaved intellectual heft. They're not a bad read.

---

9. Hodge and Warfield, "Inspiration," 237.
10. Hodge and Warfield, "Inspiration," 238.
11. Hodge and Warfield, "Inspiration," 238.
12. Marsden, *Fundamentalism and American Culture*, 18–19.

Things devolved after America declared war on Germany in 1917. Most in the growing fundamentalist movement had opposed American involvement. They were far from alone, but paranoia engulfed the nation after the declaration. Some theological modernists claimed that premillennialism, which prevailed among fundamentalists and foretold of a dim future until Christ's literal thousand-year reign, denied human responsibility and played into Germany's hands. Shirley Jackson Case, Professor of Early Church History at the University of Chicago's Divinity School, leveled severe and unfounded accusations against premillennialists: "Two thousand dollars a week is being spent to spread the doctrine . . . Where the money comes from is unknown, but there is a strong suspicion that it emanates from German sources. In my belief the fund would be a profitable field for government investigation." *The Christian Century* attacked premillennialism in a series of 21 articles.[13]

Fundamentalists responded that the fault for Germany's atrocities lay with its nation's theological modernists, which meant that modernism was bringing civilization to its collapse. They cited Carl Gustav Adolf von Harnack (1851–1930), one of Liberalism's major proponents, who had a hand in writing the Kaiser's wartime speeches.

The hostility and militancy only burned hotter in the early 1920's, when fundamentalists—especially among Presbyterians—spurred a series of anti-liberal heresy trials. They actually had the numbers for the floor votes, but the modernists often outflanked them when final decisions were referred to study committees—where, predictably, they silently died.

It all came to a head in May of 1925 in the small town of Dayton, Tennessee, and the Monkey Trial. The fundamentalists won a technical victory but lost in the public mind. Columnist H.L Mencken licked his chops: The trial "serves notice on the country that Neanderthal man is organizing in these forlorn backwaters of the land, led by a fanatic, rid of sense and devoid of conscience. Tennessee, challenging him too timorously and too late, now sees its courts converted into camp meetings and its Bill of Rights made a mock of by its sworn officers of the law. There are other States that had better look to their arsenals before the Hun is at their gates."[14]

Mencken, supposedly, was the advocate of liberal open-mindedness.

Princeton Seminary soon reorganized and John Gresham Machen, its leading conservative scholar, established Westminster and allied himself with the fundamentalists, although he was neither dispensationalist nor premillennialist. Fundamentalism mutated into a raucous caricature of its

---

13. Marsden, *Fundamentalism and American Culture*, 147–148.
14. Mencken, "Journalist H.L. Mencken's Account of the Scopes Trial," 1925.

former self as its adherents fled mainline denominations. Even theistic evolution was now anathema. The movement's center of gravity moved south and enmeshed itself with the region's civil religion.

MEANWHILE, ACROSS THE POND . . .

It didn't have to be this way. Our British cousins walked a more civil, nuanced path. It's as if its nation's theologians debated over Sherry while the Yanks threw Bibles at each other's heads.

Historian Mark Noll traced British moderation to several sources. First, most evangelicals were Anglicans and not separatists, which meant all parties knelt before the same communion rail. They kept talking. Second, most of the nation's modernist-leaning scholars rejected German radicalism, which imposed the assumptions of Georg Wilhelm Friedrich Hegel on the Bible and adjusted the Scriptures accordingly (Hegel, 1770–1831, was a German philosopher who postulated that history is an on-going process of synthesizing opposing concepts). British modernists didn't normally dismiss supernatural activity, usually affirmed Christ's historicity and resurrection, and were generally empirical and practical. Third, their fundamentalist countrymen lacked the eloquence and scholarly acumen of the American *Fundamentals* writers. The scarcity of left-wing militancy and right-wing intellectual power paved the path toward moderate civility. Fourth, heavy-handed discipline backfired. Some scholars colored outside the lines at several moments in the mid-to-late 19th century. Church traditionalists responded with adjudication, suspensions, and firings—which, of course, transformed the alleged rebels into martyrs.

Good scholarship saved the day after punishment failed. A trio of Cambridge-educated academics—textual critic Fenton A.J. Hort, commentator B.F. Westcott, and church historian J.B. Lightfoot—led the way down the prudent path. Hort and Westcott published a critical edition of the New Testament in 1881 in which they investigated manuscripts unavailable to the translators of the venerated 17th-century King James Bible. They discovered necessary adjustments, of course, but they also found that the New Testament as a whole stood firm and tall. It was "more thoroughly and more clearly attested than any other volume of the ancient world."[15]

So maybe scholarship's tools could be employed in dismantling the radical theories of F.C. Baur (1792–1860) and Germany's Tubingen school. Baur moved the authorship of Matthew, Mark, and Luke to the latter half of the second century to bolster his theory that the Gospels synthesized

---

15. Noll, *Between Faith and Criticism*, 68.

the allegedly adverse teaching of Peter and Paul, per the Hegel paradigm. Enter Lightfoot. He took aim at a volume written by J.A. Cassels, a Baur fan who questioned Westcott's integrity and argued that supernaturalism harmed religion by overpowering its ethics. Lightfoot defended his friend and showed that the Gospels stood on firmer historical ground than the Germans allowed: All evidence suggested first-century authorship. He also exposed Cassel's paltry scholarship. Cassel's book sales plummeted.

Non-evangelical British scholars accidentally, perhaps, loaned their support when they followed the lead of C.H. Dodd (1884–1973), a giant among New Testament scholars, and retained their relative orthodoxy. Civility reigned and rendered inerrancy less urgent.

This ethos nurtured C.S. Lewis, so influential among today's American evangelicals, and Intervarsity Christian Fellowship, which established Tyndale House on the Cambridge campus. F.F. Bruce and I. Howard Marshal became two dominant evangelical New Testament scholars, respected across the academy's spectrum. Bruce believed more than one author contributed to the Book of Isaiah and Marshall theorized that Paul didn't write the Pastoral epistles (1 and 2 Timothy and Titus). Neither described the Bible as inerrant.

Noll notices another key contrast between the Atlantic's two shores. In America, "a lively vibrant tradition exalting the work of the (Holy) Spirit" grew through the Methodist expansion and the ministry of Charles Finney, Dwight L. Moody, and the Keswick movement. Many Presbyterians and Baptists, however, were suspicious—and they supplied most of evangelicalism's theologians and Bible scholars. The two streams never diverged in Britain. One result: British evangelicals displayed "less concern for rational precision than one group of Americans, and somewhat more interest in learned study than the other."[16]

Britain's evangelicals would be poised to escort Americans out of fundamentalism's caves when the time came.

BACK TO THE USA

The kinder, gentler American fundamentalists emerged during World War 2 and gave themselves the neo-evangelical tag—but, for all their civility and calls for cultural engagement, historian Molly Worthen wondered if they truly left fundamentalism: "Scratch a neo-evangelical and underneath you

---

16. Noll, *Between Faith and Criticism*, 89–90.

would likely find a fundamentalist who still preferred the comforts of purity to the risks of free inquiry and collaboration."[17]

Neo-evangelicalism evolved more than it suddenly materialized. There was the formation of the National Association of Evangelicals in 1942 and Carl Henry's 1947 call for cultural engagement. There was the all-important launch of Fuller Theological Seminary that same year, with radio broadcaster Charles Fuller providing much of the funding and land in Pasadena. Harold Ockenga served as its off-campus president; Billy Graham sat on the board; Carl Henry taught there for the first few years before transferring to Washington DC to edit *Christianity Today*.

Henry and Ockenga personified the new evangelicalism's amalgam and tensions. Neither was a dispensationalist. Both were thoroughly Reformed but saw underlying unity with pentecostals and Arminians (there was that Wesley portrait on Ockenga's wall). Both clung to Warfield-like inerrancy and, true to the great Princeton theologian, advocated interpretative nuance.

Some high-powered minds gravitated to this nascent movement, which was re-defining itself even as it grew. Edward John Carnell (1919–1967)—a Baptist and Fuller's second president—was educated at Wheaton College, Westminster, and Harvard. He wrote several books and would have brandished greater influence had he not suffered a debilitating breakdown. Eventually, he would die from a medication overdose. Bernard Ramm (1916–1992), an American Baptist and Barth student, wrote *The Christian View of Science and Scripture* in 1954. He argued against a young Earth and viewed his mentor favorably. Ramm's sway rivaled Henry's in the early 1970's. Another was Geoffrey W. Bromiley (1915–2009), a British native and ordained Anglican. He taught at Fuller from 1958 to 1987, translated Gerhard Kittel's *Theological Dictionary of the New Testament* (a multi-volume affair conquering a couple shelves in pastor's offices, usually unread), Karl Barth's *Church Dogmatics,* and works by Helmut Thielicke and Jacques Ellul. There was George Eldon Ladd (1911–1982) and Timothy Smith (1924–1997), a Nazarene historian and director of the American Religious History doctoral program at Johns Hopkins University. He wrote *Revivalism and Social Reform* in 1957, which convincingly argued that 19th-century evangelicals led the fight against slavery and poverty. Ralph Martin (1925–2013) was another British New Testament scholar who found his way to Fuller after teaching in his native land. And we cannot pass by Britain's John Stott (1921–2011), whom American evangelicals universally acclaimed—not least because of his gracious godliness.

---

17. Worthen, *Apostles of Reason*, 46.

Behold the opportunity for convergence. Many European Christians were backing out of modernism and following Barth and Brunner—and neither Ramm nor Bromiley read Barth through Van Til's jaded lens.

The influx of British-educated scholars at evangelicalism's American capital, Fuller, exposed the vulnerability of meticulous inerrancy. Many were beginning to agree with Ramm, who examined Protestantism's original creeds in 1970 and found that

> . . . the churches have accepted the *infallibility* of the Bible in all matters of faith and morals. Men may depend on the doctrines and morals of the Bible with complete certitude of their truthfulness. Going yet another step, these churches have accepted the *inerrancy* of all the historical and factual matters of the Scriptures which pertain to matters of faith and morals. This is demanded by the very historical nature of the Biblical revelation, and the plan of redemption . . . What is actually proposed is that the major historical features of the Scriptures are reliable. The Bible is errant in historical, factual, and numerical matters which do not affect its faith and morals . . .

Ramm argued against "a precise literalness to the number usages of the Bible." Such an exercise is an "illustration of an artificial theory of inerrancy." An example of the Bible's lack of scientific precision:

> Some interpreters have insisted that Jesus had to be in the grave exactly seventy-two hours because he said he would be buried for three days and three nights. But the expression "three days and three nights" *must be determined by Jewish usage*. In fact to insist on exactly seventy-two hours creates confusion. If Jesus were crucified on Friday, as practically all competent scholars agree, then the resurrection would not be till late Monday afternoon. In fact, if the burial were in the afternoon-as is stated in the Scriptures that it was before sundown-the resurrection had to be just seventy-two hours later in the afternoon. If one insists that the crucifixion were on Wednesday then the seventy-two hours ends before sundown on Saturday, and not on the Lord's day.[18]

An internal debate over inerrancy brewed at Fuller for years. A committee chaired by theologian Paul Jewett proposed the change in the statement of faith and it was finally adopted in 1970.

Any faculty member not bracing for controversy would have been naive—and some worries were legitimate. Jewett even stretched the seminary's

---

18. Ramm, *Protestant Biblical Interpretation*, 201–202.

new statement when he tried to tackle the Apostle Paul's enigmatic teaching on women in his *Man as Male and Female* (Paul seems egalitarian in Galatians 3:28 and Romans 16:1,7 while chauvinistic in Ephesians 5:22, 1 Timothy 2:12, and 1 Corinthians 14:34). Jewett's conclusion: We must distinguish between Paul the rabbi and Paul the Christian. The rabbi errs; the Christian is enlightened.

Jewett played into fears of a slippery slope—especially since careful exegeses reveals that Paul's supposedly chauvinistic passages aren't so chauvinistic after all.[19]

THE BATTLE IS ON

So Lindsell had a point. He now feared that his beloved institution, which he helped establish, was teetering over the same cliff off of which Princeton fell in the 1920's. Surely this called for a response.

But he ventured far beyond legitimate worry and into the realm of paranoia. *The Battle for the Bible*, which marked inerrancy as a "watershed question"[20] is a case study in Van Tilian bullying. The book lifted historical references out of context, made arguments from silence, and stirred an atmosphere of fear and alienation when the times called for engagement and legitimate, pointed, and civil debate.

No doubt Lindsell was sincere when he said, "However sincerely and however deeply I believe in infallibility, I will not inscribe a diatribe against those who do not agree with my viewpoint."[21] But the book quickly descended into the raw polemics he disclaimed. The Gospel's spread was at stake: "As men retreat from inerrancy, they lose any vital interest in evangelism and missions. Their zeal for finishing the job of world evangelization is replaced by socio-political-economic concerns."[22] He asserts this early: "In dealing with infallibility, there is one pitfall we must avoid by all means. We must not determine the rightness or wrongness of a man's position by his personal life."[23] But, later, he asked: "How is it that when errancy begins to creep in among evangelicals it always is accompanied by moral deceit and ethical failure?"[24]

---

19. See Payne, *Man and Woman, One in Christ*.
20. Lindsell, *The Battle for the Bible*, 23.
21. Lindsell, *The Battle for the Bible*, 24.
22. Lindsell, *The Battle for the Bible*, 206.
23. Lindsell, *The Battle for the Bible*, 206.
24. Lindsell, *The Battle for the Bible*, 206.

Those accusations fly in the face of the facts. Fuller established its School of World Mission even as it shed inerrancy from its statement of faith—and splitting social concerns from evangelism is a 20th-century American fundamentalist idiosyncrasy, not shared with historical evangelicals or evangelicals abroad. Besides, later developments proved Lindsell's assumptions wrong: We're now painfully aware of inerrantist moral slippage.

Lindsell weakened his argument even while he exercised it. He rightly claimed that few throughout Christian history questioned inerrancy. Both heretical Arians and Orthodox upheld the doctrine in their fourth-century dispute over Christ's nature; Pelagius and Augustine assumed it as they argued over Original Sin. "All sorts of heretical groups and reactionary and reforming parties arose in the church and were dealt with. These included the Ebionites, the Gnostics, the Manicheans, the Montanists, the Novatianists, the Donatists, and others."[25] None of them questioned inerrancy.

Which renders inerrancy a flimsy protective fence against doctrinal vandals.

Lindsell cites clusters of Christian VIP's from second-century heroes to Augustine and onto Luther and Calvin and beyond. "Anyone who reads Calvin and Luther and compares them with modern writers who deny biblical infallibility cannot fail to note the difference in attitude of the Reformers and that of the modern objectors to infallibility. The latter unfailingly seek to denigrate Scripture, to humanize it, to swallow a camel to strain out a gnat. The Reformers did not react in that way. Their attitude toward the Word of God was one of reverence, humility, and positive acceptance of it as authoritative and infallible."[26]

Really? Has any Fuller professor emulated Luther and called the Book of James "an epistle of straw?" Has any Free Methodist? How about non-inerrantists like Michael Bird? I. Howard Marshall? F.F. Bruce? C.S. Lewis? N.T. Wright?

Lindsell totally lost his moorings when he ridiculed Robert H. Mounce's article in Eternity Magazine *defending* inerrancy. Mounce proclaimed confidence in the Bible: "Are there errors in the Bible? Certainly not, so long as we are talking in terms of the purpose of its authors and the acceptable standards of precision in that day . . . It is a counsel of despair to hold such variations (as e.g. the 23,000 and the 24,000 of 1 Corinthians 10:8 and Numbers 25:9) did not exist in the autographs. For the purpose that

---

25. Lindsell, *The Battle for the Bible*, 42
26. Lindsell, *The Battle for the Bible*, 62

Paul had in mind it made no difference. This concern was to warn against immorality, not to give a flawless performance in statistics."[27]

But Lindsell couldn't live with that, so he twisted into a harmonizing acrobat to prove numerical precision. For example, Mounce said the measurements of the molten sea of 2 Chronicles 4:2 are an approximation; Lindsell counters with an elaborate, migraine-inducing explanation of how the measurement is scientifically precise. The migraine booms as he resolves the seeming difficulty over how many times the cock crows before Peter denied Christ: Peter, he says, actually denied Christ six times.[28]

Not even Hodge and Warfield would meet Lindsell's inerrancy definition, but that didn't stop him from leveling charges of theological deviance against the Lutheran Church's Missouri Synod, the Southern Baptists, and, of course, Fuller. The non-inerrantist "infection" was spreading.

Then comes his final appeal: "It is my conviction that a host of those evangelicals who no longer hold to inerrancy are still relatively evangelical. I do not for one moment concede, however, that in a technical sense anyone can claim the evangelical badge once he has abandoned inerrancy."[29]

A new line in the sand was now drawn—and it excluded most evangelicals outside the United States and many within, including the National Association of Evangelicals. Its statement of faith on the Scriptures reads, "We believe the Bible to be the inspired, the only *infallible*, authoritative Word of God" (emphasis added).

AFTERMATH

At first, it seemed Lindsell's book fell flat. Even inerrantists demurred. Carl Henry said the doctrine shouldn't determine "evangelical authenticity" and J.I. Packer said Lindsell failed to distinguish the inerrant text from his own interpretation. Others rushed in to pan it outright. Wesleyan theologian Donald Dayton criticized Lindsell's historical research and even his ethics: "In his zeal for the cause Lindsell has not hesitated to use private correspondence without permission, taking material out of context for his own purposes in a way that distorts intentions."[30] Fuller President David Allan Hubbard responded with a three-pronged chapel message: a new inerrancy squabble might imperil evangelical unity, priorities, and contributions to

---

27. Lindsell, *The Battle for the Bible*, 163.
28. Lindsell, *The Battle for the Bible*, 176.
29. Lindsell, *The Battle for the Bible*, 210.
30. Dayton, "The Battle for the Bible: Renewing the Inerrancy Debate," 976–980.

the larger church.[31] The late Duke McCall (1914–2013), then president of Southern Baptist Seminary in Louisville, Kentucky, was dismissive: The book "stirs up the snakes but kills none of them. The author will neither destroy the heresy he opposes nor divide the Southern Baptist Convention with this silly game with words."[32]

Not so fast.

McCall displayed a hallmark of denominational academics and leaders: He was out of touch with the rank and file. The fundamentalist-modernist controversy finally embroiled the nation's largest Protestant denomination before the television cameras. Americans watched the actors play their roles from a script written in the 1920's: Shocked "moderates," some of whom actually leaned to the theological left, invoked Baptist magnitudes such as "soul liberty" and "autonomy;" blustering fundamentalists inveighed inerrancy. The moderates seemed so enlightened and diplomatic, veritable ladies and gentlemen with southern drawls; the back-water fundamentalists seemed so uncouth.

Things were actually more complicated and some fundamentalist complaints were valid. Robert S. Alley, a tenured professor at the Baptist University of Richmond, reportedly told a small atheist gathering that Jesus never claimed he was the Son of God.

This time, the Fundamentalists won. The conservatives eventually overthrew the self-styled moderates and overtook the denomination's schools. Many faculty members fled. Albert Mohler, an aggressively doctrinaire Calvinist, now presides over the Southern Baptist Theological Seminary in Louisville, Kentucky.

The issue burned hot outside the Southern Baptist fold. In 1978, the newly-formed International Council on Biblical Inerrancy gathered 200 scholars in the Windy City and issued The Chicago Statement on Biblical Inerrancy, which affirmed: "Being wholly and verbally God-given, Scripture is without error or fault in all its teaching, no less in what it says about God's acts in creation, about the events of world history, and about its own literary origins under God, than in its witness to God's saving grace in individual lives."

Firm, non-negotiable stuff.

But then comes a list of affirmations and denials. Note Article XIII: "We deny that it is proper to evaluate Scripture according to the standards of truth and error that are alien to its usage or purpose. We further deny

---

31. Hubbard, "The Good Ship Fuller: Chapel Message," 1976

32. Dayton, https://www.religion-online.org/article/the-battle-for-the-bible-renewing-the-inerrancy-debate/

that inerrancy is negated by Biblical phenomena such as a lack of modern technical precision, irregularities of grammar or spelling, observational descriptions of nature, the reporting of falsehoods, the use of hyperbole and round numbers, the topical arrangement of material, variant selections of material in parallel accounts, or the use of free citations."

Robert Mounce was vindicated.

Inerrancy has since become an American evangelical credential, perhaps even a shibboleth—and it conveys different meanings in different settings. In academia, it signals that the entire Bible is true in its original autographs. The word is almost always qualified, such as at Asbury Theological Seminary and in the Lausanne Committee of World Evangelization (the Bible is the "only written Word of God, without error *in all it affirms*," italics added). Even John Piper, the modern-day Calvinist par-excellence and Bible champion, felt compelled to supply a long explanation while affirming the word. He tied the doctrine with the purpose of a given biblical writer.[33]

More nuance came with the 1980 publication of *Inerrancy and Common Sense*. Eight evangelical scholars contributed essays endorsing the doctrine while affirming non-literalistic interpretations of certain passages. John Jefferson Davis, for example, probed Genesis 3–4 and found that the Adam-and-Eve story is stylized: two historical, once-innocent prototypical human beings rebelled at a vague point in our primordial past. We don't know how the actual event unfolded.[34]

But Roger Olson points up a dilemma. Most lay people think inerrancy conveys "technical, precise, exact correspondence with reality with no room for estimates, rounding up or down numbers, reliance on errant sources, etc. etc." He's shown the Chicago Statement on Inerrancy to conservative students. Their inevitable reply: "That's not inerrancy."[35] Such has been my experience in Bible studies and in churches. The word becomes weaponized whenever someone argues for interpretive nuance and complexity. Pastors risk heresy trials upon the accusation: "You don't believe in inerrancy!" The accusers have often read the late Norman Geisler (1932–2019), who tarred the reputation of solid teachers. One recent victim was Denver Seminary's Craig Blomberg.[36]

It didn't help that some gave a bad name to open-mindedness. Robert Gundry sparked flames with his 1982 publication of *Matthew: A Commentary*

33. Piper, "How Are The Synoptics 'Without Error'?" 10/7/1976.

34. Davis, "Genesis, Inerrancy, and the Antiquity of Man," *Inerrancy and Common Sense*, 137–159.

35. Olson, "Further thoughts on why 'inerrancy' is problematic," 6/11/2012..

36. Geisler, Farnell, "The Erosion of Inerrancy Among New Testament Scholars: Craig Blomberg, 2012"

on His Literary and Theological Art. He felt the Gospel writer threw in outright fiction in his account of Christ's ministry. This was too much for the Evangelical Theological Society, which expelled him. J. Ramsay Michaels was already making life uncomfortable at my alma mater, Gordon-Conwell. He tipped the scales in *Servant and Son*, published in 1981, when he seemed to suggest that some of the accounts of John the Baptist were unhistorical and that Jesus had to be shocked out of ethnocentrism. The book offered compelling thoughts on Jesus's self-understanding, but it also displayed the near-sightedness of scholars spending hours with their texts: Small differences in the Gospel accounts swelled into major dilemmas. Perhaps worse, Michaels plunged into those differences without supplying a helpful interpretive method. He resigned under fire in 1983, with egg smearing the seminary's face as well: Administrators knew he'd been teaching this material for years.

Most evangelical inerrantist and infalliblist thinkers have settled in peace. After all, both parties argue for the Bible's truthfulness and authoritativeness; both agree that our current Bible is merely infallible; both agree that time-honored doctrines stand tall; both write articles for *Christianity Today*; both can sign on with the National Association of Evangelicals. And, very often, they find total agreement. Olson recalls a conversation with an "officer of a leading evangelical professional society that required affirmation of biblical inerrancy for membership:" He recalls: "I told him I did not think the word "inerrancy" fit the phenomena of Scripture, but that I do believe in Scripture's full authority. After sustained discussion we realized that, given his qualifications to inerrancy, he and I agreed on our view of the Bible! Then I asked if I could join his professional society. He said no; one must not only believe in the Bible's inerrancy (as he defined it) but must also affirm the word.[37]

Welcome to our hostile world, where sabers rattle even upon agreement.

MY LITTLE NEST

It seems there's a not-so-hidden resolution to this debate. Evangelicals of all stripes should have no trouble affirming this statement: "All Scripture is God-breathed and profitable for teaching, for reproof, for correction, and for training in righteousness." Just make 2 Timothy 3:16 our doctrine. It's good enough for God. Why not us?

But altering statements of faith risk another battle for the Bible.

Instead, I'll merely sign my denomination's inerrancy statement for the same reason Olson won't: We're all talking about the same thing. No

---

37. Olson, "When did evangelicalism start to go wrong (right)?"

heretic hunter in my denomination threatens if I don't interpret Genesis 1 literally; no war looms over the pre-tribulation rapture or pre-millennialism or a-millennialism or post-millennialism or any other ism over which some love to brawl. And I think of the Christians I admire: Timothy Keller, Ed Stetzer, Vineyard pastors, professors at Asbury Theological Seminary and Gordon-Conwell. They're inerrantists and they're my kin.

Perhaps I'm a soft inerrantist. I'm comfortable with the language of the Lausanne Covenant (". . . without error in all that it affirms, and the only infallible rule of faith and practice"), but I cannot agree with anathema-hurling hard inerrantists. Surely we're theological hombres with those affirming the entire Bible's inspiration.

It seems we can position ourselves on a doctrinal continuum rather than partitioning ourselves behind walls. The fundamentalists would teeter over the far right; inerrantist evangelicals would still be ranked among the conservatives, with infallibilist Fuller edging toward the evangelical left. Next would come orthodox Protestants like C.S. Lewis, then Barth and his neo-orthodox colleagues. Theological liberals would venture beyond the leftward edge.

Viewing the continuum allows us to see similarities as well as differences and helps us form alliances as well as man battle stations.

CONCLUSION

Hard inerrantists inevitably portray themselves as the Bible's protectors. All others, including soft inerrantists like me, are wishy-washy at best. We don't love the Bible enough.

I hereby bristle. My love for the entire Bible grows exponentially even as I've yielded to 21st-century pressure and bought a smart phone. I walk the neighborhood with buds in my ears, lost in the podcast world. I hear lectures and sermons from John Piper, Timothy Keller, the Vineyard Christian Fellowship of Evanston, Illinois, the Gospel Coalition, the good people at Fuller, Asbury and Gordon-Conwell seminaries, and the teachers at biblicaltraining.org, founded by New Testament scholar Bill Mounce (Robert's son). I love it. But none of those talks compare with my Bible ap. I've listened to books I've read countless times and they come alive. The podcasts, while stimulating, shrivel when compared with the Word itself. I cherish that Word and I defend it—and I know many others do as well, even though they're uncomfortable with that word, inerrancy. There is no reason why evangelicals cannot engage in a civil discussion or even pointed debate. We don't need to fight a battle.

7

The Beat Goes On

The fire from the *Battle For The Bible* era still burns as Van Til's legacy lingers, complete with evangelical orthodoxy's self-appointed guardians leveling inaccurate charges. Intimidation rules. Reputations are needlessly marred.

Perhaps John MacArthur grabbed the bully prize after the 1992 publication of *Charismatic Chaos*, which heaped inaccuracy upon caricature in an anti-Pentecostal/charismatic harangue. Even non-charismatic reviewers winced. They winced again in 2013 when he parroted similar charges in *Strange Fire: The Danger of Offending the Holy Spirit with Counterfeit Worship,* and again after a conference in the fall of 2019, when he was asked to sum up his thoughts in two words on Beth Moore, the Houston-based Bible teacher who has called Southern Baptists to task over sexual abuse. His verdict: "Go home." Female preachers seemed to scandalize him more than predatory pastors.

But most are on to MacArthur. He barely makes a dent beyond his dwindling tribe of fundamentalist cessationists. Even many fans of his sermon broadcasts filter his condemnations.

Far more troubling are the esteemed, well-reputed scholars writing footnote-laced broadsides. They're not household names, but they wield behind-the-scenes influence because of their laurels. Take Donald A. Carson, for instance. Born in 1946 and reared in Canada, Carson received his Ph.D.

in New Testament studies from Britain's Cambridge University in 1975 and was hired at Trinity Evangelical Seminary near Chicago in 1978, where he's served as a research professor. He's written or edited some 57 books and contributed hundreds of articles to popular and scholarly journals.

The rub: Carson deserves many of the accolades ladled on him through the decades. His 1984 commentary on the Gospel According to Matthew in the *Expositors Bible* series is commendable, especially since he wrote it in a pressure cooker: His editors rejected drafts submitted by Robert Gundry, whose novel interpretations eventually led to his ouster from the Evangelical Theological Society. Then there's his useful *Commentary on the New Testament Use of the Old Testament*—published in 2007 and edited with Greg Beale—and his efforts in co-founding the Gospel Coalition along with Timothy Keller. The coalition pools evangelical Reformed thinking via an on-line hub, podcasts, blogs, panel talks, essays and conferences. It's often helpful, although it ails from Calvinism's hereditary disease: Its writers often snub other Christians.

I thought twice about singling Carson out. I sympathize with him on many levels. Like him, I'm wary of trendy fads and gimmicks. Like him, I'm convinced we don't need new theologies. And I can't help but notice that many of my icons—like Timothy Keller—admire him. But Carson also wears a perpetual, he-swallowed-a-lemon frown while waging a decades-long battle against real and imagined Pied Pipers. He lacks the grace of the founders of the evangelical resurgence and, like Van Til and Lindsell, he commits the scholar's most grievous sin: He doesn't get his facts right.

I've seen his carelessness in three instances.

First, there's his hatchet job in a 1992 jeremiad edited by Michael Horton: *Power Religion: The Selling Out of the Evangelical Church?* Various Reformed authors probed the evangelical movement of the late '80's and early '90's and found it wanting. Misaligned "power," they claimed, had snaked into American pulpits and was strangling a full-orbed faith. They railed against power politics (the idolization of political power), power evangelism (believers were supposedly bent toward unhealthy spiritual power and dependence on dubious signs and wonders), power growth (everything bad in the mega-church movement), power within (pop psychology was erasing the Bible), power preachers (anti-cultural paranoia transformed churches into fortresses), and the power switch (Sunday worship now catered to secular America's entertainment cravings).

Many of the punches were well-aimed. Pact-with-the-devil partisanship was and is suffocating Christ's message; *some* church growth champions venerated numbers over people and thinned Christianity into a sweetened, culture-pleasing paste; cultural paranoia burned bridges with secular America. But the book sagged under the weight of its own jaundice. Everything was bad. Nothing was good. And the authors missed something amid the hand-wringing: A mini-renewal was sweeping the Church, with the Vineyard movement providing a solid theological core. The Toronto Blessing loomed in the near future and, for all its weaknesses, displayed the Holy Spirit's direct touch. Perhaps a full-throttled awakening loitered just around the corner, accompanied by the usual mess?

Alas, the renewal fizzled and the revival never fully flamed, but that was hardly predictable.

The book fell into outright inaccuracy in its three essays on power evangelism. John Armstrong, Carson, and the late James Montgomery Boice fixed their crosshairs on John Wimber and the Vineyard. They were so mistaken that Vineyard leaders abandoned their usual silence in the face of criticism. None other than Wayne Grudem, then Carson's Trinity colleague who occupied an office across the hall, wrote a response. Grudem, as I point out in other chapters, is as Reformed and conservative as they come. He also replied to Armstrong's series of attacks published in *The Standard*, the journal of the Baptist General Conference.

To review: Wimber, a former musician and Quaker pastor, abandoned his cessationist leanings under the teaching of George Eldon Ladd and founded the church that would eventually be called the Vineyard Christian Fellowship, which, in turn, spawned hundreds of others. He did not mandate speaking in tongues or a second work of grace; he repeatedly said not all were healed; he emphasized the need for holiness. He taught a gentle prayer method that cued off God's activity. No one proclaimed health and wealth.

And Wimber's favorite book was the Westminster Confession.

I guess it's too much to remember all those nuisance verses reproving false accusation. Skip Exodus 20:16 ("You must not testify falsely against your neighbor") and Deuteronomy 5:20 ("Do not give dishonest testimony against your neighbor") and Proverbs 3:30 ("Do not contend with someone for no reason, when he has done you no harm"). And, please, don't deliberate over the implications of Revelation 12:10, where the great dragon—or Satan—is described as the "accuser of our brothers and sisters" (hint: false accusers align themselves with the devil, called "the father of lies" in John 8:44)."

Anti-Vineyard denunciations and insinuations and innuendos swept the Christian press and beat on to this very day—and Carson fanned the flames. He politely tipped his hat to the Vineyard's strengths, then growled through its perceived flaws, beginning with the picky and debatable: At a "purely linguistic" level, he said, the Vineyard's "signs and wonders" didn't match the Bible's. "Most of the events that the Bible designates as 'signs and wonders' are miraculous, redemptive-historical acts of God,"[1] alluding to the Exodus in the Old Testament. Thus the New Testament backdrop: "At least some Christians saw the coming of Jesus as a major redemptive-historical appointment, on par with the Exodus . . . combining in the one event great salvation and judgment."[2]

I've surveyed Vineyard literature and I can only wonder: Where's the heresy? Wimber and his colleagues say that miracles point to Christ. Besides, the New Testament's terminology *does* refer to those everyday acts the Holy Spirit performed through Jesus and his followers. Read John 6:2: ". . . and a great crowd of people followed (Jesus) because they saw the signs he had performed by healing the sick." Or Peter's speech in Acts 2:22: "Fellow Israelites, listen to this: Jesus of Nazareth was a man accredited by God to you by miracles, wonders and signs, which God did among you through him, as you yourselves know." Or Acts 14:3: ". . . they spent a long time speaking boldly with reliance upon the Lord, who was testifying to the word of His grace, granting that signs and wonders be done by their hands." Read Acts 2:43, 4:30, 5:12, 6:8, 8;6–13, 15:12, Romans 15:18–19, 2 Corinthians 12:12. "Signs and wonders" can refer to great, historical events or to the simple Kingdom in-breaking that validates evangelism and illuminates Christ's compassion (see Matthew 9:35–37).

Carson moved from the picky to the serious: He pointed out that not all miracles receive Scriptural praise.[3] The Egyptian magicians, after all, met Moses and Aaron miracle for miracle; the "lawless one" of 2 Thessalonians 2:9–10 performs counterfeit miracles. Even demons do them. Reports of miracles come from Christian Science, Islam, and Hinduism.[4] Indeed, false miracles can draw us to idol worship—even if the idol worshipers claim they serve the god of Israel. "The contemporary application is pretty clear," he says. "The question is not first of whether the miracles reported by the Vineyard movement are real (though that is an important question), nor even whether people are drawn to renewed love for 'Jesus.' There are, after all, many Jesuses around: the Mormon Jesus, the Jehovah Witness Jesus, the Muslim Jesus, and so forth. The question, rather, is whether the movement

---

1. Carson, "The Purpose of Signs and Wonders in the New Testament," in *Power Religion*, 91.

2. Carson, "The Purpose of Signs and Wonders in the New Testament," in *Power Religion*, 92.

3. Carson, "The Purpose of Signs and Wonders in the New Testament," in *Power Religion*, 94.

4. Carson, "The Purpose of Signs and Wonders in the New Testament," in *Power Religion*, 95.

draws men and women to renewed love for the Jesus of God's great, redemptive-historical act, the Jesus of the cross and the resurrection."[5]

Grudem said it well: "This is an extraordinarily serious charge. And it is simply false."[6] He testified: "I have been in Vineyard churches for three years now and the Jesus preached and prayed to and trusted and worshiped is Jesus Christ 'the Son of God who loved me and gave himself for me' (Gal. 2:20), who 'died for our sins in accordance with the scriptures,' and who 'was buried,' and 'was raised on the third day in accordance with the scriptures' (1 Cor. 15:3–4)."[7]

Carson poured ambiguity over the insinuation: Perhaps Vineyard teaching was so insidious that gullible believers won't decipher its veracity or lack thereof. Grudem replied: "Therefore many readers will be frightened that the Vineyard is a false religion even when they have no hard evidence that it is a false religion."[8]

Other charges ran the gamut: The Vineyard isolates God's activity to the miraculous and, thus, it holds a "secular" view of everyday life (Grudem: "It is a rather strange turn of logic that belief in miracles is now said to be a 'profoundly secular world-view.' By that logic, I suppose we should conclude that people who don't believe in miracles have a profoundly *Christian* world view."[9]); miracles are "central" to the Vineyard (wrong: Christ's teaching on the Kingdom is); the Vineyard is arrogant (an ironic charge from a Calvinist); the cross "scarcely registers on the scale of what's important" (Grudem itemized many songs and teachings in which the cross reigns paramount); there is little or no teaching on suffering (Wimber wrote a booklet on suffering) or holiness (the Vineyard has held entire conferences on holiness); its reports of healings are "badly skewed" (Carson provides no evidence for this and Wimber's Anaheim church kept detailed records).

The bottom line: Instead of amassing facts and rendering sage and helpful assessments, Carson fed the rumor mill. He alienated a potential ally and bad-mouthed his brothers and sisters in Christ. This was raw bullying, made worse because it emanated from a respected scholar.

The essay's effect lasts. As recently as 2011, Michael Horton praised it as "excellent" and lumped the Vineyard with Peter Wagner (whom he mistakenly dubbed the movement's "theologian"), the Kansas City prophets, the

---

5. Carson, "The Purpose of Signs and Wonders in the New Testament," in *Power Religion*, 96–97.
6. Grudem, "Power & Truth," 5.
7. Grudem, "Power & Truth," 5.
8. Grudem, "Power & Truth," 6.
9. Grudem, "Power & Truth," 4.

Toronto Blessing, the prosperity Gospel, and the eccentric New Apostolic Reformation Movement.[10] The Vineyard has never preached prosperity and had long since distanced itself from Wagner and those other movements. Wimber died in 1997, before the NAR crystallized, but current Vineyard leaders are far from thrilled with it.

MORE GRIST FROM THE MILL

All might be sanguine if Carson's Vineyard mauling were isolated, but he was at it again in his thick 1996 screed, *The Gagging of God: Christianity Confronts Pluralism*, which paints a grim portrait of the West's descent into postmodernism and pluralism. Many evangelical Christians, he claimed, were plunging in. He took special aim at the now-late Stanley Grenz (1950–2005), a prolific Baptist theologian and consulting editor to *Christianity Today*. Grenz wrote dry essays and tomes about ethics, postmodernism (with sympathy), and evangelicalism's relationship with the world. He stressed narrative and community and, some would argue, de-emphasized the Bible's propositional passages. The dawning emergent church movement loved him while many of its leaders were still evangelical.

Carson, of course, saw only dangers. He claimed Grenz "prefers the direction illumined by (Friedrich) Schliermacher (1768–1834, the father of liberal theology), arguing that the three sources or norms of theology are Scripture, tradition, and culture. This is, to say the least, decidedly unhelpful. Quite apart from the extraordinary complexities of linking Scripture and tradition in this way, the addition of culture is astonishing . . . With the best will in the world, I cannot see how Grenz's approach to Scripture can be called 'evangelical' in any useful sense."[11]

Indeed, Grenz would have shredded his own evangelical credentials had he matched Carson's caricature—especially if he leveled culture with the Bible. But he didn't. Not even close. Sample the theologian himself:

> As the attempt to articulate the unchanging faith commitment of the church—the Christian confession 'Jesus is Lord'—in a specific historical-cultural context, the theological task must be carried out with a view in three directions. The three 'pillars' or norms of theology form an ordered sequence of (1) the biblical message, (2) the theological heritage of the church and (3) the thought-forms of the of the historical-cultural context in which the contemporary people of God seek to speak, live and act.

10. Horton, "The Politics of Enthusiasm," *The White Horse Inn*, 8/19/2011.
11. Carson, The Gagging of God," 481.

He emphasized: "Of first importance to the theological task is the Bible as canonized by the church. More specifically, the primary norm for theology is the biblical message. The theologian must look first and above all to the kerygma as inscripturated in the Bible."[12]

Pare away the academic and theological jargon, which weighs Grenz's writing and renders it inaccessible to most readers, and he's merely saying this: We obey the Bible as God's Word with an eye to historical orthodoxy, then translate it to the contemporary culture in its language. And, of course, we keep an ear open to the truths within a culture (theories on democratic government, for example are not found in the Bible). That's hardly controversial. Preachers do that every Sunday. But, again, Carson leveled a false but serious charge based on a misunderstanding—and he missed his opportunity to engage in a worthy debate (is postmodernism a friend or foe?). Once again, he fed a vicious rumor mill and needlessly assailed a colleague's orthodoxy.[13]

SHORT AND NASTY

But all that's so 1990's. Perhaps Carson learned from his mistakes and now trims his attacks to mere constructive criticism.

Alas, no. He did it again, this time in a book-cover blurb endorsing John Piper's *The Future of Justification*, published in 2007. Piper was attempting to reply to British scholar N.T. Wright, who *seemed* to question Protestantism's traditional take on the doctrine of justification by faith. Wright's challenge arose under the *New Perspective on Paul* umbrella, which houses a scholarly clique confronting long-held assumptions about the Apostle's response to first-century Judaism.

Christianity Today summed up the Wright-Piper debate. Wright defined justification in this way:

> God himself, in the person of Jesus Christ (the faithful Israelite), has come, allowing the continuation of his plan to rescue human beings, and, through them, the world. The Messiah represents his people, standing in for them, taking upon himself the death that they deserved. God justifies (declares righteous) all those who are "in Christ," so that the vindication of Jesus upon his resurrection becomes the vindication of all those who trust

---

12. Grenz, *Revisioning Evangelical Theology*, 93.

13. Olson described the fierce defamation against Grenz here: "Memories of Stanley J. Grenz with Special Attention to Criticisms of His Theology (and Some Hitherto Unrevealed Facts)," *My Evangelical Musings, 12/5/2014*.

> in him. Justification refers to God's declaration of who is in the covenant (this worldwide family of Abraham through whom God's purposes can now be extended into the wider world) and is made on the basis of faith in Jesus Christ alone, not the "works of the Law" (i.e., badges of ethnic identity that once kept Jews and Gentiles apart).[14]

Piper in this way:

> By faith we are united with Christ Jesus so that in union with him, his perfect righteousness and punishment are counted as ours (imputed to us). In this way, perfection is provided, sin is forgiven, wrath is removed, and God is totally for us. Thus, Christ alone is the basis of our justification, and the faith that unites us to him is the means or instrument of our justification. Trusting in Christ as Savior, Lord, and Supreme Treasure of our lives produces the fruit of love, or it is dead.[15]

I can't help but ask: Are these two views are mutually exclusive?

But I digress. I only bring up the Piper-Wright debate to highlight Carson's inflammatory blurb: "The so-called 'New Perspective on Paul' has stirred up enormous controversy. The issues are not secondary, and, pastor that he is, John Piper will not allow believers to put their trust in anyone or anything other than the crucified and resurrected Savior."

Once again, Carson implies a severe charge: Wright teeters on universalism. Once again, he is wrong. Read Wright's words: ". . . the vindication of Jesus upon his resurrection becomes the vindication of all those who trust in him" . . . "Justification refers to God's declaration of who is in the covenant . . . and is made on the basis of faith in Jesus Christ alone."

NT Wright responded directly: "The implicit charge that the Pauline theology I have articulated might lead people to put their trust in 'anyone or anything other than the crucified and resurrected savior' . . . is seriously misleading."[16]

Fact is, Carson bullied the Vineyard, Grenz, and Wright. He blew down straw men in the process and needlessly tarnished the reputation of fellow Christians. A casualty is legitimate debate: Both John Jefferson Davis and Michael Bird raise valid questions over Wright's New Perspective exegesis,[17] but few hear their sober analysis amid the neo-fundamentalist fury. Equally

---

14. Wax, "The Justification Debate: A Primer," *Christianity Today*, 6/26/2009.

15. Wax, "The Justification Debate: A Primer," *Christianity Today*, 6/26/2009.

16. Wright, *Justification*, 239.

17. Davis, *Practicing Ministry in the Presence of God*, 150–157; Bird, "What Is There Between Minneapolis and St. Andrews?" *JETS*, 6/2011, 299–309.

tragic, potential alliances are damaged: The Vineyard, Grenz, and Wright have resisted the progressive temptation to veer left on every issue. They disagree with those who would alter sexual morals, for example.

WHY THE FUSS?

Why isolate a single academic? He's hardly a household name.

The problem: Carson, along with others, breeds disciples in the "Young, Restless, and Reformed" movement, of which Colin Hansen sympathetically wrote in 2008. Hansen portrayed an up-and-coming evangelical generation of evangelicals eschewing baby-boomer trivialities and embracing Calvinism's supposed sophistication. They flock to *Passion* conferences featuring Piper; they populate Reformed schools and laud such Calvinist luminaries as the late R.D. Sproul and Albert Mohler.

Hansen highlighted one young-restless leader as a harbinger of the future: The ever-resourceful Mark Driscoll, who was surfing his popularity's crest as the pastor of Seattle's Mars Hill megachurch. Indeed, Driscoll is an organizational and oratorical virtuoso. He co-founded Mars Hill and established The Resurgence (a Mars Hill theological cooperative) and Acts 29 (a church planting network). He was a founding board member of the Gospel Coalition and wrote books and toured the speaker's circuit while supervising a multi-site church. He admittedly burned out in 2007 and resigned from several positions while Mars Hill overhauled its bylaws.

But hints suggested all was not well. He fired two staffers in 2007 after they disagreed with him, leading to accusations of authoritarianism. And there were his cavalier statements: The mainstream church had transformed Jesus into a "Richard Simmons, hippie, queer Christ," a "neutered and limp-wristed popular Sky Fairy of pop culture . . ."[18] There was a 2011 Facebook post, later deleted: "So, what story do you have about the most effeminate anatomically male worship leader you've ever personally witnessed?" There was his tweet about Barak Obama on the day of his second inaugural: "Praying for our president, who today will place his hands on a Bible he does not believe to take an oath to a God he likely does not know" and his environmental statement at a 2013 conference: "I know who made the environment. He's coming back, and he's going to burn it all up. So yes, I drive an SUV." He later claimed he was just yucking it up: "According to people who, unlike me, go on the Internet, some did not understand I was telling jokes and people were laughing."

Perhaps the bright lights blinded him to some who walked out.

18. "Mark Driscoll Says Just Grow Up," *Relevant*, 9/9/2010.

Things imploded in the summer of 2014 amid a feud with MacArthur, plagiarism charges, and formal complaints from his Mars Hill staff. The Acts 29 board removed him and recommended he leave the ministry, which he did in October. The Mars Hill network disbanded the following year. Driscoll has since moved to the Phoenix area in Arizona and planted another church. So far, his tweets focus on grace and relationships. I honestly wish him well.

I only dredge up the Driscoll tragedy to point out this: Few Reformed magnates publicly criticized his bullying. Piper said he sent him a critique in a long letter, but no one knew that.

Perhaps it's time for the leaders of this aggressive, resurgent Calvinism to look in the mirror and see the acne. After all, they shake the accusing finger at everyone else—partly because their opponents supposedly welsh on total depravity. They should ask the uncomfortable question of themselves: What about *our* depravity? Has bullying entrenched itself into our culture? Are we even aware of our tradition's belligerent dark side, which hastily slaps the heretic label on all others? And why are we so "restless?" Maybe just "Young and Reformed" will do—or, better yet, "Young, Gracious and Reformed." We've got the role models within our own tradition. There's the irenic Dutch theologian, Herman Bavinck (1854-1921); there's J.I. Packer; there's Henry; there's Ockenga; there's Timothy Keller. Did we lay a dark spawning ground for Driscoll's crudeness? And were we so busy attacking Barth, infallibilists, Wimber, Grenz, and Wright that we failed to see the real adversaries, who were twisting the evangelical name into a mere partisan label while dropping time-honored convictions?

Settle down. Cool it. View the scene soberly. Thinkers standing in the broad evangelical heritage are often looking over their shoulders, fearful of heresy accusations. Meanwhile, real adversaries have hijacked the label and twisted it beyond recognition.

8

Moderate Complicity

IT'S TIME TO ASK: Where were those conscientious and gentle moderate evangelicals in whom many vested their hopes? We hear they diligently recycle their tinfoil and sponsor World Vision children and hold prayer meetings in their suburban living rooms. Articles and books told us they'd soon rise up in a kind-hearted revolution. It was just round the next bend. Maybe the protests during the 2016 presidential campaign foreshadowed the uprising.

No such luck. Some brave moderates kept at it, but most shivered like frightened fawns while counseling patience, love, and understanding. They smoothed ruffled feathers and silenced any meaningful response to the bullying—all under the banners of unity and peace. The result: Intimidators interpreted the silence as weakness. They exploited it, tagging anyone raising objections as "liberal" (that feared word again) and imposing a partisan orthodoxy over Christianity's time-honored creeds.

Call the strategy for what it is: Enablement.

Probing the moderate evangelical dilemma forces me to go where I don't want to go. Again. Good people, from whom I have learned and whom I deeply admire, have unwittingly fed the intimidation machine by retreating from the necessary battle. They think of peace as the mere absence of conflict and unity as everyone getting along. Conflict is Enemy Number One, so the moderates dash in to quench any perceived clash, often equipped with a mob of Bible proof texts divorced from an overall peace-making theology.

One commendable organization epitomizes all the ironies wrapping the moderate evangelical response to bullying. *Peacemaker Ministries* is packed with earnest people longing to do God's will. It's a great ministry. I recommend it despite my criticisms. I've benefited from its training and taught Bible studies using its materials. As I've said, I even led an entire church through a *Peacemaker* course and seriously explored the possibility of obtaining certification as one of its Christian Conciliators.

But I eventually found that the Peacemaker remedy ailed with the moderate evangelical disease. Its approach isn't so much wrong as incomplete. I probe it here as a case study in how well-meaning people can offer an insufficient response by misdiagnosing a problem.

A GOOD IDEA

The subject of conflict has become all the rage as beleaguered pastors stumble through the dissonant din of spats and power plays. Enter the refreshing Ken Sande, a lawyer from Billings, Montana, the author of *The Peacemaker* and founding president of *Peacemaker Ministries*, which he left in 2012 to establish another organization, *Relational Wisdom 360*. Dale Pyne took the helm immediately after him and remained at the post until 2017, when leadership was handed to Brian Noble.

Sande welded himself to the Bible while bringing in the insights of Alternative Dispute Resolution, which offers more consensual mediation and arbitration methods than our adversarial courts.[1] He discovered that believers, churches, and ministries were hauling each other before secular judges, which violates 1 Corinthians 6:1–11 and mars our witness for Christ.

I've come to see that ADR is not enough. Indeed, the concept of dispute *resolution* gives us only a glimpse of a wider, multi-layered biblical approach encapsulated in the term, *conflict transformation*. The goal of conflict resolution is to resolve, or settle, the clash; conflict transformation

---

1. Sprangler, "Alternative Dispute Resolution (ADR)." *Beyond Intractability,* June, 2003. Sande and others in Peacemakers often point out the differences between their methods and those of ADR, but their mediation process involving Greeting and ground rules, Opening statements, Storytelling, Problem clarification, Explore solutions, and Lead to agreement (note the GOSPEL acronym) bears striking similarity to ADR patterns and processes advocated by Roger Fisher, William Ury, and Bruce Patton in *Getting to Yes: Negotiating Agreement Without Giving In* (New York: Penguin, 1991). Bringing in those insights is by no means bad—indeed, Sande and his colleagues are to be commended—but they should do some footnoting and attribution.

brings justice and shalom and transforms the scene. Conflict itself is not only an "opportunity" to glorify God, as Sande says, but God's transforming agent when properly stewarded. Those involved in ADR anchor their experience in one-on-one disputes. Transformation's practitioners, such as John Paul Lederach, have spearheaded national and regional peace efforts and are more familiar with sociological and group dynamics.[2]

I should emphasize that Peacemaker Ministries sincerely seeks to get at root causes within an ADR framework—and, because its leaders refuse to "put down the book" (they're strenuously biblical), they dig far deeper than secular mediators. Conflict resolution is very proper as a crucial stage in conflict transformation—and there are few better organizations than Peacemaker Ministries for that task.

VEILED WEAKNESSES

Mediation's and ADR's limitations are subtle but real. For one thing, I've seen manipulators stage-manage the mediation process itself. Second, there is almost always an implied assumption of moral equivalency: both parties are equally wrong and right, which sounds even-handed but is often not true. Genuine victims remain victimized because their legitimate grievances have not been addressed. Third, the very goal of ADR is to "resolve" the interests and issues of the conflicted parties so the conflict will end. Meanwhile, the feud's underlying cause—often involving power plays and relationship webs of which the issues are only a symptom—remains unaddressed. Conflicts resurface. Only the labels and names have changed: The interests and issues are different and the actors play musical chairs. Fourth, I attended a two-week seminar in which I learned that most mediators test as conflict avoiders, which means ADR is not as neutral and benign as it initially appears. The mediators themselves fall prey to manipulators. They're blind to nasty head games; they may not see passive aggressiveness and they may shrivel beneath a bully's onslaught. Conflict avoidance may temporarily bring calm, but it does long-term damage by circumventing something absolutely necessary for real peace: The truth. A lawyer once told me he dreads the involvement of mediators because "they'd rather be fair than true."

Anthropologist Laura Nader saw deep flaws in ADR. The process imposed a "coercive harmony." She explained: "The powerful tend to become advantaged by alternative dispute resolution . . . Studies revealed alternative

---

2. See Lederach's essay on "Conflict Transformation." *Beyond Intractability*, October 2003, and *The Little Book of Conflict Transformation*.

dispute resolution's practice of controlling the definition of the problem and the form of its expression, including the prohibition of anger."[3]

Nader's jadedness should not blind us to her genuine insights: The preponderance of psychological language stifles worthwhile debates over truth and justice. We're mired in never-ending arguments over hurt feelings, with discussions weighted on whether this person was insensitive to that person: so-and-so should have anticipated that what's-his-name would have been offended. We're forever correcting the delivery of a given viewpoint rather than debating the argument's merits. Whether we know it or not, we invariably view conflict as intrinsically wrong—and anyone who offends someone else needs correction. We're nomads in the labyrinth of passive aggressiveness while limping under the weight of the tyranny of the sensitive.

Behold the moderate evangelical's plight: We bite our tongues lest we hurt the feelings of Raging Joe or Josephine. Joe and Josephine interpret the silence as an endorsement and fume even more.

MY OWN AWAKENING

My growing leeriness of exclusive reliance on ADR methods surfaced amid a series of controversies while serving that hostile church. All my statements offended nebulous, nameless groups of "people." The fracturing escalated even after the entire body threw itself into The Peacemaker Church study. Every issue—no matter how unimportant—was analyzed through conflict resolution's lens. We could never just disagree or debate; everything was a "conflict" and each conflict had to be resolved. The inevitable resolution involved statements along these lines: "I feel like you could have phrased things in such a way that people would have been less offended" ... or, "You should have anticipated that people would have felt this way ..."

Then came my fatal question: "How did Jesus handle controversy?" As I said, I began reading the Gospel of Mark with an eye for his approach. I was stunned. I saw familiar passages as if for the first time. First came 1:40–45, where he healed a leper via his touch, making himself ceremonially unclean (see Leviticus 13:45–46 and 5:2). Jesus wasn't playing by the rules. Things got worse in 2:1–12. A group brings a paralytic to Jesus and he forgives his sins (verse five), fully knowing that the audience's teachers would see blasphemy (verses 6–7). I could almost hear the whispers among the crowd's conflict resolvers: "You could have been more sensitive, Jesus. You should have anticipated their offense and taken a different course." But

---

3. Nader, "Controlling Processes," *Current Anthropology*, December, 1997, 713–714.

Christ made no apologies. Instead, he proclaimed healing to show he had the "authority on earth to forgive sins" (verses 10–12).

Mark this: Jesus knowingly sparked a conflict. He showed no interest in placating the Pharisees in 2:13–22, and he was offensive again in verses 23–27 when he advocated a different view of proper Sabbath behavior.

But Mark 3:1–6 was the real shocker. Jesus entered a synagogue on a Sabbath and found a man with a shriveled hand. He told him to stand, knowing that "some of them were looking for a reason to accuse" him. He asked his opponents a loaded question: "Which is lawful on the Sabbath: to do good or to do evil, to save life or to kill?" Their stubbornness distressed him. He healed the man. The Pharisees "went out and began to plot with the Herodians how they might kill Jesus" (verse 6).

There was no way around it. Jesus actively *sparked* controversy.

Imagine the moderate second-guessing: "Jesus, you showed no respect for the religious authorities . . . Jesus, you could have ingratiated yourself and gotten on their good side . . . Jesus, you could have healed him the following day and thus not have offended anyone . . . Jesus, you could have used more 'I' statements . . . Jesus, Jesus, Jesus . . . If you're at all interesting in advocating your cause without stirring up trouble . . ."

But therein lies the quandary. Trouble was unavoidable and, indeed, necessary in this circumstance.

It seems the moderate instinct to settle every conflict beneath pithy language ("so-and-so has a good heart . . .") must be resisted. In fact, it seems moderates are culpable patrons in evangelical Christianity's moral, doctrinal, and spiritual collapse.

BEYOND MY OWN STORY

But perhaps my own autobiography fails to convince. So I'll appeal to history—specifically, to April 12, 1963. Martin Luther King and Ralph Abernathy were arrested during the Birmingham Campaign, which featured segregationist Commissioner of Public Safety Bull Connor, attack dogs, and water cannon aimed at children. One outcome was King's *Letter From A Birmingham Jail*, in which he responded to a group of white clergymen calling for a halt to the demonstrations. The earnest whites used the language of resolution as they penned a classic in conflict avoidance. King answered with one of conflict transformation's most eloquent testaments.

The clergymen never addressed whether King, Abernathy, and their colleagues were right or wrong. They fell back on the you're-not-doing-it-right phraseology. Recalling a previous appeal in January, they said: "We expressed understanding that honest convictions in racial matters could properly be pursued in the courts, but urged in the meantime that decisions of those courts should be peacefully obeyed." They naively assumed that Alabama's judges mirrored blindfolded Lady Justice with no interest in perpetuating discriminatory methods and laws. They continued: "Since that time there has been some evidence of increased forbearance and willingness to face facts. Responsible citizens have undertaken to work on various problems which cause racial friction and unrest."[4]

Notice how they framed the issue. The problem was the "friction and unrest," not America's apartheid, and those sparking such friction were not "responsible citizens." In other words, conflict is intrinsically wrong.

They kept at it as they puzzled through the controversy gripping their beloved city, which they viewed as southern hospitality's fulcrum. Birmingham seemed trouble-free until they were "now confronted by a series of demonstrations by some of our Negro citizens, directed and led in part by outsiders."

"Resolution" language laces the letter. The white leaders positioned themselves as "peaceful:" they agreed with "certain Negro leadership which has called for honest and open negotiation of racial issues in our area." Local people—"white and Negro"—are best at handling the difficulty, "meeting with their knowledge and experiences of the local situation."

The implicit accusation: King incited black "hatred and violence" (never mind white hatred and violence) because his actions spur aggression "however technically peaceful those actions may be" (this was a no-win for King). They said Birmingham stood on the verge of an era of "new hope," rendering "extreme measures" unjustified. They appealed for "calm" and "restraint" and pleaded to the "Negro community" to withdraw support for the demonstrations and to "unite locally in working peacefully for a better Birmingham."[5]

And, please, again, use the courts and local leadership for redress. Avoid "the streets."[6]

Laura Nader is relevant after all. The white church leaders were just that: white, southern society's mainstream, blind to African America's Hell and only dimly aware of the nation's institutionalized defiance of justice and shalom. They did not understand that King, Abernathy, and their colleagues only brought a pre-existing conflict to the surface so all could see it in its living brutality.

4. A Group of Clergy Men, "A Letter To Martin Luther King," April 12, 1963.
5. A Group of Clergy Men, "A Letter To Martin Luther King," April 12, 1963.
6. A Group of Clergy Men, "A Letter To Martin Luther King," April 12, 1963.

King's response was brilliant. He hailed his colleagues as "men of genuine good will" whose "criticisms are sincerely set forth" and immediately addressed their "outsider" remarks: the local leaders, members of a wider organization of which he was the president, began their home-grown campaign and called him in for help. He then appealed to the Bible: "Just as the prophets of the eighth century BC left their villages and carried their 'thus saith the Lord' far beyond the boundaries of their home towns, and just as the Apostle Paul left his village of Tarsus and carried the Gospel of Jesus Christ to the far corner of the Greco-Roman world, so am I compelled to carry the gospel of freedom beyond my home town." He pointed out that we're all interrelated. His organization's local affiliate had already negotiated with the whites and reached an agreement, only to see it violated. And again, the courts were hardly regal halls of justice: "Negroes have experienced grossly unjust treatment in the courts. There have been more unsolved bombings of Negro homes and churches in Birmingham than in any other city in the nation."[7]

And there's that poignant, famous paragraph in which he alludes to moderation's veiled weaknesses: "I have almost reached the regrettable conclusion that the Negro's great stumbling block in his stride toward freedom is not the White Citizen's Councilor or the Ku Klux Klanner, but the white moderate, who is more devoted to 'order' than to justice; who prefers a negative peace which is the absence of tension to a positive peace which is the presence of justice; who constantly says, 'I agree with the goal you seek, but I cannot agree your methods of direct action.'"

Here's the crucial line delineating conflict transformation from mere resolution: "The purpose of our direct action program is to create a situation so crisis-packed that it will inevitably open the door to negotiation. I therefore concur with you in your call for negotiation. Too long has our beloved Southland been bogged down in a tragic effort to live in monologue rather than dialogue."[8]

The entire campaign—including breaking unjust laws—aroused "the conscience of the community over its injustice."[9]

The white clergymen sought calm; King sought justice. The whites wanted resolution; King wanted transformation. To the whites, any conflict brought disruption and was therefore wrong; to King, properly stewarded conflict—done nonviolently, always with an extended hand to his enemies, never seeking their harm, understanding that they needed healing because

---

7. King, *A Letter From A Birmingham Jail*, April 16, 1963.
8. King, *A Letter From A Birmingham Jail*, April 16, 1963.
9. King, *A Letter From A Birmingham Jail*, April 16, 1963.

they, too, were unwitting victims of the very injustice they inflicted—is useful. A properly stewarded crisis can lead to *genuine* negotiation and resolution. Injustice is addressed and true peace—more akin to Hebrew shalom—is established. In Birmingham, the conflict shocked the nation and Congress passed the Civil Rights act in 1965.

As Daniel Buttry says, "sometimes conflict resolution must begin by heightening the conflict."[10]

THE AIM: JUSTICE AND PEACE

How does this bear on the evangelical moderate? Peacemaker Ministries then-CEO Dale Pyne unwittingly showed us in a blog post dated July 15, 2016 and entitled, "When Difficult People Interrupt the Peace."[11] It was a what-to-do article on handling problematic people.

Time out. "Difficult people" come in all shapes and sizes and mentalities, from the schizophrenic to the manic depressive to the braying political partisan, with each demanding a different approach. Some need counseling; others need a sincere friend; still others need confrontation. Many need a blend. But Pyne generalized from one obscure biblical story and—while filing the necessary disclaimers—fell back on the inevitable moderate reflex: Relent. He calls us to emulate Isaac, one of Israel's three patriarchs and the favored son of Abraham, in Genesis 26:12–33. Isaac had lied about his beautiful wife and said she was his sister while they lived among among the Philistines (Abraham had done the same thing; both feared local leaders would kill them and take their wives). Abimelech, the Philistine king, was none too pleased when he discovered the truth. He scolded Isaac, then assured him of safety: "Anyone who molests this man or his wife shall surely be put to death" (verse 11).

God displays his provision and faithfulness within the intricacies of jealousy, feuds, and quarrels over water rights in an arid land. Isaac planted crops, which yielded a hundred-fold harvest "because the Lord had blessed him" (verse 12). His wealth sky-rocketed, his herds multiplied, and he commanded a burgeoning multitude of servants. The Philistines responded with envy and sabotage (they stopped up wells dug during Abraham's life), whereupon Abimelech, exercising his right as a Middle Eastern despot and backed by an army, ordered the patriarch to leave. Isaac had no choice.

---

10. Buttry, *Christian Peacemaking*, 31.

11. Pyne's blog post, "When Difficult People Interrupt The Peace," was once on T*he Everyday Peacemaker*, https://grow.peacemaker.training/ , but seems to have been taken down.

He followed orders and settled in the Valley of Gerrar. His clan reopened other Abrahamic wells, which prompted more objections from neighboring herdsmen. Isaac fled again. His followers dug another well and met more quarrels, so they moved on and finally dug a well over which no one protested. Isaac named the place Rehoboth (meaning, "open spaces"), then journeyed to Beersheba and met God in the night. Verse 24, where the Lord assures Isaac, reveals the story's finale: "I am the God of your father Abraham. Do not be afraid, for I am with you; I will bless you and I will increase the number of your descendants for the sake of my servant Abraham."

God *will* remain faithful to his tiny nation, now confined to Isaac's extended family, even as it wandered among jealous and hostile goyim (non-Hebrews). That's the message. This foreshadowed a time of greater peril some 400 years later, when envious Egyptians coveted the prosperity of the patriarch's descendants and enslaved them. Moses and Aaron held hostile negotiations with Pharaoh and prevailed. Pharaoh didn't do too well.

Pyne, unfortunately, strains for a conflict-resolution narrative, revealing the moderate's conundrum in the process. He sees that Isaac yielded to Philistine demands and generalizes: "When someone interrupts our peace, often our first impulse is to respond in kind. Yet, when he encountered such adversity, he didn't demand his rights. He laid them down. Although this came at a great personal price, God honored his quiet perseverance."

He misses the story's theme, which is not about conflict resolution. It's about God's provision.

Thus my frustration with moderate evangelicals. We tip our hat to biblical passages calling for boldness, but all our illustrations and stories tell of quiet, nice people persevering in silence, yielding all the way until God miraculously intervenes. We neglect such prophets as Elijah, Isaiah, Amos, and the ever-blunt John the Baptist, who boldly confronted Israel's corrupt leaders. We forget the Munich Conference in 1938, when Hitler bullied the allies into surrendering portions of Czechoslovakia. The Nazi tyrant, typical of despots, was unimpressed when British Prime Minister Neville Chamberlain conceded. World War 2 came a year later.

THE WHOLE BIBLE

There's a more sophisticated approach. We keep the biblical goal in mind when ministering in conflict, which is encapsulated in the two Hebrew words for justice: *mishpat* and *tsedaqah* (the latter is often translated as righteousness). The goal is never mere settlement. If that were the case, Elijah should have received sensitivity training vis-à-vis Ahab and Jezebel; John the Baptist should have apologized for his slurs—and so should his cousin, Jesus; Martin Luther should take back those 95 theses; John Calvin was too impolite; John Wesley and George Whitefield were impertinent. And let's all race to John 17 without understanding that Jesus articulated his prayer for unity in the middle of a conflict culminating in the cross. If Jesus had not engaged in the conflict, we'd be condemned and remain unreconciled.

So much for Isaac's "quiet perseverance."

We see the goal of justice and righteousness in a swarm of passages, including Amos 5:24 and 1 Samuel 15:22–23. There's Psalm 72 for a description of the just and righteous king, whose governance spawns the righteous community. Jesus commends those who hunger and thirst for righteousness in Matthew 5:6.

The word, *tsedaqah*, used 157 times in the Old Testament—along with its masculine form, *tsedeq*, used 119 times—has intriguing roots that clue us into its implications: It means to "make straight."[12] Properly stewarded conflict surfaces that which is pulling the community off course. It shows what does not line up.

Understanding the true nature of the Hebrew word for peace, *shalom*, underscores the need for genuine justice. The word means "'completeness', 'soundness', 'well-being,'"[13] which is far more positive than the mere absence of discord. We can now grasp the strange story in Numbers 25:6-13, where Phinehas kills a couple violating the law. A plague stops and God makes a "covenant of peace" with him. Phinehas actually brought justice (he made things straight in the eyes of the law) and completeness upon Israel with his violent act, which we would not emulate today. What's more, we can now understand how the following verses dovetail with peacemaking: "Those who sin are to be rebuked publicly, so that others may take warning" (1 Timothy 5:20); ". . .Therefore, rebuke them sharply, so that they will be sound in the faith" (Titus 1:13). We can begin to grapple with the aggressive language of Matthew 11:12 (see also Luke 16:16), although not necessarily solve the legitimate debate over translation and interpretation: "From the days of John the Baptist until now, the kingdom of heaven has been forcefully advancing, and forceful men lay hold of it."[14]

All these passages illuminate the deep harm of conflict avoidance, especially when it comes in the guise of resolution. Resolution only arises when the roots of a dysfunctional organization—or an entire movement—have

---

12. See Brown, Driver, Briggs, and Gesenius (BDBG) 841. See also Payne, "Justice," 634–636; Sider, *The Scandal of Evangelical Politics*, 101–126.

13. Foulkes, "Peace," *New Bible Dictionary,* 891. See also BDBG, 1022.

14. See the discussion in Ladd, *The Presence of the Future,* 159–164.

been exposed. To use more theological language, the hidden institutional sin must be laid bare. There simply is no such thing as peace without justice and righteousness.[15] Conflict avoidance enables and perpetuates an unjust and unrighteous condition, so it is no exaggeration to call it an act of disobedience.

AN ASSESSMENT

To be fair, Sande and Peacemaker Ministries attempt to guide pupils away from avoidance. They delineate "attack" responses (assault, litigation, and murder) and "escape" responses (suicide, flight, and denial)—and, while attack and escape are occasionally needed (we must sometimes leave the scene, temporarily, for our own safety or to gather our composure), they prefer the more unifying "peacemaking responses." In "personal peacemaking," we can overlook an offense, seek reconciliation, and engage in negotiation—depending on the degree and depth of the conflict. In "assisted peacemaking," we seek mediation, arbitration, and accountability—with the "Four G's" (Glorify God, Get the Log out of your eye; Gently restore, and Go and be reconciled) serving as the underlying principles.

My guess is that Sande is calming the adversarial, attack-dog world of attorneys. Bless him. But, in the process, he has left little room for the redemptive conflict and its consequent, necessary controversy. We must carve a notch for legitimate debate and the essential rebuke and for the naturally animated. Make space for those nurtured in cultures encouraging enthusiasm—cultures in which the raised voice is heard as engagement rather than animosity.

Real debate and argument are necessary peacemaking responses. Pastors and other leaders must pack them into their tool boxes. I've seen instances in which debate itself is called an "attack," where the mere emphasis of a point is deemed "harsh." In his quest for gentility, I fear Sande has unwittingly wrapped leaders in straight jackets. Conversation becomes stilted. Creativity dies.

---

15. Some have difficulty with the use of "righteousness" because of what they hear when the word is used. First, they may hear "self-righteousness" and judgment. We're not talking about that. Others may hear condemnation. We're not talking about that either. Still others may hear "legalism" or "earning" our salvation. We're not talking about any of those things. We're merely talking about what Paul advocates in Romans 6:1–7, where we live the resurrected life, and verses 15–23, where we are freed from the life of sin so that we can be "slaves of righteousness" (see verse 18). We can also throw in Ephesians 2:10 and the entire letter of James.

Sande did give leaders more tools in his book's first edition: his second "G" was "go" and show your adversary his fault. That may sound rough, but it's biblically sound (see Matthew 18:15, which compliments Paul's statements in 1 Timothy 5:20 and Titus 1:15). He relented in his second edition and used the language of Galatians 6:1: "Brothers, if someone is caught in a sin, you who are spiritual should restore him *gently*" (emphasis added). The shift in the second "g" may have been advisable in the attorney's world, but he may have armed passive aggressors.

A DIFFERENT APPROACH

Christian writers on conflict resolution often portray aggressors as well-meaning souls needing empathy. Which is ironic. All branches of evangelical theology hold a high view of Original Sin. We're sinister creatures who fall prey to the those tempting words: "You will not surely die. For God knows that when you eat of it your eyes will be opened, and you will be like God . . ." (Genesis 3:4–5, ESV).

Jesus viewed the ministry more soberly. Remember how he prepared his own apostles before commissioning them: "I am sending you out like sheep among wolves. Therefore be as shrewd as snakes and as innocent as doves. Be on your guard against me; they will hand you over to the local councils and flog you in their synagogues." (Matthew 10:16–17, NIV). And remember Paul's oft-quoted warning: "Finally, be strong in the Lord and in his mighty power. Put on the full armor of God so that you can take your stand against the devil's schemes. For our struggle is not against flesh and blood, but against the rulers, against the authorities, against the powers of this dark world and against the spiritual forces of evil in the heavenly realms" (Ephesians 6:10–12, NIV).

Denominations and other organizations prepare their leaders to ward off conflict by teaching them how to be nice. Jesus and Paul prepared their ministers for war, knowing that conflict does not necessarily arise from a wrong. It may come because someone did something morally and spiritually righteous. Witness Mark 5:1–20, where the Gadara asked Jesus to leave after he healed Legion. Witness Jesus and the cross. Witness Acts 16:16–24: Paul and Silas cast out a demon from an exploited slave girl. The owners, who were manipulating her fortune-telling capabilities for profit, had the apostolic team arrested, imprisoned and fettered in the deepest, darkest cell. Luke, the author of Acts, does not comment: "Paul and Silas re-assessed their situation and apologized for their insensitivity. They agreed to wait until the Philippians were more psychologically prepared." Instead, Paul and

Silas sang in the prison. An earthquake led to the salvation and baptism of an entire family (see verses 25-34). Paul then had the gall to invoke his Roman citizenship and embarrass the authorities (verses 35-40).

The scene in Acts 16 bears study. A conflict "resolver" would usher in negotiation and mediation techniques at the moment of arrest; a "transformer" would investigate the conflict's surfaced issues: exploitative business practices, hasty arrest procedures with no evidentiary proceedings, a mob mentality, and an immediate assumption of guilt. The conflict was also used for redemptive ends (the salvation of the jailer and his family). Negotiation came once the sins were exposed and justice, at least in part, was done (verses 37-40). In this instance, the negotiation was not win-win. The injustice was exposed. There was no moral equivalency because the opposing parties were not morally equivalent. Paul's tactics were more similar to the non-violent actions of Gandhi and King than they were to ADR.

A GOLDEN OPPORTUNITY

A soft breeze of possibility blew through the evangelical scene early in 2018, when Doug Birdsall, honorary chair of the Lausanne Movement—an international evangelical alliance—invited over fifty pastors, organizational leaders, writers, and academic officials to meet at Wheaton College in Illinois for a two-day consultation on the movement's Trumpian takeover. He said the meeting was "prompted by the challenges and distortions to evangelicalism that have permeated both the media and culture since the 2016 election." The consultation would, he said, release a pastoral letter speaking to the movement's partisan alinement, although "our purpose . . . is neither political nor centered on public policy."[16]

Maybe the moderates would finally act.

Or not.

Fuller Theological Seminary President Mark Labberton saw evangelicalism's moral catastrophe. He told the gathering: "This is not a crisis imposed from outside the household of faith, but from within. The core of the crisis is not specifically about Trump, or Hillary, or Obama, or the electoral college, or Comey, or Mueller, or abortion, or LGBTQIA+ debates, or Supreme Court appointees. Instead the crisis is caused by the way a toxic evangelicalism has engaged with these issues in such a way as to turn the gospel into Good News that is fake. Now on public display is an indisputable collusion between prominent evangelicalism and many forms of insidious racist, misogynistic, materialistic, and political power. The wind and the

16. Beaty, "At A Private Meeting In Illinois," 4/26/2018,.

rains and the floods have come, and, as Jesus said, they will reveal our foundation. In this moment for evangelicalism, what the storms have exposed is a foundation not of solid rock but of sand."[17]

Powerful stuff.

But, once again, it was all duck and cover. Birdsall ladled assurances even before the consultation's opening: This summit should not be seen as opposing a pro-Trump gathering of a thousand evangelicals scheduled in June, and the pastoral letter's release would be postponed until after that date. Meanwhile, the right-wing evangelical press immediately leaped into action, with some pasting the consultation with "leftist" and even "Marxist" labels. Complaints were filed against Birdsall's failure to invite members of Trump's evangelical advisory council.

We've read from this script before: The zealots leveled ridiculous charges and the conflict-avoiding moderates yielded in their illusive quest for unity. At the conference, a generation gap soon yawned even as two conservatives walked out. Katelyn Beaty, who had been tweeting quotes from on-record speeches until she was asked to stop, rightly mourned in the *New Yorker*: "With a few exceptions, the older, white cohort stressed civility and unity. What the movement needed, they said, was a gentler evangelicalism that reached across partisan aisles for the common good. Others, especially the leaders of color, stressed repentance; there could be no real unity without white evangelicals explicitly confronting the ways in which they had participated in the degradation of persons of color and women."[18]

And so it devolved. Fewer attended on the second day, when conferees kept balking at calls for repentance. One longtime leader of an "evangelical umbrella group" said donors protested his mere attendance. Gabriel Saguero, the president of the National Latino Evangelical Coalition, denounced white evangelicalism's "idolatry of safety."

The upshot: There would be no pastoral statement.

Beaty concluded: "Without a statement, and with the bewildering skittishness about getting political, my time at Wheaton left me feeling deeply unsettled about the moral and political fortitude of my spiritual community in the era of Trump and beyond."[19]

Welcome to the world of moderate complicity, where the supposed "peacemakers" avoid risks at all costs.

---

17. Labberton, "Political Dealing: The Crisis of Evangelicalism," 4/16/2018.
18. Beaty, "At A Private Meeting In Illinois."
19. Beaty, "At A Private Meeting In Illinois."

A POST-FINAL WORD

I fear that I've been unfair to Peacemaker Ministries. So I reiterate: Peacemaker Ministries is a good organization and Ken Sande is a godly man. I'm thankful that he has brought in ADR's insights. As long as we understand that conflict resolution is only part of conflict transformation—albeit a crucial stage—I'm convinced we can use Peacemaker material constructively.

PART III

Beacons of Hope

9

Introducing the Real Jesus People

BUT THERE'S HOPE. REALLY. No fooling. It lingers beyond the growling reek. It even pokes its head on center stage and waves hello—and we needn't drift beyond our creedal pool to find it.

Seeing genuine hope stopped me from joining the ever-dour ex-evangelicals, who've fled the tribe and yell at it from afar. They wear bitterness like a warm sweater and join trendy movements like the Emergent Church, which was all the rage in the 1990's and in this century's early years. Gurus like Brian McLaren, Doug Pagitt, and Rob Bell invoked terms like "generous orthodoxy" and "conversation" and "dialogue." They presented themselves as an evangelical subset at first, more eager for insights from postmodernism (a nebulous intellectual school rejecting the 18th-century Enlightenment's cold rationalism).

That sweater soon itches. We scratch so hard we flare welts and our screams drive people away. Just look at the Emergents. The vague movement fizzled amid bickering even as it promoted dialogue—and Bell and McLaren wandered off orthodoxy's path, psychoanalyzing their opponents all the way as they dismissed legitimate theological concerns.[1] Its on-line hub, the Emergent Village, went defunct.

---

1. McKnight, "Brian McLaren's 'A New Kind of Christianity,'" *Christianity Today*, 2/26/2010..

Many now gather in the twitter flock surrounding John Pavlovitz and thumb tweets beginning with "if only evangelicals would . . ." and "why do evangelicals think ..?" They seem unaware of Roger Olson, Scott McNight, Katelyn Beaty, Timothy Keller, Beth Moore, Richard Mouw, Russell Moore (no relation to Beth), the Creation Care Network, and Christians for Biblical Equality, all of whom resist the bully onslaught. They've forgotten that traditional evangelicalism spans a theological range from Arminiasm to Pietism to Calvinism to Dispensationalism to Charismatic-Pentecostal-Third Wave, and those 81–19 2016 election-year results shed more fog than light: Again, many of those self-identified white evangelicals disagree with the tradition's historic beliefs. They're evangelical in name only. And remember: Those polls only refer to *white* evangelicals who voted for president. Trump's evangelical landslide plummets when we bring in the minority vote, which represents one third of Americans with evangelical beliefs.[2]

I knew a few now-popular ex's before they wrote books and complained of flight delays between speaking engagements. Common threads weave through their stories: They often grew up in a hermetically sealed neo-fundamentalist subculture, feathered with its shibboleths like so many chicks in a nest. They knew nothing but their fundamentalist and neo-fundamentalist worlds until calamity unveiled the horrible truth: Evangelicals aren't always nice and, shock of shocks, there's a vast universe of committed Christians beyond their coalition's pale. They discover dedicated Catholics and Eastern Orthodox believers who sincerely praise Jesus. They even unearth supposedly evil "secular humanists" who are deeply humanitarian. They sicked-up their grim neo-fundamentalism and now heap poxes on the entire evangelical house, failing to grasp that they lived in one of the movement's cobwebbed closets, usually painted in strict Calvinist and Dispensationalist hues.

They were scathing neo-fundamentalists back in the day; now, they're the caustic enlightened ones.

I briefly tried on that sweater. It didn't fit.

Something strange happened after I took it off: I listened to podcasts from evangelical institutions like Asbury and Fuller theological seminaries; I heard Keller and the debaters in the Veritas Forum; I listened to the preaching at Vineyard Christian Fellowship of Evanston, Illinois, an interracial congregation that resettles refugees and implements the so-called charismatic gifts. All reminded me that historical evangelicalism is a broad alliance that's neither anti-science nor politically partisan. Several of my

---

2. Stetzer, MacDonald, "Why Evangelicals Voted Trump: Debunking the 81%," *Christianity Today*, 10/18/2018.

favorite outlets are Reformed, which forces a smile: God is compelling me to learn from those with whom I disagree.

I re-discovered my home: I am, indeed, an evangelical—*as that term has been historically understood*. Like Keller, I normally don't use the "e" word in everyday banter because it's lost its meaning.

I'm still angry over the hijacking of the evangelical name and I know there's a place for legitimate, prophetic severity. I've exercised it here, remembering how Jesus chased out the Temple's money-changers—but he didn't do that every day and he found room for grace.

A welt-riddled life is no fun, so I'm glad I've thrown off bitterness's sweater and see the wisdom in Mahatma Gandhi's satyagrahi resistance philosophy: "The satyagrahi's object is to convert, not to coerce the wrongdoer."

We'll convert no one if all our words burn like acid.

Besides, bitterness blinds us to the real hope found in ministries led by Keller, Ed Brown, and Steve and Cindy Nicholson of the Vineyard Church of Evanston, Illinois. I devote a chapter to each because they meet three qualifications: First, they've marked me personally; second, they've ministered for decades and have maintained the character and doctrinal prerequisites so necessary for renewal. Worthy younger ministers dot the landscape, of course, but I'm playing it safe and following Proverbs 16:31 ("Gray hair is a crown of glory; it is gained in a righteous life," ESV). Third, they've thrived in the belly of the beast. They're older white American evangelicals, and yet they've yielded to neither partisan bullying nor bitterness. Their winsome, irenic path leads away from bitterness and into grace.

They're far from alone, of course, so I'll drop in some honorable mentions.

There are those minority evangelicals, who deserve another book. Or three. Or five. Don't be surprised if the morally bedraggled movement resurrects through African American and Hispanic communities.

And there's the effervescent Beth Moore. The Houston-based Bible teacher and speaker still talks the evangelical talk, complete with a drawl and invocations of a personal Satan (I find that refreshing and I agree with her). She didn't retreat after unveiling her thoughts in the wake of Trump's *Access Hollywood* tape. Read her tweet on November 14, 2017: "It's been a harrowing trip to Oz for many evangelicals this year, the curtain pulled back on the wizards of cause. We found a Bible all right, seemingly used instead of applied, leveraged instead of obeyed, cut and pasted piecemeal into a pledge of allegiance to serve the served." And there's another tweet: "It will become increasingly vital that we learn to distinguish between what is pro-Christian and what is actually Christ-like." And her anti-tyrant tweet: "There's a sick line of shared reasoning on perpetual repeat in the minds of racists, bigots, white supremacists, misogynists, & sexists: If we give them an inch, they'll take a mile. Here's the shocker: It's not your inch. Claiming ownership over God's property is perilous hubris."

I'm now a Beth Moore fan.

Finally, there are many evangelical academics. Many never joined the religious right and cry out against the bully hijacking. They, along with other faithful leaders, were especially appalled when President Trump dismissed certain African and Latin American nations as "shithole countries" in January of 2018. Fuller President Mark Labberton replied in a tweet:

> As a fellow human being, as a citizen of the United States, as a seminary president, and specially as a disciple of Jesus Christ, I am horrified by and ashamed of Trump's comments about Haiti and African countries, and their peoples. It is shocking, though not surprising, that Trump holds such views since his track record has been long and clear. Our history and our system has brought us to this horrific point, leaving us stunned and humiliated by the vile statements and actions of our elective leader. May this moment awaken a profound national lament, true repentance of racist hearts, and a fresh commitment to personal and systemic change that honors all human beings as creatures made in the image of God.

Kent Annan, a senior fellow at Wheaton College's Humanitarian Disaster Institute, wrote this in Christianity Today: "I'd hope that Americans, including those in power, would recognize the beauty of these countries and the contributions their immigrants make to our country. Our neighbors, who are especially vulnerable right now, deserve our continued welcome without disparagement and without hesitation."[3] Karen Swallow Prior, a Liberty University English professor at the time, responded via social media: "I've been privileged to travel to Africa four times, and fell in love more each time with the land and the people. I have never been treated more hospitably than when I was in that beautiful continent. What an example you set for America, dear #Africa!"

And the presidents of Calvin College and Calvin Theological Seminary signed a joint proclamation:

> Calvin College and Calvin Theological Seminary, higher education institutions founded by immigrants, are composed of students, faculty, and staff from more than 60 nations. While 600 of us may claim citizenship in another country, we are all prime

---

3. Annan, "Why We Need to Talk about Trump's Haiti Remarks," *Christianity Today*, 1/12/2018.

citizens of the Kingdom of God and share in a brotherhood and sisterhood that transcends all borders. It is for this reason, this love for our brothers and sisters, that we are deeply troubled and offended by the disparaging comments attributed to the President of the United States in recent days about people who come from Africa, Haiti, and Latin America. These comments sow fear and hatred in our country, and they are wrong.[4]

Not to mention Russell Moore, who often chides evangelicals from his post as president of the Southern Baptist Ethics & Religious Liberty Commission.

There are, indeed, signs of hope all over the evangelical map. Think of the three ministries I'm about to probe as beacons of many more. They, and others, allow us to rephrase a famous line from Bill Clinton's first inaugural address: "There is nothing wrong with evangelicalism that cannot be cured with what is right with evangelicalism."

---

4. Le Roy, J. Medenblick, "Joint Statement from Calvin Seminary and College," 1/15/2018.

10

Gotham's Good Calvinist

Note: Timothy Keller issued a sobering announcement just before this book rolled into production: He discovered he had pancreatic cancer. I'm praying for his full recovery.

HELL HATH NO FURY like the wrath of the open-minded.

Witness the roil in March 2017, when Princeton Theological Seminary researchers unveiled their pick for an annual $10,000 award. The school's Abraham Kuyper Center For Public Theology deemed Timothy Keller, the retiring pastor of Manhattan's Redeemer Presbyterian Church, worthy of its prize for "Excellence in Reformed Theology and Public Life." And why not? Keller is the poster child for an engaging brand of Calvinism hailing from the late 19th-century Netherlands, often called neo-Calvinism, led by a multi-tasking dynamo named Abraham Kuyper (1837–1920). Kuyper saw Christ everywhere and urged cultural involvement. The Center grants the award "to someone who has excelled in his or her chosen sphere, and as a result won recognition for the continuing cultural relevance of the Reformed tradition. The Abraham Kuyper Lecture and Prize opens the annual conference on a theme related to the winner's work."[1]

Keller, whom Kate Shellnut described as "the most popular Reformed preacher and author in America today,"[2] shuns the stereotypical Calvinistic

---

1. See the seminary's library web site at: https://library.ptsem.edu/newsletter/the-research-centers#1235;.

2. Shellnutt, "Princeton Seminary Reforms Its Views on Honoring Tim Keller," *Christianity Today,* 3/22/2017.

frown even as he sinks his roots deep into Reformed theology. He's actually a gracious Calvinist. He's dodged the culture war while upholding traditional values, making him a beacon of hope to the Reformer's heirs and the larger evangelical community. He's even supported The BioLogos Foundation, founded by geneticist Francis Collins to promote classical Christianity's reconciliation with evolutionary science.[3]

Some, naturally, suspect he's slid down the slippery slope. My prayer: "Almighty God, transform all Calvinists into Keller Calvinists."

FROM ALLENTOWN TO MANHATTAN

Born in 1950 in Allentown, Pennsylvania, Keller came to Christ through the guidance of InterVarsity Christian Fellowship and the writings of C.S. Lewis as a Bucknell University undergraduate (class of '72). He signed on with InterVarsity's staff in Boston for three years, attended Gordon-Conwell Theological Seminary (where he met his wife, the former Kathy Louise Kristy of suburban Pittsburgh), was ordained by the Presbyterian Church in America (not to be confused with the more theologically progressive Presbyterian Church of the United States of America, or PCUSA, with which Princeton affiliates), and did a nine-year pastoral stint in Virginia. He earned a Doctor of Ministry degree at Westminster Theological Seminary, joined the faculty, moved to the Philadelphia area, and implemented the neo-Calvinist vision: He involved himself in Muslim evangelism, chaired an organization reaching out to homosexuals and AIDs victims, and advised a group aiding jobless Philadelphians.

His career seemed set. The professorial role fit him like a snug blanket. He even looked and acted the part: wire-rimmed glasses, a balding pate, and a head crammed with enough tomes to declare his brain a fire hazard. But he found himself wooed by New York City's strange allure. His Atlanta-based denomination asked him to do the field research for a church plant in the heart of America's Gomorrah, where a 50-member team was planning and praying. He discovered some spiritual vitality in the city's outer boroughs, but Manhattan itself was a Sahara sprouting a lonely oasis: The Upper East Side, where a Campus Crusade For Christ offshoot was guiding executives into the faith. They now needed a church. Keller's first two pastoral choices declined the offer, and he grew convinced that God was calling him, his wife, and his three "hellion" sons (Kathy's description) to the crime-riddled city (remember, this was the 1980's). Not all onlookers were sure. Tim Stafford

---

3. See the BioLogos web site, https://biologos.org/. Keller presented a paper to BioLogos in which he defended evolution. See Keller, "Creation, Evolution, and Christian Laypeople," not dated.

quoted a Keller acquaintance: He "doesn't know what he has on most of the time, and Kathy is pure Pittsburgh."[4]

The couple defied the doubters. An evening service was launched in April of 1989 at a Seventh-Day Adventist church, where attendance climbed to 250 by Christmas. Three staff members were added by the church's anniversary. A non-profit mercy ministry, Hope For New York, opened in 1992. The church outgrew the Seventh-Day Adventist sanctuary by 1993 and moved to Hunter College's auditorium. Eventually, Redeemer met at three sites and achieved accumulative attendance levels of about 5,000 (45% are of Asian descent, which displays the Kingdom's inter-racialism[5]). Keller shuttled among the services. Redeemer planted daughter churches throughout the area and spawned other ministries—including the Center for Faith and Work, which mentors artists, entrepreneurs, and young professionals. In 2001, Keller unveiled *Redeemer City to City*, which trains church planters and has helped start 381 churches in 54 urban areas.[6]

Savor this: Keller embraces "catholicity and nonsectarianism ." He believes in Christian unity across denominations. He explains:

> If we are not united, the world writes us off, and perhaps, in light of Jesus' high priestly prayer in John 17:23 ('May they be brought to complete unity to let the world know that you sent me'), they have a right to do so. While we must continue to align ourselves in denominations that share our theological distinctives, at the local level our bias should be in the direction of cooperation with other congregations. Because of this belief, Redeemer Presbyterian Church has for a number of years given money and resources to churches of other denominations that are planting churches. We have helped start Pentecostal churches, Baptist churches, and Anglican churches, as well as Presbyterian churches. For our efforts we have received sharp criticism and a lot of amazed stares. We believe this is one clear way to practice the kind of catholicity that turns a city of balkanized Christian churches and denominations into a movement.[7]

---

4. Stafford, "How Tim Keller Found Manhattan," *Christianity Today*, 5/5/2009. Also, see "Redeemer history" at https://www.redeemer.com/learn/about_us/redeemer_history; Hooper, "Tim Keller Wants to Save Your Yuppie Soul," *New York Magazine*, 11/29/2009.

5. Zylstra, "The Life and Times of Redeemer Presbyterian Church," *The Gospel Coalition, US Edition*, May 22, 2017.

6. See the City-to-City web site: https://www.redeemercitytocity.com/about/.

7. Keller, *Center Church*, 368–369.

Mark this: A committed Calvinist sees the validity and orthodoxy of Arminian Pentecostals.

And he's written a kazillion books. His apologetical works, such as *The Reason For God* and *Making Sense of God*, defy today's conventional wisdom and employ rational argumentation. We're not supposed to do that anymore, what with everyone purportedly spinning in the postmodernism vortex, where meta-narratives swallow linear thinking and all dwell in their own truth. Yet Keller pulls it off. In *Generous Justice*, he dispenses with the false choice between personal and societal redemption: We steep in God's compassion for the poor and oppressed when we come to Christ. A yearning for societal justice should be inevitable.

Redeemer intentionally split into three sister congregations upon Keller's 2017 retirement (he's still a member and leads seminars). Each shares common, generous-justice goals: long-term, poverty-ending community development; integrating faith and work for university graduates; affordable day care and after-school programs; neighborhoods welcoming churches; and churches armed with expertise in faith, work, social justice, evangelism, and community building. All seek to "change hearts and form new communities of believing individuals united in serving their cities with the love and hope of Christ."[8]

Keller also teamed-up with D.A. Carson in 2005 and founded the Gospel Coalition. My reviews are mixed. I've listened, read, and found myself pleasantly surprised. Its writers, who take the Bible seriously, call Trump to task. But one of its leaders, John Piper, wandered into near misogyny even as the #MeToo Movement swelled: Women, he said, should be barred from the police force and seminary faculties.[9] To their credit, some coalition members distanced themselves from Piper's remarks,[10] but the hub seems to live in a complementarian, Calvinist paddock. Jonathan Merritt's criticism bears legitimacy: "Pop the hood, and you'll find that (the Gospel Coalition's) modus operendi combines harsh critiques of those outside its tribe with a bunker mentality that silences any who dare to question their thinking."[11]

Advice to the Coalition: Lean more toward Keller and less toward Carson. And remember: Calvinism occupies only one enclave in the Protestant house.

---

8. See the "About" page on the Redeemer City-to-City web site

9. See desiringGod.org posts on 8/23/2015 and 1/22/2018.

10. See Thompson, "Women on a Theological Faculty?," *The Gospel Coalition Australia Edition*, 7/02/2018.

11. Merritt, "The Gospel Coalition and how (not) to engage culture," *Religion News Service*, 6/6/2016.

Nevertheless, Keller's gems gleam. First, there's his homiletics—which, perhaps, can be described as "all substance but no style." His Sunday sermons bore the aura of fascinating lectures—or, as Stafford put it, "Keller speaks like a college professor, absorbed in his content, of which there is a lot. When longtime friend and founding member Dee Pifer invited colleagues from her Manhattan law firm, she would say, 'I want you to hear a really good litigator.'"[12] Joseph Hooper marveled over his refusal to pull punches: "Keller doesn't speak in theatrical, over-the-top tones but in a soft, conversational manner, as if he's sharing a confidence with a friend," but: "He notes that tennis legend Chris Evert once admitted in an interview that she was driven to win because 'winning made her feel pretty' and that Madonna confessed she felt special only when she was breaking through to new levels of fame. Whether we're athletes, artists, businesspeople, or preachers, Keller says, we all suffer from the same malady—trying to fill our empty spaces with achievement when only accepting God's grace can do the job. 'We want to feel beautiful, we want to feel loved. We want to feel significant and that's why we're working so hard and that's the source of the evil.' In another sermon, on another Sunday, he asks the congregation point-blank: Why are you in New York? Deep down, you think something is wrong with you.'[13]

He litters his sermons with Flannery O'Conner quotes and Robert Bellah references and allusions to the Puritans. No dumbing down here.

And there's his graciousness, which shines as he fields skeptical questions in Veritas Forums or before Google workers (find the talks on YouTube). And his traditionalism, for lack of a better word. He doesn't shrink from Christianity's less palatable doctrines. He argues for Hell's reality (I agree with him), and says the Bible teaches marital complementarianism and exclusively male church leadership (I disagree agree with him there).

Hear the explosion as commonplace platitudes blow up. There's no way such a church should thrive in cynical New York, but it does.

APPLAUSE FROM THE LAND OF TULIPS

I can imagine the beaming smile of Abraham Kuyper, the Dutch pastor, theologian, journalist, educator, politician, university founder, and prime minister. Perhaps he's passing cigars in Heaven and declaring: "That's my kid."

Kuyper plumbed Calvinism's past and felt the pulse of its great theologians: Everything and everyone sprawls flat before the transcendent

---

12. Stafford, "How Tim Keller Found Manhattan," *Christianity Today*, 6/5/2009.
13. Hooper, "Tim Keller Wants to Save Your Yuppie Soul."

Being—including monarchs, dictators, CEOs, generals, and Type A alphas. We're all microscopic before the Almighty, say the tradition's theologians—and yet, we're important. God created all and touches everything with His common grace. Each believer is a priest and everyone is responsible, with civil government given the vital role of protecting all citizens in a well-ordered society. The office of the magistrate, said Calvin, is "specially assigned" by God.[14] Thinking developed through the centuries: The law restrains kings and queens. If absolutely necessary, citizens must depose rogue monarchs, which is why Congregational and Baptist churches spurred revolutionary fervor in the American colonies.

Calvinism's societal repercussions crystallized in Kuyper's roaring intellect and his claim, "No single piece of our mental world is to be hermetically sealed off from the rest, and there is not a square inch in the whole domain of our human existence over which Christ, who is sovereign over all, does not cry, 'Mine!'"[15] Richard J. Mouw sums it up: "When God saves us, (Kuyper) insisted, he incorporates us into a community, the people of God. And this community, in turn, is called to serve God's goals in the larger world."[16] Kuyper reasoned: "If thinking is first in God, and if everything created is considered to be only the outflowing of God's thought so that all things have come into existence by the Logos—i.e., by divine reason or, better, by the Word—yet still have their own being, then God's thinking must be contained in all things. There is nothing in the whole creation that is not the expression, the embodiment, the revelation of a thought of God."[17]

Genesis 1:28 implies a "cultural mandate" in which God delegated his rule to humanity, a rule implemented through distinct but interconnected spheres. There's the sphere of religious institutions; there's the sphere of politics; there's science, the arts, and so on. Each sphere must honor the others. Clerics cannot mandate their practices via law and politicians must respect religious liberty. The separation of church and state thwarts both secular domination and theocracy, giving Christians a theoretical basis for political participation in a pluralistic society: We advocate our positions while co-ruling with others. We do not dominate.

Mouw cautions that "there is plenty in Kuyper that needs updating and even serious correcting"[18] (pa-lease look away from his racism and sympa-

---

14. Calvin, *Institutes of the Christian Religion*, IV, 20:9.

15. Quoted Van Til, "Subsidiarity And Sphere-Sovereignty: A Match Made In . . .?," 623–624.

16. Mouw, *Abraham Kuyper: A Short and Personal Introduction*, 5.

17. Van Til, 622–623.

18. Mouw, xi.

thies for his Dutch cousins, the South African Boers), but he bequeathed us a framework for envisioning societal engagement. Calvin College took up the mantle in its mission statement: "We aim to develop knowledge, understanding, and critical inquiry; *encourage insightful and creative participation in society*; and foster thoughtful, passionate Christian commitments" (emphasis added). Kuyperian minds bred thoughtful declarations on social and ecological justice in the Christian Reformed Church and planted roots for The Center for Public Justice, a Christian think tank with origins in the 1970s Evangelical Left. His framework has spread into evangelical academia and mainline Protestantism via Princeton's Center.

A TEMPEST OVER A GENTLE MAN

So surely the amiable Keller deserved the Center's award. Even theological progressives respect him. The Center's directors probably expected polite applause in 2017 when they said the scholar-pastor "is widely known as an innovative theologian and church leader, well-published author, and catalyst for urban mission in major cities around the world."[19]

The ensuing squall opened a rare public peephole into progressive Christianity's double-speak: Everyone's welcome as long as they tip-toe on the politically correct tightrope.

The first tremors shook through a student organization. Representatives of the school's LGBTQ alliance submitted an "Open Letter to the Abraham Kuyper Center for Public Theology and (seminary president) Dr. Craig Barnes." The letter, which was polite, didn't cry for boycotts or the award's withdrawal. Instead, the signatories worried: "Rev. Keller's exclusionary and prohibitive stances on the ordination of women and LGBTQ persons is diametrically opposed to the mission and values of Princeton Theological Seminary." They cited a Keller quote: "I affirm and support the PCA's belief in male headship in the home and church. I would never want to see our denomination compromise its support of this biblical complementarianism. Along with Ligon Duncan, I have never seen a credible biblical case made for the ordination of women to be elders or pastors. And when I see some of my friends try to make such a biblical case, I find their use of Scripture alarming and disturbing."[20]

---

19. Gibson, "Princeton Seminary Taking Some Heat for Honoring Redeemer's Tim Keller," *Religion News Service*, 3/22/2017.

20. Calvo and signatories, "Open Letter To the Abraham Kuyper Center for Public Theology and Dr. Craig Barnes," accessed, 10/12/2018. The quotes were taken from Keller's essay, "The Case for Commissioning (Not Ordaining) Deaconesses."

I'm a little alarmed and disturbed that Keller is so alarmed and disturbed. Some of his own Gordon Conwell professors—including the late Roger Nicole, a respected Calvinist—presented sound arguments for women's ordination, and a close reading of Ephesians 5:18–33 reveals mutual service in marriage, not male dominance. Still, it must be said: The quote is snatched from its context. Keller was arguing for an *expanded* ministerial role for women in his denomination.

They also quote Keller's view on gay marriage: " . . . male and female have unique, non-interchangeable glories — they each see and do things that the other cannot. Sex was created by God to be a way to mingle these strengths and glories within a life-long covenant of marriage. Marriage is the most intense (though not the only) place where this reunion of male and female takes place in human life. Male and female reshape, learn from, and work together . . . Without understanding this vision, the sexual prohibitions in the Bible make no sense. Homosexuality does not honor the need for this rich diversity of perspective and gendered humanity in sexual relationships. Same-sex relationships not only cannot provide this for each spouse, they can't provide children with a deep connection to each half of humanity through a parent of each gender."[21]

This was, essentially, the PCUSA's formal stance until 2014. Now everyone must toe the line despite two thousand years of unified Christian doctrine—and requiring every award recipient to bow before the PCUSA on marriage effectively bans all Catholics and Eastern Orthodox Christians, as well as most American Protestants and almost all outside the post-Christian west.

Still, the petition was civil. The signatories had no qualms with inviting Keller to speak ("It is one thing to uphold academic freedom by allowing campus groups to invite certain speakers whose views may not reflect all the values of the institution . . ."); but the school should not esteem him with Princeton's name (" . . . it is wholly another to honor Rev. Keller by awarding him a prize as significant as this one when he has actively and personally championed the exclusion of women and LGBTQ persons from sharing in the full ministry of the Church"). They asked the Center to take a closer look in the future.

I understand the LGBTQ community's concerns even while I disagree. I'm less sympathetic with those who complained, "I wonder if I really belong here."[22] Really? Does your entire sense of home hinge on one award

---

21. Keller, "The Bible and same sex relationships: A review article," *Redeemer Report*, June 2015.

22. Barnes, "What I Learned From Our Seminary's Conflict About Hosting Tim Keller," *The Christian Century*, 8/9/2017.

granted to one individual? Is seminary a crib for coddling? If so, good luck in the tumultuous church at large.

The protests escalated in the blogosphere. Traci Smith, a San Antonio PCUSA pastor and Princeton alumnus, wrote: "It boils down to this: *an institution designed to train men and women for ministry shouldn't be awarding fancy prizes to someone who believes half the student body (or is it more than half?) has no business leading churches.* It's offensive and, as I have taught my four and five year olds to express, *it hurts my feelings*" (her emphasis).[23] Carol Howard Merritt—usually a thoughtful writer, pastor, and teacher—cried apocalypse on her *Christian Century* blog, getting Keller wrong in so many ways: "Princeton Seminary, the flagship seminary of the Presbyterian Church (U.S.A.), is giving an award for *Excellence in Reformed Theology and Public Witness to Tim Keller*, one of the loudest, most read, and most adhered-to proponents of male headship in the home . . ."

Loudest?

She continued: "I am literally shaking with grief as I write this. I have spent years with women who have tried to de-program themselves after growing up in (complementarianism's) baptized abuse . . . *Complementarianism means married women have no choice over their lives at all*" (her emphasis).[24]

Merritt lumped all complementarians into one heap. Granted, some are blind to the industrious woman of Proverbs 31:10–31 and would lock women in the kitchen. Most, however, are making an honest attempt to obey 1 Timothy 2:12: "I do not permit a woman to teach or to assume authority over a man; she must be quiet" (NIV) and Ephesians 5:22: "Wives, submit to your own husbands as you do to the Lord" (see my previous replies). And some of the most vocal opponents of marital egalitarianism and female leadership are assertive women. Read Kathy Keller's blunt essay: *Jesus, Justice, & Gender Roles*. She was gearing up for the pastorate until she met seemingly prohibitive passages. She halted her ordination process (I disagree with her exegesis; I admire her integrity). What's more, women did occupy ministerial offices at Redeemer and played crucial roles. Again, read Kathy Keller. She called herself Redeemer's co-founder and was the assistant director of communications and media. And Timothy Keller is anything but the domineering husband. All attest to Kathy's boldness. A friend, Scott Sherman, said, "he really depends on her . . . They were both nerds who read Tolkein, and probably know more Elvish than they would like you to know.

---

23. Smith, "Princeton Theological Seminary, Rev. Dr. Tim Keller, and the Abraham Kuyper Lecture," *Faith & Family & Spirit*, 3/10/2017.

24. Merritt, "Does teaching submission encourage abuse?," 3/17/2017.

He's inexplicable apart from her. She has her fingerprints all over his brain, and I mean that in a very good way."[25]

Merritt plunged into despondency: "So as Princeton Theological Seminary celebrates Tim Keller's theology, I will be in mourning. As he presents his lecture and receives his $10,000 award, I will lament for my sisters who have been maligned and abused. So much of my ministry has been dedicated to aiding the victims of these poisonous beliefs. In these difficult days, when our president says that women's genitalia is up for grabs by any man with power and influence, I hoped that my denomination would stand up for women, loud and clear. Instead we are honoring and celebrating a man who has championed toxic theology for decades."[26]

Meanwhile, Barnes and Keller were chatting. The seminary president recalled: "Tim Keller and I talked about this three times over the phone, and then finally we just agreed — it was his suggestion, actually — to say, 'Let's just set aside the prize. It's just gotten to be too much of a distraction.'"[27]

Underscore: *Keller* suggested the prize's withdrawal. He'd simply give the lecture.

Unfortunately, Barnes didn't say that when he conveyed news of the decision on March 22. He wrote, "In order to communicate that the invitation to speak at the upcoming conference does not imply an endorsement of the Presbyterian Church in America's views about ordination, we have agreed not to award the Kuyper Prize this year."[28]

The inevitable conclusion beyond the seminary's walls: Princeton's leaders swooned before the identity-centered onrush. The backlash was predictable. Jonathan Merritt, no back-holler fundamentalist, wrote this: "I've had the pleasure of being with Tim Keller on two occasions. Each time, I recognized areas where his theology and mine did not align. But I also walked away feeling I had been in the presence of someone who was eminently reasonable, thoughtful, kind. Tim Keller is no extremist. He is no misogynist. He is no bigot. He is not hateful. Anyone who has paid attention to his Manhattan ministry can attest to this. If Christians like Tim Keller are unworthy of honor and deserve to be marginalized, American Christianity is in serious trouble. Keller is like the tens of millions of American Christians who hold to traditional interpretations of the Bible on these issues. Most of them do not hate gay people (though some do). Most do not believe

25. Stafford, "How Tim Keller Found Manhattan," *Christianity Today*, 6/5/2009.
26. Merritt, "Does teaching submission encourage abuse?"
27. Williams, "Princeton Seminary President Talks Tim Keller, Women's Ordination, and How One Award Ignited Christian Twitter," *Sojourners*, 4/12/2017.
28. Barnes, "Update on the 2017 Kuyper Lecture and Prize," 10/13/18.

women are inferior (though some do). They are doing their best to love their God and love their neighbors and live their lives according to what they believe the Bible teaches."[29]

Britain's Ruth Jackson, the editor of Premier Youth and Children's Work and head of Youth Apologetics, described herself as "fiercely, unequivocally, unapologetically egalitarian" but a "huge" Keller fan. She said of Merritt: "Not only is her post grossly hyperbolic by equating Keller with Trump's womanizing, it is also a heinous misrepresentation of the church leader's ministry which has focused on urban transformation and reaching skeptics, not fighting the culture wars of right-wing politics. Her use of words such as 'maligned', 'abused' and 'victims' are incredibly offensive to individuals who have experienced genuine abuse both inside and outside the Church. Likewise, I would rather reserve terms like 'poisonous beliefs' and 'toxic theology' to those preaching a message antithetical to the gospel. Extremist jihads who kill innocent people in God's name, harsh task masters who negate grace and oppress individuals through staunch legalism, selfish dictators who refuse to help the poor and downtrodden—these beliefs and practices are poisonous and toxic."

She pointed out: "Many have noted the irony of the fact that Abraham Kuyper himself, the theologian after whom the award is named, would now be ineligible to receive it."[30]

Richard Mouw, a former award recipient, commented: "Just last week I talked to a journalist who told me how much Keller had encouraged her in her calling to be a strong voice in her profession. 'I see him as one of my key mentors,' she said. She is not alone in this. I have heard similar testimonies from women in the banking world, academic life, and other areas of public service."[31] Fifteen Kuyper Prize recipients threw in their protest: "In this decision, Princeton Theological Seminary gives evidence of a policy unworthy of its history of free academic debate and diversity that characterizes this great institution."[32]

---

29. Merritt, "Why Princeton's snub of Tim Keller should outrage progressives," *Religion News Service*, 3/22/2017.

30. Jackson, "I'm an egalitarian female preacher who believes Tim Keller has been treated horribly," *Premier Christianity*, 3/24/2017.

31. Mouw, "From Kuyper to Keller," *Christianity Today*, 3/27, 2017.

32. Carnes, "Princeton Theological Seminary is 'Unworthy' of its traditions, says Kuyper Conference alumni," *A Journey Through NYC Religions*, 4/ 5/2017. The signatories were: Dr. James D. Bratt, Professor of History Emeritus, Calvin College; Dr. Ad de Bruijne, Professor of Ethics and Spirituality, Theologische Universiteit Kampen; J. Daryl Charles, Affiliated Scholar, John Jay Institute; James Eglinton, Meldrum Lecturer in Reformed Theology, University of Edinburgh; George Harinck, Professor of History, VU University Amsterdam / Theologische Universiteit Kampen; Marinus de Jong

So the Internet lit up, with no end of I-told-you-so comments from evangelicals. I had fun on the HuffPost: "Should We Tag Tim Keller With a Trigger Warning?"[33]

Keller smiled through everything. He didn't play the martyr or impugn anyone's motives or speculate over conspiracies from the theological left. He simply gave the Princeton lecture—an interesting talk on missiologist Leslie Newbigin (1909–1998), who returned to Great Britain from India and found a pagan society. The Church, said Newbigin, must engage in a "missionary encounter with Western culture."

I watched the lecture on YouTube and loved it. But I'm prejudiced. I'm a Keller fan. Perhaps it's better to view the talk through the eyes of Jeff Chu, a gay former evangelical and Princeton student:

> On the night of the lecture, Keller showed up as the nice guy that nearly everyone expected him to be. His talk, less polished than his typical Sunday sermon, zipped serviceably through "seven ways to have missionary encounters in Western culture," building on the work of 20th-century British missiologist Lesslie Newbigin.
>
> A well-mannered guest, Keller criticized his own family more than his hosts, repeatedly citing evangelicals' flaws. When he critiqued the mainline (for overemphasizing the gospel's horizontal, social axis at the expense of the vertical and salvific), he did so winsomely, saying, 'Let me just for a moment dump on the mainline—it won't be long.'

Keller said he prepared the talk before the controversy. "Still," said Chu, one suggestion seemed relevant: "'You can't disagree with somebody by just beating them from the outside,' he said. 'You have to come into their framework. You critique them from inside their own framework; you don't critique them for not having your framework.'"[34]

MA, PhD candidate, Theologische Universiteit Kampen; Andrew Kloes, independent scholar; Cornelis van der Kooi, Professor of Systematic Theology, VU University Amsterdam; Andrew Ong MDiv, PhD candidate, University of Edinburgh; Alvin Plantinga, Professor Emeritus of Philosophy, University of Notre Dame / Calvin College; Stefan Paas, Professor of Missiology, VU University Amsterdam / Theologische Universiteit Kampen; Gregory W. Parker Jr. BS, MDiv student, Gordon-Conwell Theological Seminary; Nathaniel Gray Sutanto MAR, PhD candidate, University of Edinburgh; Nicholas Wolterstorff, Noah Porter Professor Emeritus of Philosophical Theology, Yale University; John Halsey Wood, Jr., independent scholar.

33. Redfern, "Should We Tag Tim Keller With A Trigger Warning?" *Huffpost*, 3/23/2017.

34. Chu, "Soul-searching at Princeton Theological Seminary," *Religion News Service*, 4/12/2017.

The standing-room-only crowd enthusiastically applauded after a gracious talk in which Keller kindly stood his ground. It was a tour de force. Once again, Keller glowed as a beacon of hope.

WALK TOWARD THE LIGHT

Keller and his church help light the path out of white American evangelicalism's current darkness. His path guides us away from gutted Bibles and into Christ's radical call. Perhaps not surprisingly, jaded America finds him refreshing. He wrote articles for *The New Yorker* and *The New York Times*—veritable secular bastions—in which he defied the evangelical political caricature. He traced the varied meanings of "evangelical" through the centuries in *The New Yorker*, emphasizing its theological, non-partisan character. Now, via misunderstanding in the popular press mixed with doctrinal drift among self-identified white evangelicals, the word heralds a political and social tribe, most often associated with "hypocrite." But does that mean evangelicalism lies on its deathbed? He said answering that question requires discernment. There's "big-E" evangelicalism, to which the media flocks, and "little-E" evangelicalism, of which reporters are barely aware but which percolates in America's minority communities and flows across the world. The little-E's are far more committed to racial and social justice. "In this way, they might be called liberal. On the other hand, these multicultural churches remain avowedly conservative on issues like sex outside marriage," he said. They "resist contemporary ethical package deals" from the political partisans because they march to the beat of a different drummer. Perhaps another term may replace "evangelical" but the thinking behind it will thrive.[35]

In *The New York Times*, he addressed the burning question: With which American political party should Christians feel more at home? His answer: Neither. Our cry for justice and conservative family morals doesn't sync with any political clique. We make people freeze at cocktail parties. This doesn't mean we should abandon politics, since many moral issues bear political ramifications (think of slavery in the 19th century), but we'll sense that odd-man-out feeling wherever we wander.[36]

Lisa Miller characterized Keller as a "misfit."[37] May his brand of winsome incongruity spread far and wide.

---

35. Keller, "Can Evangelicalism Survive Donald Trump and Roy Moore?," *The New Yorker*, 12/9/2017..

36. Keller, "How Do Christians Fit Into the Two-Party System? They Don't," *The New York Times*, 9/29/2018.

37. Miller, "The Smart Shepherd," *Newsweek*, 2/ 9/2008.

11

Rescuing God's Creation

I admit it. I want Ed Brown's job—even though donation shortfalls forced him to prune one of his ministries in 2019. The Wisconsin based missionary kid and former pastor travels the world in an effort to save the Earth, convinced that "the church of Jesus Christ is the key to environmental healing."[1] He comes across a kindly grandfather who reads bedtime stories to giggling kids. They don't know he's synchronizing an international alliance of eco-friendly Bible-based Christians.

He faces no small task. As we have seen, some well-publicized evangelicals embrace an environmental philosophy extolling rancid swill and hurling suspicion on anyone agreeing with the scientific majority. Society at large can't help but see the irony: Pro-life evangelicals rightly cite science in their anti-abortion arguments but decry it on this issue.

We've also seen that such environmental hostility is an aberration in the Christian heritage, where the burden of proof lay with industrial innovators. Alister McGrath pointed out that many in the medieval church doubted the morality of mining because it altered the Earth: God's designated stewards were meant to toil in harmony with His creation.[2] They were not His tyrants. Industrialization, with all its benefits, was anchored in

---

1. Brown, *Our Father's World*, 14.
2. McGrath, *The Reenchantment Of Nature*, 55.

the humanity-against-nature thinking of the 18th-century Enlightenment. Machines could whip back the forests, slaughter wild and rabid wolves, drain mosquito-infested swamps, fill-in bays, and spread European civilization to far-flung fronts.[3]

Both C.S. Lewis and J.R.R. Tolkien carried traditional Christianity's torch. Their writings reveal suspicion of soot-laden, impersonal mechanization that demotes human beings to economic cogs. A host of American evangelicals now run the race, and it's a pity I can't devote a chapter to each. Calvin B. DeWitt, born in 1935, is sometimes hailed as "the modern-day father of Christian environmentalism."[4] He served as the first executive director of the Au Sable Institute of Environmental Studies, helped establish the Evangelical Environmental Network in 1993, wrote reams of essays and books, lectured the world over, and taught for decades at the University of Wisconsin. Canadian-reared Katharine Hayhoe, an atmospheric scientist at Texas Tech University and pastor's wife, tours the Christian college circuit and gives forceful, data-driven arguments for action on human-induced climate change. *Time Magazine* listed her among the one hundred most influential people in 2014. There's the Au Sable Institute itself, which began its pre-natal infancy in 1961 as a nature-study summer youth camp in northern Michigan.[5] It blossomed into its present state in 1979 and, today, offers courses to students from sixty Christian colleges, with campuses on the Pacific rim, in India, Costa Rica, and, of course, Michigan. Many ecologically-aware evangelicals have passed through Au Sable and now write books. One is Dorothy Boorse, a Gordon College biology professor at the forefront of pro-science evangelicals. She's written a text on environmental studies,[6] speaks at gatherings, and serves on Au Sable's board. Another is Ben Lowe, who led Young Evangelicals For Climate Action until he aged out of the position when he passed thirty.[7] And never forget the Evangelical Environmental Network, now led by Mitch Hescox. Ronald Sider's Evangelicals For Social Action founded EEN in 1993 and eventually spun it off into its own entity. Among other things, EEN personnel lobby senators and congressmen for sound environmental policies.

So many unheralded, worthy people, laboring in under-funded ministries and often blasted with hate mail. Others include Lowell Bliss of Eden

---

3. McGrath, *The Reenchantment Of Nature*, xv-xviii.

4. See the Au Sable web site (https://www.ausable.org/our-story) and Brown, *Our Father's World*, 14.

5. See Au Sable's web site, https://www.ausable.org/our-story.

6. Wright and Boorse, *Environmental Science*.

7. Lowe's books: *Green Revolution*; *Doing Good Without Giving Up*; *The Future of Our Faith: An Intergenerational Conversation*

Vigil; Peter Illyn of Restoring Eden; Matthew and Nancy Sleeth of Blessed Earth; and John Elwood of Beloved Planet—to name a paltry few.

THE MOVEMENT MAKER

Brown is bringing them together. He's the C.E.O. of Care of Creation in Madison, Wisconsin, which fell victim to those funding cuts, and head of Creation Care in the Lausanne movement (an international network of evangelicals forged in the 1970s under the leadership of Billy Graham and Great Britain's John Stott). Brown is a genial organizational hombre and cat herder. He must be. His alliance encompasses introverted biologists, physicists, environmental scientists, academics, and disgruntled writers, teachers, and speakers composing evangelicalism's creation care movement. The Lausanne idea for environmental care: Awaken all to the Scriptural call for ecological nurture.

That's ambitious. Scientists and academics are often more at home in the lab or sloshing through swamps. Rallying believers involves . . . *people*.

Two characteristics render him uniquely qualified to spur a global movement of loners. First, he knows the mindset. "I'm strong on the introvert scale," he told me in a 2018 e-mail interview. "I was painfully shy in high school—no one would have or could have predicted my career trajectory." Second, he's been a world trekker for as long as he can remember. He was the first of five children and born in 1953 in Fitchburg, Massachusetts, a city of about 40,000 near the New Hampshire border and 45 miles northwest of Boston. His family moved to Pakistan in 1954, so he wasn't in Fitchburg when it crossed paths with fame: *The Return of Peyton Place* was filmed there in 1961. His parents had signed on with the Conservative Baptist Foreign Mission Society (now WorldVenture) and worked in the southern Sind Province. He and his siblings attended school in the mountains north of Islamabad. Brown returned to America every four years for furlough, then permanently in 1969, where he finished high school and studied at Gordon College near the Cape Anne Peninsula on the Massachusetts Bay's north shore. He met his first wife, Sharon, at Gordon. They moved to Denver Theological Seminary, where doctors discovered calamity: She had brain cancer. He transferred to Gordon-Conwell, about two miles from his alma mater, so they'd live near Sharon's family during her illness. He graduated in 1979 and, alas, she died in 1981. He freely admits it "probably took several years to get back to normal."

He wedded his second wife, Susanna, in 1982, and they've remained married ever since.

Like many, Brown discovered tragedy's interwoven layers of emotions and wisdom. Surprising positives accompany the predictable mental paralysis: "Facing death in the face—your own or somebody else's—tends to put the rest of life into perspective." A question hovers over any given issue: "What's the worst than can happen?" If the worst has already occurred, "there's a bit of a sense of freedom that comes with it." And of limits: "I can remember very clearly articulating a lesson from God: 'We're not allowed to ask why something happens.' God has his reasons, and to allow him to be God in my life means accepting that his reasons are and must be good, even if I can't understand them. This also allows you to reject some of the silly 'why' answers that people bring to you, thinking they are helping or comforting." He finally declared: "I don't know why, but God has said he will bring me through, and I trust that he will do so."[8]

Brown juggled his emotions while pastoring a Conservative Baptist church in urban Lynn, a city of about 92,000, almost eleven miles north of Boston and once the world's shoe-making capital: 234 factories churned out a million pairs of shoes a day at the turn of the twentieth century. But Lynn met a familiar fate: Its main industry evaporated and the last shoe factory closed in 1981. By the time he and ailing Sharon arrived, Lynn was known for its vice, crime, and dropping wages (a family's 2016 median annual income stood at $54,711 in 2016, compared with $75,297 for Massachusetts as a whole; to be fair, Lynn's income had climbed from $37,364 in 2000).[9] A tasteless popular rhyme paid the city no compliments: "Lynn, Lynn, the city of sin, you'll never come out the way you went in . . ."

It sinks from there.

And Brown's church had plunged down a familiar spiral: It "was almost on its last legs when I had it and died after the next pastor. There were some demographic changes going on, but the reality is that they had an abusive pastor before me and never got over it. They could never trust a pastor after that, and while I was able to keep things steady for six or seven years, growth wasn't possible." Many former members now served on other church boards.[10]

He kept at it until December of 1983, when he signed on with International Students, Inc., in Providence, Rhode Island, and remained until 1990, then served at Islamabad's Protestant International Church until 1995. Eighteen months of unemployment followed when his job was eliminated, so it was back to the U.S.A., this time as personnel coordinator for

---

8. E-mail interview, 2018.
9. City-Data.com, "Lynn, Massachusetts."
10. E-mail interview, 2018.

InterVarsity Christian Fellowship's Link program in Madison, Wisconsin. InterVarsity is a parachurch campus ministry founded in Great Britain, with Link sending staff overseas to spur student movements in other countries. Gone were the days of solo ministry. Now he was a team player in a mammoth organization. He discovered his latent organizational skills as he wove a web of relationships via InterVarsity's membership in the International Fellowship of Evangelical Students, composed of 160 movements.

But he met a professional dead end after five years with InterVarsity, and Au Sable was hunting for a chief operating officer. The irony: The future creation care leader "moved because Au Sable needed my organizational skills, not because I felt any sort of strong pull toward environmental work." His family was underwhelmed. His mother-in-law celebrated by asked him: "Are you abandoning God's call?"[11]

He worked with Au Sable for five years, which gave him a front-row seat to the budding Christian Environmental Stewardship movement, as it was then called. He met students and faculty from over sixty Christian colleges and learned from scientists such as Sir Ghillean Prance, an Au Sable board member and leading British botanist and ecologist, and Sir John Houghton, then head of the Intergovernmental Panel on Climate Change. He met Jim Ball of EEN and Richard Cizik and soaked in DeWitt's wisdom in their breakfast meetings. Au Sable "transformed my perspective on God, his creation, and the urgency of the environmental crisis facing the world today."[12] He got the "environmental bug," as he put it. "I began to learn what the real issues are in the world, and I wanted to help."[13]

The movement was strong on brain power and advocacy, with spokespersons filing testimonies before House and Senate subcommittees and dropping in on Capital Hill representatives: Vital work, no doubt, but he felt more energy should be funneled into the world of pastors and church boards and Sunday School teachers. He and Susanna believed "that the whole church of Jesus Christ and the ordinary people who are its members are the best and perhaps the only hope for a true solution to the global environmental crisis." They "hold the fate of creation in their hands."[14]

And he seemed to be the man. Few others had swum in so many of evangelicalism's feeder streams: He knew the local church and scientists and the world of missions. His globe-trotter upbringing forced him to view

11. E-mail interview, 2017.
12. Brown, *Our Father's World*, 15.
13. Robinson with Chatraw, *Saving God's Green Earth*, 63–64.
14. Brown, *Our Father's World*, 15–16.

issues and events through a multi-cultural prism: "I tend to see things as if I were not an American."[15]

Circumstances converged. DeWitt would soon be stepping down and Au Sable's powers-that-be opted for restructuring. It would go without a COO and leave Brown, now over fifty with three college-age children and no savings, looking for a job. He and Susanna prayed while wiping off beads of sweat.

The life-changing e-mail arrived in December of 2004. It came from soft-spoken but determined Craig Sorley,[16] who had been promoting an innovative approach to missions in his beloved East Africa. Sorely plaintively asked, "How would you like to help us?"[17]

Brown knew his story. Sorely, a child of medical missionaries, grew up in three different East African countries. He holds two degrees from the University of Minnesota (a bachelor's in Natural Resources and a master's in forestry), where he managed to survive brain cancer in 1989. He may have coined the term, "environmental missions" after witnessing Kenya's massive ecological devastation: a noxious brew of climate change and poor farming practices left vast swaths stripped of trees and bereft of crops (in 2015, the nation lost an average of 5.6 million trees a day[18]). He envisioned teams teaching land-friendly farming methods while sharing the Gospel. They'd model themselves after medical missionaries, who heal the body and the soul; environmental missionaries would heal the *land* and the soul—highly relevant in agricultural Kenya. As Lowell Bliss puts it: "Shovel in one hand. Bible in the other. That's environmental missions."[19]

Perhaps predictably, Sorley's plea fell on deaf ears. No mission agency said yes.

Maybe Sorley was Brown's "Macedonian Man,"[20] an allusion to Acts 16:6–12 in the New Testament, where the Apostle Paul's ministry team met walls until a man from Macedonia beckoned in a dream. It made sense. Environmental Missions may ring esoteric to sandal-clad Westerners hunting

---

15. E-mail interview, 2017.

16. Sorley's gentility and devotion oozes in a 2015 youtube Wheaton College video, "Mobilizing the Church in East Africa Towards a Commitment to Land Care," found here: https://www.youtube.com/watch?v=RQQ0xU7OwVo; accessed, 3/9/2018; it also comes through in his *Christ And Creation: Our Biblical Call to Environmental Stewardship*.

17. Brown, *Our Father's World*, 13.

18. Africa-Ecpo News, "Study: Kenya Loses 5.6 million trees daily," *Capital News*, 3/26/2015.

19. Bliss, "What is an Environmental Missionary?." *Flourish,*, Spring, 2010.

20. Brown, *Our Father's World*, 13.

for asparagus in a Muzak-haunted frozen food aisle, but it's up-close and personal to Kenyan subsistence farmers tilling deforested landscapes. Agriculture employs more than 75 percent of that nation's workforce; 46 percent lives below the poverty line; 35 percent of its toddlers are stunted and 16 percent are underweight. Only 20 percent of the land is arable.[21]

Some Occidentals do see the land-soul bond. Brown discovered that when he was Au Sable's exhibitor in 2003 at Urbana, InterVarsity's triennial student missions convention. Students besieged him. "Au Sable was the only organization among hundreds present that had 'environment' in its name or ministry description, and only a handful had anything to offer students concerned with this issue."[22] He saw it again at the 2006 conference. Science and environmental students "could not understand why this problem, so apparent to them, seemed not even to exist in the world of Christian missions organizations."[23]

What better laboratory than Kenya? Roughly 80 percent of the population identifies as Christian, yet poverty intensifies amid environmental collapse. "The people don't know how to be good stewards of the land—and it's killing them," he said. Just do the math: "If Kenya is 80 percent Christian, then Christians are the best hope to reverse the trend in Kenya. If you can show them that God wants them to care for the environment and give them the tools to do so, it can change quickly."[24]

Brown and Sorely wrote up a plan and circulated it among friends. "Everyone began encouraging us to do this."[25] The eventual mission statement was impressive:

> *Mobilizing the worldwide church toward*
> *a God-centered response to the environmental crisis*
> *that brings glory to the Creator,*
> *advances the cause of Christ*
> *and leads to a transformation of the people*
> *and the land that sustains them.*

Such entrepreneurship wasn't exactly risk adverse: "Starting a brand new organization that's both evangelical and environmental is just crazy—sort of like walking on water. It would take that much faith and more. In spite of all that, Craig's invitation was intriguing and even tempting, for I agreed with his premise that the church of Jesus Christ is the key to environmental

---

21. Feed The Future, *Kenya Fact Sheet*, January, 2013.
22. Brown, *Our Father's World*, 19–20.
23. Brown, *Our Father's World*, 20.
24. Robinson with Chatraw, *Saving God's Green Earth*, 65.
25. Robinson with Chatraw, *Saving God's Green Earth*, 64.

healing. His message, 'We want to transform people and the land they live on,' went to my heart."[26]

They launched the organization in April of 2005. Brown paid the bills by helping an N.G.O. relieve Pakistani earthquake victims. Care of Creation raised sufficient funds by May of 2006.

Brown served as the organization's overall director and C.E.O. while Sorley led the East African branch, headquartered at the Moffat Bible College in Kijabe, Kenya, on the edge of the Rift Valley and a little under 38 miles from Nairobi. The work eventually fanned into Tanzania. Tracy, Sorley's wife, mothered their two sons while consulting on projects and finances. They offered extension services, seminars in "mindset transformation" and "Farming God's Way"—which employed sustainable methods first honed in Zimbabwe—and they spearheaded tree-planting efforts. In the United States, Brown and his staff linked up with like-minded organizations, led workshops for churches and groups, gave talks at Christian colleges and missions organizations, and kept tabs on East Africa. His travel schedule for the first half of 2018 included trips to South Africa, California, Australia, Poland, and Illinois.

Sorely has since written four books and Brown has written two.

Brown finds himself swimming against the people-over-ecology argument ("we'd rather help human beings than plants"), which springs from "no grid to process how caring for the environment is a value germane to the Christian faith."[27] He responds: "When you care for the land, you're caring for the people. This is even more evident in a place like Kenya where people farm the land and live off it." And then there's the we're-not-lefties argument: "I've had to wrestle with this because I speak to some very conservative audiences . . . 'We can't be environmentalists because we're conservatives.' The heart of the evangelical faith and a great deal of what we believe as evangelicals is ecological. We believe God birthed creation, and we believe God has called us to take care of it."[28]

EXPANDING INFLUENCE

His sphere swelled after October 2010, when over four thousand Christian leaders representing 198 nations descended on Cape Town, South Africa, at the Lausanne Movement's Third International Congress on World Evangelization. The majestic aspiration of the Lausanne Movement, named after

---

26. Brown, *Our Father's World*, 14.
27. Robinson with Chatraw, *Saving God's Green Earth*, 65.
28. Robinson with Chatraw, *Saving God's Green Earth*, 66.

the Swiss city in which its first Congress convened in 1974, is to unite "influencers and ideas for global mission, with a vision of the gospel for every person, an evangelical church for every people, Christ-like leaders for every church, and kingdom impact in every sphere of society."[29] At the insistence of Latin American theologians Samuel Escobar and Rene Padilla as well as John Stott, Lausanne knits evangelism and social justice under the "integral mission" banner. The second Congress met in Manilla in 1989.

Each Congress crafted a statement, with the 1974 Lausanne Covenant casting the vision and laying the theological foundation. The Manilla Manifesto proclaimed 21 affirmations, the last of which reads: "We affirm that God is calling the whole church to take the whole gospel to the whole world." Integral mission loomed larger than in 1974:

> The proclamation of God's kingdom necessarily demands the prophetic denunciation of all that is incompatible with it. Among the evils we deplore are destructive violence, including institutionalized violence, political corruption, all forms of exploitation of people and of the earth, the undermining of the family, abortion on demand, the drug traffic, and the abuse of human rights. In our concern for the poor, we are distressed by the burden of debt in the two-thirds world. We are also outraged by the inhuman conditions in which millions live, who bear God's image as we do.
>
> Our continuing commitment to social action is not a confusion of the kingdom of God with a Christianized society. It is, rather, a recognition that the biblical gospel has inescapable social implications. True mission should always be incarnational. It necessitates entering humbly into other people's worlds, identifying with their social reality, their sorrow and suffering, and their struggles for justice against oppressive powers. This cannot be done without personal sacrifices."[30]

Intriguing: World-wide evangelicalism tacked toward communal responsibility and Catholic social teaching while Americans sank into Ayn Rand's libertarianism.

And so it continued in Cape Town.

Compare and contrast: The original 1974 gathering drew 2,700 mostly white Westerners from 150 nations; Manilla drew conferees from Eastern Europe, the crumbling Soviet Union, and an influx of Pentecostals. By 2010, Americans only filled five of the 25 seats on the Congress's advisory council,

---

29. See the "about" section on the Lausanne web site, https://www.lausanne.org/about-the-movement

30. Cameron, ed., *The Lausanne Legacy: Landmarks in Global Mission*, p. 73.

which developed a theological and strategic vision for the event. Planners made sure 55 percent of the attendees were below 50 years old.

Cape Town's statement revolved around ten "we loves" (we love because God first loved us; we love the living God; we love God the Father; we love God the Son; we love God the Holy Spirit; we love God's Word; we love God's world; we love the gospel of God; we love the people of God; we love the mission of God). The seventh is halved into two parts, with the first—"we love the world of God's creation"—rooting Lausanne firmly in the creation care camp. Sample this quote: "This love [for the environment] is not mere sentimental affection for nature (which the Bible nowhere commands), still less is it pantheistic worship of nature (which the Bible expressly forbids). Rather it is the logical outworking of our love for God by caring what belongs to him." And another: "The earth is the property of the God we claim to love and obey. We care for the earth, most simply, because it belongs to the one whom we call Lord. The earth is created, sustained, and redeemed by Christ. We cannot claim to love God while abusing what belongs to Christ by right of creation, redemption and inheritance." Love for the world also embraced love for "nations and cultures." It shuns the world of sin and Satan's rebellion.[31]

The statement implores repentance for creation's destruction, pledges commitment to "urgent and prophetic ecological responsibility," supports believers "whose particular missional calling is to environmental advocacy and action" and those "committed to godly fulfillment of the mandate to provide for human welfare and needs by exercising responsible dominion and stewardship." Integral mission "means discerning, proclaiming, and living out, the biblical truth that the gospel is God's good news, through the cross and resurrection of Jesus Christ, for individual persons, *and* for society, *and* for creation. All three are broken and suffering because of sin; all three are included in the redeeming love and mission of God; all three must be part of the comprehensive mission of God's people."[32]

But a question lingered: How to prevent the Cape Town agreement from the destiny of most noble declarations? They languish in a desk drawer's darkness or, today, wallow on a ghost web site, never to make a difference.

Lindsay Brown, then Lausanne's global director, and Las Newman of Jamaica, then the movement's Caribbean head, were on it. They pushed for a "Global Consultation on Creation Care and the Gospel" as the first in a series of post-Cape Town "consultations," or pow-wows in which movers

---

31. Cameron, ed., *The Lausanne Legacy: Landmarks in Global Mission*, 116–117.
32. Cameron, ed., *The Lausanne Legacy: Landmarks in Global Mission*, 117.

and shakers could move and shake, and they tapped Ed Brown to organize it. Brown reached into his grab bag of international contacts and enlisted Dave Bookless of A Rocha International, a network of environmental organizations founded by Britain's Peter and Miranda Harris in 1983 (Miranda, alas, died in a 2019 car accident in South Africa); Ken Gnandian, a prolific writer, educator, theologian, and founder of the ACTS Group of Institutions in India; Lowell Bliss; Bishop Efraim Tendero of the Philippines, who would be appointed as the World Evangelical Alliance's general secretary; and Ruth Valerio, who was eventually tapped as the Global Advocacy and Influencing Director for Tearfund, a British Christian relief and development agency.

Newman would host the event in Jamaica.

Brown was formally appointed as Lausanne's "Senior Associate for Creation Care" (also known as a creation care "catalyst") in June, 2012, at an international leadership meeting. Lausanne announced the move in an August press release and, typical for such statements, sung him high praise, remarkable only for its priority given to ecological care. Douglas Birdsall, then the executive chairman, said this: "Ed's appointment reflects our deep commitment as a Movement to the stewardship of God's creation and our commitment to seek ways to work together as the global Body of Christ to alleviate the destruction, waste, and pollution of earth's resources." He added: "We see this in terms of the Creation Mandate, and in terms of God's comprehensive redemptive mission, which is cosmic in scope."[33]

In other words, environmental care isn't a choice. It's a divine commandment.

Fifty-seven conferees from 26 countries met from October 29th to November 2nd in St. Ann's Parish, about 50 miles north of Kingston on Jamaica's coast, while Superstorm Sandy pummeled the Eastern United States. Dorothy Boorse couldn't reach Jamaica. Her flight was canceled. The Lausanne web site dropped in one of those no-kidding comments: "The destruction and loss of life [of Sandy] was a startling reminder as to the urgency, timeliness, and importance of this Consultation."[34]

The theologians, church leaders, scientists, and environmentalists prayed and deliberated over "God's World, God's Word, and God's Work" and signed a manifesto dubbed the "Jamaica Call To Action," which articulates two underlying convictions: First, "creation care is indeed a 'gospel

---

33. Frizzell, "Lausanne Movement Appoints Senior Associate for Creation Care," 8/6/2012.

34. Lausanne Movement, *Creation Care and the Gospel: Jamaica Call to Action*," 11/20012.

issue within the lordship of Christ," and, second, "we are faced with a crisis that is pressing, urgent, and that must be resolved in our generation."[35]

These principles laid the platform for the summons itself: "We therefore call the whole church, in dependence on the Holy Spirit, to respond radically and faithfully to care for God's creation, demonstrating our belief and hope in the transforming power of Christ. We call on the Lausanne Movement, evangelical leaders, national evangelical organizations, and all local churches to respond urgently at the personal, community, national. and international levels."[36]

There were specific appeals for "a new commitment to a simple lifestyle" and "new and robust theological work" and pleas for leadership from the global south. It called for the mobilization of the whole church and engagement with society, environmental missions among unreached peoples, radical action in the face of climate change, sustainable food production (so relevant in a world of desertification, sinking aquafers, and slash-and-burn farming), an economy harmonized with God's creation, biodiversity-boosting efforts at the local scene, and "prophetic advocacy and healing reconciliation." It's all capped off with an "urgent call to prayer."

Earth-shaking stuff.

I've met many of the consultation's participants and, surprise-surprise, they don't wear Che Guevara T-shirts. They brandish marked-up Bibles. They memorize verses and say "Hallelujah" and "Praise Jesus" and "glory be to God." Some even raise their hands as they sing hymns while packing their kids' lunches before sending them off to Christian schools. Most are mild-mannered husbands and wives and mothers and fathers who'd love to emulate conflict-avoiding Isaac. But they face a problem: They know their Bibles and hear God's call to steward his creation. They see the superstorms and the spreading deserts and the drought-laced landscapes and the sinking islands, so they swallow their introversion and spend their own money on flights to those gatherings, where they lecture and sign the statements and withstand the consequent social media troll invasion.

In other words, they're following Carl Henry's 1947 summons to emerge from their fortresses and engage the culture. And, without intending

---

35. Naturally, such phraseology met criticism. While endorsing environmental care, Marvin Newell, adjunct professor at Moody Bible Institute, said this: "If we infuse the 'gospel' with good and compelling yet secondary causes, we lose the essence of what the gospel primarily is—the good news of the redemption of mankind," *Missio Nexus*, July 14, 2015. Newell's criticism is friendly—he is pro-environment—and his call to see evangelism's priority must be taken seriously. But Colossians 1:16, as well as Genesis 1–3, shows us that God is rescuing the entire world by rescuing us. This really is a "Gospel issue."

36. "Creation Care and the Gospel: Jamaica Call to Action."

to, they flourish the antidote to moderate enabling and disgruntled whining: a theologically robust, biblical, spirit-filled, classical evangelical Christianity. Or, if the "e" word is now too hot, just call it Classical Christianity, which was the goal of Luther, Calvin, the pietists, Wesley, Edwards, and all those Protestant VIPs.

GOING WORLD-WIDE

Of course, the Jamaica Call stood in immediate peril: the desk drawer; the ghost web site.

Not to worry. There was a plan. Brown recruited Dave Bookless again and they wrote up a proposal for a three-year, nine-conference drive "to bring the message of Jamaica to the rest of the world," as he said in one of our e-mail interviews. "As things turned out, we are now completing our fourth year and have done eight conferences, with four more in the planning stages over the next year [2018–2019], so it will have turned out to be a six-year, twelve-conference campaign and will have touched almost one hundred countries."

The idea is to "jump-start or strengthen evangelical creation-care movements" across the globe.

Conferences were held in Africa, Asia, North America, South America, Australia, France, an other environs. I attended the meeting for North America in early August of 2015 at Gordon College. It was a time warp. I was strolling through evangelicalism's golden days—before intimidators laid their trip wires. There were lectures, of course (brainy academics and intellectuals give them in their sleep), with topics ranging from climate science to environmental missions to communication techniques to creation care's theological underpinnings. And there was prayer. And singing. And laughter. And biblical exposition. And field trips to local wetlands and Singing Beach, where my wife and I once strolled during seminary study breaks. And I drove the two miles to Gordon Conwell and visited one of my favorite professors, Garth Rosell. He gave me a bear hug.

It was all scented with God's presence. I felt light and free, no longer weighed by the passive aggressiveness and inertia rampant in the feuding, self-destructive churches I shepherded. I longed to be part of this movement. Perhaps I'd offer my oratory skills and serve as a spokesman.

Cancer benched me, but the movement pressed on. A team, led by Brian Webb, Houghton College's Sustainability Coordinator, represented climate-friendly evangelicals at the United Nation talks in France later that year, out of which emerged the landmark Paris Agreement. A 2016 book,

Creation Care and the Gospel, featured essays from 31 international authors. Partnerships were formed with A Rocha and Tearfund, and the campaign merged with the WEA (it's now known as the Lausanne / World Evangelical Alliance Creation Care Network, or LWCCN). Together with Care of Creation, the organizations surveyed 18 countries and found 55 Jamaica-stimulated environmental projects throughout the world.

Yes. God uses once-shy missionary kids. Power to the introverts.

Bookless was appointed as another Lausanne Global Catalyst for Creation Care early in 2018. He shares responsibilities.

SEEING THE POSSIBILITIES

Brown views the scene and sees hope. He said in 2016: "The sleeping giant that is the evangelical church is indeed waking up to the importance and urgency of caring for God's creation."[37] In 2018, he admitted to me that the awakening is slower than he had anticipated, but he still rung optimism's bell: "Seminaries are signing on; *Christianity Today* now regularly covers creation care topics; many mission organizations have devoted at least some staff time to this issue." As for the Trump earthquake: "In some ways, his election has helped to energize the creation care community both here and in other countries." He saw the mercurial president through his international eyes: "At this time, I think the greatest danger is within the US, in terms of long-term damage that will come from changed regulations, unless those can be reinstated relatively quickly after he goes." But "as in Narnia, the wind is coming from the south, and spring will come."[38]

Maintaining hope can be difficult in the precarious non-profit world. In May, 2019, Brown e-mailed his supporters: "Big changes are coming to Care of Creation and our affiliated ministries." Such statements usually signal staff cuts, and this e-mail did not disappoint. Mounting financial challenges, including drops in giving from major donors, forced an organizational split. The Sorleys would "transfer out of Creation Care, Inc.," and secure their own funding; responsibility for Creation Care's Tanzania branch would be "assumed by our Austrian ministry partners;" staff in Wisconsin would be trimmed, the office would be closed, and Ed would zero-in on his work for the Lausanne-WEA network.

So the ministry chugs on.

---

37. Brown, *The Lausanne Global Campaign For Creation Care and the Gospel: A Mid-Campaign Update Report*, 2.

38. E-mail interview, 2018.

Brown would wince if I lionized him or portrayed him as a hero—and that's not my aim. The fact is that he's one of many godly evangelicals living and working beyond the television camera's range. He and others show us that the solution to white America's evangelical debacle lies within evangelical Christianity itself, where humble ministers meekly deny their humility and take up their cross. They're signposts to hope.

Another ministry, located just north of Chicago, drills that point home as it embraces the power of the Holy Spirit and the Bible's call to befriend the sojourner. We now turn to it.

12

The Whole Gospel in the Midwest

I FINALLY PLUGGED INTO the 21st century in the winter of 2017 on a neighborhood walk, with buds in my ears and a smart phone in my pocket. There it was: The podcast universe, a veritable nerd's paradise of political lectures, philosophical talks, and theological debates galore. And I re-discovered that familiar, gentle voice, comforting a traumatized congregation just north of Chicago the Sunday after the 2016 electoral upheaval. The church was an inter-cultural and immigrant cornucopia, with worshipers from tyrant-riddled lands remembering life in the old country, where hatred's lingo signaled new prison wings for political inmates.

    I first heard that voice in the early 1990's as I stood quivering in a church sanctuary near Boston, eyes closed, as brave as a squirrel facing a barreling pick-up truck. Steven Nicholson, the featured speaker and pastor of the Vineyard Christian Church in Evanston, Illinois, was praying for conferees in a three-day forum on the power of the Holy Spirit. The scene looked like a casualty-littered battlefield. Almost everyone was sprawled on the floor. Some even twitched. Many Pentecostals call this experience "slain in the spirit;" Vineyard leaders are less dramatic and call it, "falling down."

    Whatever. I yearned to run away heroically. My history of epilepsy left me with no longing to lose body control—and an incongruity messed me even more: Nicolson didn't fit the stereotype. There was nary a drop of hairspray on his head and he shouted over no one. He seemed more like an insurance actuary than a preacher, even donning the requisite heavy-framed glasses under a full head of brown hair (it's white now).

Maybe I should sneak out of line and flee this mayhem.

But my hunger for God's touch overpowered my fright, so I remained, frozen like that befuddled squirrel. The conferee ahead keeled over and now the jeans-clad Nicholson stood before me. Suddenly, I was engulfed in a surge of electricity-like energy vaguely resembling an epileptic aura—but not quite. It was somehow therapeutic. I begged God for more even while I refused to fall, and Nicholson stood there for what seemed like minutes (it was probably thirty seconds). He watched. He said nothing. He saw my name tag and commented: "Wow, Chuck. The Holy Spirit's all over you," then watched some more. The energy kept surging (*I will not fall! I won't!*). Then came his reassuring voice: "Your prayers have been answered, Chuck. You *will* hear God's voice."

That was uplifting. I had, indeed, been praying for divinely-inspired dreams and visions and impressions. I longed to *know* this Lord in whom I believed. Nicholson stepped away and the energy surge tapered, leaving me with the sense that I shared the same experience as those floor twitchers. God understood my fear and allowed me to stand.

I would never forget Nicholson. He guided me through one of my first encounters with the Spirit's power.

He was unknowingly comforting me again through the podcast and shining a light on my path toward hope. Both he and his wife, Cindy—the church's assistant pastor—were wary of Trump's nationalism. And no wonder. His church, which they've served for over forty years and from which 16 others have been planted,[1] is now a microcosm of post-2045 America, that demographic landmark when whites of European decent are slated to step aside as the US majority. The Evanston Vineyard's weekly attendance averages 1,296 in four services at two locations, with the a racial-cultural data profile breaking down to 35% white, 10% African-American, 2% Asian Indian, 9% Pacific Islander, 9% Black African, 2% Black West Indies, 21% Hispanic-Latin, 1% Middle Eastern, 6% multi-racial, and 2% "other."[2] Its ministries include a care center featuring a clothes closet, help for area residents from everything to finding diapers to apartment hunting to child care to information on affordable legal counseling, English as a Second Language courses, a jobs program, a food pantry, and safe family training.

---

1. See the church's website as of 6/29/18: https://evanstonvineyard.org/overview/. Seven other churches have branched off from those sixteen.

2. See the church's 2017 annual report and Nicholson, "I Said 'Yes' To God," 5/30/2013.

The Nicholsons are among many Vineyard leaders guiding the association toward multi-racialism and multi-culturalism. Others include Kevin Fisher in Miami, whom Steve called a "pioneer" in a 2018 e-mail interview; Rich Nathan of Columbus, Ohio; and Geno and Shannon Olison, an interracial couple leading the South Suburban Vineyard in Flossmoor, Illinois. Geno grew up on Chicago's largely African American south side and discovered the lily-white church world in college, which spurred multiculturalism into his vision for a church plant. And there's Josh and Tina Williams of The Elm City Vineyard in New Haven, CT. Tina—a mother and worship leader—practices immigration law at the Esperanza Center for Law and Advocacy. Josh serves on the association's executive committee.

I'll focus on the Nicholsons with apologies (they're not interested in the limelight) because they meet all my gauges: They've unknowingly touched me personally; they've survived the decades and boast the white hair to prove it (indeed, they're almost retired); they're theologically orthodox; and the odds are they won't preach heresy or perp-walk with raincoats over their heads. Suffice it to say that the Evanston church is a beacon among beacons. It hosted conferences in 2016 and 2018 called, "Better Together: Race, Reconciliation, and the Multi-Ethnic Church," to which a slew of ministers flocked.

A WIDER VISION

It seems the entire Vineyard found its way into deeper, more holistic ministry after Wimber's 1997 death. The association has expanded its kingdom vision to include social and environmental justice (its church in Boise, Idaho, has blazed the trail in environmental ministry; the Vineyard Justice Network was established in 2013).

Wimber actually anticipated this and spurred service to the poor. Which is intriguing. Critics once disparaged the Vineyard for carving cookie-cutter white suburban enclaves mirroring Mother Anaheim. They were veritable caricatures of the church growth movement's "homogeneous unit principle" (a church won't grow unless its people bear the same ethnic and cultural characteristics). Thirty-seven percent of its churches now meet the sociological standard marking them as multi-racial—a benchmark met only by 13% of all US congregations.[3] What's more, many leaders see links with Catholic piety and practice spiritual direction, development, and contemplative prayer.

3. See Strout in the trailer for *Better Together: Race, Reconciliation, and the Multi-Ethnic Church, 2016*.

All this vivacity defies the rumor-mill, which portrayed the Vineyard was a shell of its former self, a whiff of leftover smoke from the Wimber-era fire, a numbers-crunching church-planting machine and nothing more. I bought that fable, but I now see that the Vineyard offers even more hope than in those "spotlight years," as Nicholson calls them, when Anaheim—dubbed "Wimberland" by Jackie Pullinger[4]—was a Mecca for signs and wonders.

The all-important question: Are we willing to listen? Or will we, once again, heap our own fears on the Vineyard and bury it in ill-founded accusations?

TACKING TO THE RADICAL MIDDLE

The association's popularity among charismatics dropped in the wake of its two controversial decisions—uncoupling from the Kansas City Prophets and the Toronto Blessing—but those verdicts steered it clear of hyper-spiritual fads. Its leaders found their way back to Wimber's original path: the "radical middle," which mixes the best of orthodox evangelical theology with charismatic practice. A gulf now separated the Vineyard and apostolic-prophetic eccentricity. And, according to Nicholson, the image of a tremoring, post-Wimber Vineyard was overblown. He told me, "Wimber's death didn't shake us as much as you think. He'd been sick for a number of years beforehand and the national board had already been running things without him. When Wimber died, it got us out of the national spotlight, which in my opinion was a welcome relief."

He assessed the controversial 1980's and 1990's: "A lot of those challenges were essentially what I would consider 'teenage years' for the Vineyard movement—a time of figuring out who we were and who we weren't. In the end, we settled down to a more thorough acceptance that we're not ever going to be Pentecostal, but would be truly a Kingdom of God movement."

MATURITY'S PATH

Steve and Cindy themselves are an inter-cultural mesh. One was raised among pentecostals in Montana ranch country; the other grew up on Connecticut's gold coast and knelt before the Episcopalian communion rail.

Steve, born in 1952, is the son and grandson of Assembly of God pastors and was reared in Livingston, a Montana town of 7,400 about 55 miles

---

4. Pulliinger, "Chased by the Dragon," in *Power Encounters*, 198–210.

north of Yellowstone National Park. Livingston's 2018 median household income was $42,635.[5] Google photos reveal red-brick stores and businesses, parked pick-ups, and Independence Day parades with mule teams and horses. He told the 2016 Better Together conferees: "The big diversity that we had in our town was between the cowboys and the townies." The fishing-riding-hunting culture didn't thrill him: "I just wanted to read books and get out of there at the first opportunity."[6]

Cindy's roots sink deep into New England (she's a descendant of Torey Hancock, John Hancock's father). She was born in 1953 in Springfield, Massachusetts. After a stint in Illinois, her family settled in Darien, CT, when she was in kindergarten, a suburb of about 20,000 some 47 miles from New York City on the Long Island Sound. Its 2018 median household income stood at $210,510.[7] Palatial homes and boating marinas rim the cul-de-sacs. She even attended a private school. Her parents helped establish Saint Paul's, which would evolve into a magnet for Anglican renewal under the leadership of the late Rev. Terry Fullam (1930–2014). Cindy's family was there in the church's pre-glory days, when fifty families assembled in a school cafeteria led by a trio of second-career priests.

Each can trace their spiritual awakenings to the AOG.

"Like a good Pentecostal, I got saved hundreds of times," Steve told me. He was forever walking forward at altar calls. His final decision came as a high school senior "through my own inner thought process regarding how I would spend the rest of my life." He had already donned the Pentecostal uniform when he spoke in tongues at 11 ("a late bloomer by their standards"). He was a straight-A student with no longing to follow in his father's footsteps, so he enrolled in Minnesota's exclusive Carleton College in Northfield, Minnesota, about 43 miles south of Minneapolis, majoring in government and international relations. He dreamed of an attorney's career, but "Jesus messed that up by giving me something better to do with my life."

Cindy remembers the evening her "on fire" husband-wife youth leadership team brought St. Paul's middle and high schoolers to an AOG church in a neighboring town. She told me, via e-mail, how the organ wheezed and the preacher rambled. But then came the altar call. "I can't remember if (the speaker) said 'to receive Jesus into your heart' or 'to receive the Holy Spirit' or 'to receive a blessing,' or none of those things," but the entire youth group walked forward and knelt at the rail. Images flashed in her head: "I had

---

5. See the census figures at: https://www.census.gov/quickfacts/livingstoncitymontana

6. Nicholson, "Where Do We Go From Here?," *Better Together Diversity Conference Recordings*, November, 2016.

7. See the US census figures at https://www.census.gov/quickfacts/fact/table/darientownfairfieldcountyconnecticut/PST045219

always felt that I was OK with Jesus because I was such a good little girl," but the images floodlit her disdain for others. She saw her sin—and "I saw how much Jesus loved me. I wept and wept with repentance and with relief that Jesus loved me and forgave me."

"That night," she said, "I think almost every one of us gave our lives to Jesus."

The Pentecostal bookworm from a cowboy town met the upscale New Englander at Carleton's InterVarsity Christian Fellowship chapter (she felt she'd only meet cultural mirrors if she enrolled in an East Coast School and the West Coast was too far away, so she chose arctic Minnesota). He was a year ahead of her and on the chapter's leadership team—at the height of the Jesus Movement, which swept America after the counter culture careened from the 1967 Summer of Love and crashed into disillusionment and mounds of spent syringes. The Jesus Freaks recoiled from Churchianity's suits and ties and hats and pink dresses and ten-minute sermons and hymn-laden Sunday services ending at precisely 11:58 a.m. They asked, What if we did innovative *this* instead of the usual dead-on-arrival *that*?

Cindy remembered the era. She appreciated the Episcopal liturgy's theological poetry, but "I also love the way that the Jesus movement put those same cookies on the low shelf where everybody could find them, with simple worship in my generation's own style, with simple Bible studies, and with lots of opportunities for connecting in powerful and personal ways with Jesus."

The IVCF chapter provided a church-planting training ground (Steve: "we grew from three students to 140, which represented 10% of the student body")—and, according to Cindy, forty to fifty of those original leaders are now heavy-hitters in various ministries.

Sparks did not immediately glitter between them. As Cindy put it: "He was single-minded and radical, I was interested in all sorts of things and predisposed toward 'decently and in order.' God does have his sense of humor. He spent six years nudging us from polar opposites toward the middle!" Their initial wariness edged toward "grudging and then willing" respect.

The IRS hired Steve as an auditor trainee in its office in Skokie, Illinois, upon his 1974 graduation, so he moved to neighboring Evanston, a city of 75,643 about twelve miles north of downtown Chicago on Lake Michigan and the home of Northwestern University's 22,019 students.[8] Area residents lump it with other affluent North Shore communities, but it's actually

---

8. See the university's official registration profile at, "Northwestern University Fall Quarter 2017 Enrollment Statistics," https://www.registrar.northwestern.edu/documents/records/enrollment-graduation-statistics/fall_2017_enrollment.pdf.

not as rich. Its median household income stood at $71,317 in 2016, above the national average but paltry compared to Lake Forest's $152,658.

Cindy graduated the following year, moved back to Darien, and then to the Boston area, where she typed and edited academic papers in a Harvard program founded by Henry Kissinger: "Heaven for a political science geek like me." She also helped start a church that survives to this very day.

Steve relished Chicago's diversity. As he said to the 2016 Better Together conferees, he was a "fish who finally found water." It was "fun," a "grand adventure."[9]

But he met an all-too-familiar routine. Churches claimed they wanted young adults—as long as they silenced themselves and groaned hymns played to organ-grinder monkey tunes. Finally, he and a crop of new graduates found a Skokie Pentecostal church with a welcoming pastor doubling up as a college professor. They imported their enthusiasm and were soon breeding small groups and leading worship—until the beloved pastor-professor left for full-time teaching. The stakeholders followed the time-honored script: They re-occupied their church. The young people scattered.

Steve quipped in 2016: "I always laugh. People say, 'Why did you start the church?' I say, 'So I could have a church that I could stand to go to.'"[10] He elaborated a little with me: "I wanted a church that worshiped with guitars that was open to the Holy Spirit—hard to find then!" Cindy supplied more details in her e-mails: "God spoke to Steve about starting a church for the people who could not find a welcome anywhere else, a church that was a hospital for the broken, a place where worship could be in a style that would resonate with all those young people for whom hymns and liturgy were foreign . . ., a community that could be family for all different kinds of people with different stories."

Steve presented his vision at a Friday night prayer meeting. The young diaspora signed on, and about forty launched the independent Christ Church of the North Shore in 1976, governed by five consensus-driven male elders—one of whom was Bill Hanawalt, the recently-retired executive pastor. The name stuck until the church joined the Vineyard ten years later.

So a group of mostly college-educated Caucasian charismatics, led by Jesus Movement para-church organizers, met in a common room at Northwestern University. They strummed their guitars in long worship services with biblically-centered sermons, bolstered by strong small groups. How could it not grow? Donald A. McGavran (1897–1990), a church growth guru and dean of Fuller Theological Seminary's School of World Missions,

---

9. Better Together conference, 2016.
10. Better Together conference, 2016.

would have smiled a broad smile. The church came close to advertising his homogeneous unit principle.

But not quite. Early tokens hinted of the future, with sprinklings from Africa, the Middle East, and Central Asia—as well as Hispanics, African Americans, and Asian Americans. Some joined hands with World Relief—the National Association of Evangelicals' humanitarian arm—and resettled Cambodian and Vietnamese refugees in the late '70's.

Northwestern's common room was soon too small, so they blazed the typical church-plant trail and worshiped in rented church halls and school auditoriums, always within the university's tram-riding range. Students flocked. They gathered for meals and picnics and spent holidays together and hosted weddings and showers and graduation parties and birthday parties.

Meanwhile, Steve and Cindy grew closer as they met at weddings of college friends. As she puts it, "in the summer of 1978 the penny finally dropped for the both of us." They were married in October of the following year.

Two key church issues lingered. First, filtering all decisions through a consensus-driven board grew cumbersome; second, they saw independent, charismatic churches annihilated on the anvils of immorality, theological eccentricity, and spiritual abuse. They knew they should bond with a larger fellowship. But with whom? The search took years. "During this time," said Steve, "we had a need to figure out our stance on healing, in particular contra the 'faith healers.'"

Faith healers often preach a guilt-kindling "Gospel" linking ailment to a lack of faith, inevitably brewing disillusionment and pain.

They also led a team into inner-city Chicago and planted a church in 1981, which remained stagnant for four years until it finally grew. It still exists and is named the Urban Vineyard Church.

THE LONG-LOST FAMILY

Then came Wimber—first through a magazine series on his famous seminary course and then through his tapes on healing. Cindy remarked: "We had never heard anything like it!" Wimber "talked like a normal person, not like a televangelist." He didn't twist Scripture and he told stories "that just made us cry or laugh or both . . . We didn't have to lose our brains to walk in the supernatural . . . John gave us whole new way to look at being filled with the Spirit and walking in the (Spirit's) gifts . . . We could be *naturally supernatural*, and that was such a relief!"

Steve also invoked the "naturally supernatural" phraseology in his emails as well as Wimber's theological and biblical integrity. "But most importantly we just felt like they were us and we were them: they were our long-lost family finally found."

He traveled to Anaheim for a closer look and tasted the experience dismissed by skeptics but affirmed by history-of-religion scholars: He felt the divine touch. The air weighs heavy and the atmosphere seems charged and the room is filled with overpowering life. God is no longer a concept. He's dynamically present.

Steve spent hours on the floor.

This touch—this dynamic presence of the Holy Spirit—struck his church at its annual meeting when he returned. Again, skeptics would chalk it all up to manipulation or group hysteria; history-of-religion professors would nod their heads.

His own wife admits she wasn't thrilled: "At first it was quiet, and that was OK. Then metal folding chairs started flipping in this gym space as people fell over under the power of the Spirit, or were bouncing or shaking. Then from the back of the room there was this blood-curdling wailing that somehow carried over all the other noise. (Later I realized that it was the sound of a broken heart from a betrayed fiancé finally receiving a touch of God's love.) Then a lady sitting next to me keeled over on top of me. My reaction was, 'Oh great. It's going to take a year to clean all this up!'"

Cindy and other leaders saw Wimber at a 1984 conference in Columbus, Ohio. She heard the solid theology; she saw a friend's back healed of scoliosis (unfortunately, the malady returned years later); she saw other healings. "But what was more wonderful was the quiet." Wimber eschewed manipulation and told everyone to wait and see what God was doing, then go with the flow. "It was revolutionary for us."

They and others met with Todd Hunter and pitched questions—including how their respective churches might join the Vineyard. She echoed her husband: "In some ways . . . what attracted us was how much the *same* the Vineyard was; that somehow we were coming home."

Wimber was no fan of consensus-driven elder boards, since such structures strangle decision-making and stymie church growth. But the time was ripe anyway and the choices were obvious: Steve was the visionary and the discernible senior pastor; Hanawalt could employ his organizational skills as executive pastor (a CFO-like manager who oversees the staff and implements the church's vision); another was headed for graduate school; still another aspired to plant another church; and a fifth, sadly, had died of a heart ailment when he was 30.

They joined the Vineyard in the summer of 1985.

The church tuned itself to the association's ethos. It opened its home groups, made room for the "ministry of the Holy Spirit" (focused prayer with an eye on God's direct activity), and allowed prophets to prophesy. Some were uncomfortable and a few left, "but," said Cindy, "like in the Gospels, for the folks who knew their need of Jesus and healing, this was all very good news." Many got "unstuck" from emotional and spiritual traps. They invited friends.

INFLUENCERS AND MOTIVATORS . . .

The Vineyard eventually tapped both for leadership roles. Steve, of course, ministered in the Spirit's power in churches across the land—thus my encounter—and was appointed national director for church planting. He'd write a manual along with Jeff Bailey[11] and travel the world in that capacity, bringing back stories of multi-cultural dynamics. Both sat on the association's board of directors and, with many others, helped usher the association into its post-Wimber maturity.

The children honored their late Dad but were now thinking for themselves. Take women's ordination, for example. Wimber unwittingly supplied quotes for both sides. Dianne Leman, the Champaign-Urbana pastor and a national executive member, said he "always treated women with incredible dignity and respect, and I am eternally grateful! In 1985, when Carol shared that all of us, both men and women, were called to the ministry of Jesus, my life as a disciple changed forever."[12] That was liberating. She grew up "in a faith that believed women should be silent and submissive."[13] The Vineyard's current egalitarian statement quotes a Wimber article, written in 1994: "I encourage our women to participate in any ministry, except church governance. A woman can preach, teach, evangelize, heal, prophesy, nurture, and built the flock of God."[14] Its authors could also cite two examples in which he approved female pastors.

But that same article supplied fodder for Sam Storms, who quoted Wimber in the complementarian *Journal of Manhood and Womanhood*: "I believe God has established a gender-based eldership of the church." And: "I endorse the traditional (and what I consider the scriptural) view of a unique leadership role for men in marriage, family, and in the church." And, "this [view] ultimately reflects the hierarchy of the Trinity."

11. Nicholson and Bailey, *Coaching Church Planters,* 2001.
12. Wassink and Wilson, *One In Christ*, 4-5.
13. Leman, "About Dianne," at Dianne Leman's web site.
14. Wassink, Wilson, 5.

Storms writes, "His conclusion is clear and unequivocal: 'Consequently, I personally do not favor ordaining women as elders in the local church.'"[15]

Such was the overall policy until 2001, when the board loosened the reins after a meeting in Boise, Idaho. Women's ordination was left to the conscience of individual congregations. But unanswered questions needled: What about regional and national positions? Leaders spurred a focused study in 2005–2006. Rich Nathan, the author, former attorney and senior pastor in Columbus, Ohio, argued vigorously for women's ordination and, along with others, won the day.[16] The board unanimously approved a statement leaving little confusion: "the Vineyard movement will encourage, train, and empower women at all levels of leadership both local and translocal. The movement as a whole welcomes the participation of women in leadership in all areas of ministry.[17]

The board offered on olive branch to the unconvinced ("Each local church retains the right to make its own decisions regarding the ordination and appointing of senior pastors"), but the overall policy was cemented. In 2008, Leman and Cindy Nicholson began leading a national task force for women in leadership; in 2013, three women served on the association's executive committee, two served as regional leaders, and 54 as senior pastors.[18]

Some craved their founder's consent, as is often true of movements with forceful late founders (hear Wesleyans: "If John Wesley lived today . . ."; or Calvinists: "What Calvin really meant was . . ."; or Lutherans: "Luther really didn't mean it when he said . . ."). They quote Carol Wimber's letter to *Charisma* in which she said her late husband would have approved: "Our daughter-in-law and son, Christy and Sean Wimber, have planted a Vineyard. Christy is the senior pastor . . . Although John did not live to see this, I know he is a part of it."[19]

Maybe. Maybe not. We'll never know. As Douglas Erickson wrote, "the question of 'What was John's view' was no longer the definitive answer to any particular question. In place of Wimber's dynamic presence, arose a diverse, corporate, and communal decision-making process, based on dialogue, interaction, and mutual biblical and theological reflection."[20]

---

15. Storms, "Women In Ministry in the Vineyard USA," *The Journal of Manhood and Womanhood*, 21

16. Nathan, "Women in Leadership: How to Decide What the Bible Teaches?"

17. Wassink, Wilson, p. 6.

18. Wassink, Wilson, 6.

19. Wassink, Wilson, 6.

20. Erickson, *Living The Future*, 32–33.

Far more intriguing is the association's expanded vision of healing: It's swelled from the micro to the macro. The *whole church* is an eschatological society, a token of the future age in which "there is neither Jew not Gentile, neither slave nor free, nor is there male and female"—because we are "all one in Christ Jesus" (Galatians 3:28). Healing isn't confined to physical bodies or wounded psyches or even family relationships; healing brings shalom to embattled ethnicities and cultures. Babel's curse, which sundered humanity into different language groups (see Genesis 11) is reversed. Acts 2:5–12, featuring a gathering from all tribes and nations, reverberates into the 21st century.

There's no doubt Wimber would have smiled over the Vineyard's escalated justice ministry and service to the poor, values he imported from Quakerism and etched into his movement's so-called "genetic code." He told his wife while he worked at Fuller: "If God ever has me pastor a church again, I pray we will devote ourselves to the poor." His Anaheim church launched one of the area's largest food banks. Many Vineyard churches now do the same and throw in language and job training.[21]

DURING A STALIN DOCUMENTARY . . .

Evanston's multi-cultural metamorphosis reveals intimacy's practicality. Once again, Steve had that experience over which skeptics guffaw: God talked to him in his living room—while he was watching television, no less. The message: The Lord was about to take back his church and circumvent the homogeneous unit principle.

Steve wasn't thrilled with the principle in the first place ("Why did I ever do that? I never did. I never went for the homogeneous unit principle."),[22] but he was dubious of the multi-cultural church's practicality. He described his doubts at that 2016 *Better Together* conference. Ecclesiastical carcasses of would-be "integrated churches" (the in-vogue term of the '70's and '80's) littered the landscape, victims of the era's tension. He could only respond to proponents: "That sounds like heaven, but I'm not sure it's possible on this Earth."[23]

The gauntlet slammed on a Saturday afternoon in the summer of 1990 as he wallowed in his secret pleasure: "I was at home watching a documentary on Joseph Stalin, which sounds really bizarre, but if you know me you know that if there's a documentary on anything history, like I'm

21. Erickson, *Living The Future*, 22–23.
22. Better Together conference, 2016.
23. Better Together conference, 2016.

on it." History is "my failing, my weakness, my hobby." While the narrator described one of history's worst xenophobic sociopaths, "all of a sudden, as clear as a bell . . . as unmistakable, as loud as any time I heard from God" the Almighty informed him of the church's destiny. God told him, "by the time I get done with it, there won't be a majority group." Steve added: "And he wasn't even asking my permission. He just said He's going to do it."

Steve could only respond: "I don't know how you're going to do that . . . but I will do my best to be a part of this. And if you bring the people, I will give myself to this goal and this process. I don't know how to do this, but we will do it . . . And God started bringing people."[24] Cindy said in her e-mails that they became "intentional," which "made something we would have said we believed but didn't do anything about into something prayerful and thoughtful and deliberate."

It seems God wasn't only speaking to Steve. There was the humble, incredible, and determined Eloise McDowell, an African American who had climbed the rags-to-riches ladder and now lived in the North Shore's professional heights. Burgin, Kentucky, her home town of 1,120 residents, lies about 31 miles southwest of Lexington and featured a 2017 median household income of $37,148.[25] Her graduating class of 23 was the largest in the hamlet's history up to that point. No matter. She earned a Ph.D. from Penn State, taught at Bowling Green State University and, from 1987–1990, managed customer services at Kraft General Foods, headquartered in Northfield, which neighbors Evanston.

And God, in a dream, commanded her to resign and head-up the church's children's ministry. She obeyed.

Steve went with it, and, for over two decades, this crush-the-barriers leader developed and selected curriculum for grammar-school kids, recruited and assisted teachers, planned daddy-daughter and mother-son nights, led small groups, sat with mothers as they birthed their babies, and traveled to South Africa, Kenya, Uganda, and Asia to train teachers.

As she said at her retirement party, "This has been a ride."[26]

Her priority was the children, of course, but she also functioned as a key turning point while the church implemented other measures. Slowly, an intercultural face was presented as more non-Europeans were tapped for announcements and leadership positions. The church looked less like Babel and more like Acts 2: Worshipers from 65 nations now attend on Sunday.

---

24. Better Together conference, 2016.
25. See the Data USA profile, Bergin, KY.
26. See Jim Teague's youtube video, *Eloise McDowell Retirement Celebration*.

"The Church that we are now is not the church I envisioned," said Steve, "but it's the church God envisioned."[27]

PUTTING IT ALL TOGETHER

He saw America's obliterated dreams in 2016. A jarring presidential campaign had already "ripped off all our illusions" and exposed the nation's inter-ethnic bridges as quivering chimeras. Americans meet on factory floors and in offices and small-talk their way through the day, but then drive home to their mono-cultures. The United States, he said, needs the inter-ethnic church because "multi-cultural churches are one of the few places where genuine bridges are built."

But those bridges must be real and firm, which means self-challenge. Congregants must force themselves into inter-cultural small groups, where they taste each other's food and challenge assumptions and dismantle their hubris. There's "nothing quite so powerful to change your perspective than the first time you sit down with somebody who is your brother or your sister and they're coming from some background that is not like yours, and they start telling you what their experience of life really is," said Steve. "That's when change happens." White Anglo Saxon New Englanders listen to Chinatown-reared San Franciscans and inevitably reply, "Wow, I never saw it that way before."

"I don't know where else that's going to happen if not in the church," he said.

If raw patriotism isn't a motive, think of this: Multi-culturalism enriches discipleship. He repeated: "You have to stretch and embrace someone else's perspective . . .You're not being stretched if you're comfortable with where you are." Or this: "multi-cultural churches are the wave of the future." He recalled Wimber's ministry philosophy: See what God is doing and do that. "What kind of future does any church have if it doesn't embrace America's multi-cultural future?" The fact is, "multi-cultural churches illustrate the power of the gospel for all people in a way that almost nothing else does." They're living displays of the Kingdom. "How can you say the gospel has any power if it's not bringing people together ..? Because that's the kingdom . . . I don't know how you believe in the kingdom of God and not do this."

The homogeneous unit principle may pave the path to trouble-free church growth, but it offers no Christ-like counter-culture and implicitly promulgates a severed society. Perhaps a few drawbridges drop at

27. Better Together conference, 2016.

inter-church gatherings, but that's as far as it goes. It's not the kingdom of God, and Steve said he's "one hundred and fifty percent" into the already-but-not-yet kingdom.

He recommended "four simple commitments" to would-be multicultural leaders.

First, *listen*. Hear the stories; read histories; feel feelings.

Second, *learn*, which never stops. New cultures will always introduce themselves, "so you don't get ahead of this thing; we're constantly playing catch-up." But anyone can do it: "It's not that hard, actually. . . it is kind of fun sometimes—really, a lot of fun—if you decide to let it be fun."

He remembered discovering wisdom at a meeting in Chile. "The Chileans can't do anything without a whole lot of hugging and kissing." The hugging and kissing swept the room whenever someone arrived or left, "and if somebody comes late to the meeting—which, of course, they do—the meeting stops so everybody can hug and kiss everybody in the room." Like most efficient Americans, Steve couldn't fend off the enough's-enough feeling. Some "really contentious issues" awaited and they were rewarding the late-comers.

But maybe not: "When we got to the contentious issues that I thought would take a whole day, they cut through those issues like a hot knife through butter." He assessed: "Maybe there's more to be said for hugs and kisses than I thought—and you get to enjoy the hugs and kisses along the way. It's a lot more fun."

The third commitment, *Love*, evolves as we express it in language that others understand. "I can't love them on my terms. That's the deal. I have to love them on their terms. It's incarnational." That means learning new skills—but then again, "who would want to be done with that?"

The fourth: *Share*. The Evanston church was originally his "baby," a church in which '70's kids "could worship in a Jesus Movement way." What if he handed it back to God and it mutated? "But, for the life of me, I couldn't figure out how to say to Jesus, 'no, I'm going to keep your church for myself." So he gave the church back to God, and God "began to change everything." Not surprisingly, "His ideas are much better than mine, and it's been a real joy."

He hasn't done everything perfectly, of course, but he has learned to kiss and hug and clap on the after-beat—and he's been practicing subtly singing a few sermon paragraphs (an African American tradition).

"If I could do (multi-culturalism), then you can do it," he said. "And it's really important for us to do it. It's important for the Gospel. It's important to Jesus. It's important for us. It's important for our discipleship. It's important for our country. It's important."

PASSING THE BATON

In May, 2018, the church announced a three-year transition plan culminating in Steve's retirement, beginning with a year-long search for a new associate pastor. The associate would immerse himself in the congregation's ethos, including multi-culturalism, then take on more responsibility. The plan is unfolding as I write in 2020. Hanawalt retired in 2019; Ted Smith was hired and now bears the title "senior pastor; and Steve is now called the founding pastor.

It's all good, of course, given the truth behind those annoying clichés: We baby boomers are no longer crisp. It's time we take our rightful place among the coffee shop's "regulars" and manage baseball teams from afar. Or, just maybe, the less jaded among us can coach and mentor and teach. Some can still be pastors—as long as we grasp what the Nicholsons grasp: The Church is not ours to keep.

Still, I wax sentimental. The Nicholsons, along with the Evanston church and the Vineyard as a whole, light the path toward genuine renewal—a path worn by Jonathan Edwards, John Wesley, the German Pietists, and historic evangelicals who embrace orthodox doctrine and experience. It veers away from trendy theologies and civil religion and personal bitterness. It brings us back to God's Word and intimacy with the Spirit, whose fruits ripen as we unwrap his gifts and participate in his present-day future.

Many disaffected-disgruntled evangelicals spread their acidity over Twitter and Facebook. I've been among the guilty. Researching Evanston and the Vineyard has brought me back home to grace, and grace is a lot more fun. I hope I stay here. Meanwhile, I wouldn't be the least surprised if God is already whispering in the Nicholsons' ears even as they enter a new chapter of fertile ministry, whatever that is.

Conclusion

Rowing at the Confluence

I OFTEN GRUMBLED THROUGH this book's opening question while walking through my neighborhood in 2009 ("What do I do when the river that swept me into the life of Christ now empties into a toxic swamp, crammed with an attack-dog army?"). The answer seemed obvious: American Christianity begs for sanity's strong advocates. I vowed I'd be one. I sprayed the internet and publications with articles and populated panels and spoke at gatherings. I was even exploring the podcast and YouTube universe. It seemed only right. Many told me I was a decent public speaker with a well-endowed "radio voice" (an overabundance of flaws keeps me humble), so I should stop shrouding my lamp under a bushel (see Matthew 5:15) and hone a well-crafted message: Don't flee theological orthodoxy, especially since it's not the culprit. Run back to a *genuine* evangelical faith emulating Christ's radical, counter-cultural kingdom. We need no new doctrines.

But then tongue cancer struck in 2015 after a 27-year hiatus. Surgeons sliced off sixty percent of my body's strongest muscle and remolded it with skin from my forearm. I'm told I'm understandable, but the consequent speech impediment smothered my YouTube and podcast dreams. Swallowing is difficult, so most meals add up to nutritious mush. Goodbye sirloin (not that I ate it that much).

Then came recurrences. And then metastasis, which seems to have been beaten back.

I view the scene as a frustrated observer and I grow even more convinced: Now is not the time for inventive doctrines. It's time to plumb historic Christianity's depths, where we rediscover God's nature and radical kingdom living. It's time to go back to the Bible, back to God's intimacy, and back to the social actions anchored in the Scriptures. History's renewal movements inevitably row at the confluence of those three streams (biblically-informed teaching; life in the Spirit; and social justice). Our beacons of hope row at that confluence in varying degrees. Biblical teaching motivates Manhattan's Redeemer Presbyterian Church into urban renewal; the same Bible spurs Ed Brown's attempts to rescue the Earth; it prompts the Evanston Vineyard to seek inter-culturalism and social action as it pursues the Holy Spirit.

We'll rediscover salient passages as we tack back to Scripture and Scripture's God. Mark 10:42–45 is especially apropos for king-of-the-hill intimidators. James and John requested thrones on Jesus's right and left. The passage describes Jesus' reply: He "called them together and said, 'You know that those who are regarded as rulers of the Gentiles lord it over them, and their high officials exercise authority over them. Not so with you. Instead, whoever wants to become great among you must be your servant, and whoever wants to be first must be slave of all. For even the Son of Man did not come to be served, but to serve, and to give his life as a ransom for many" (ESV).

Let the alpha personalities tame themselves.

And there's Galatians 5:22–23: "But the fruit of the Spirit is love, joy, peace, forbearance, kindness, goodness, faithfulness, gentleness, and self-control. Against such things there is no law" (NIV). And Galatians 6:1: "Brothers and sisters, if someone is caught in a sin, you who live by the Spirit should restore that person *gently*. But watch yourselves, or you also may be *tempted*" (emphasis added, NIV). And Matthew 7:1–5: "Do not judge, or you too will be judged. For in the same way you judge others, you will be judged, and with the measure you use, it will be measured to you. Why do you look at the speck of sawdust in your brother's eye and pay no attention to the plank in your own eye? How can you say to your brother, 'Let me take the speck out of your eye,' when all the time there is a plank in your own eye? You hypocrite, first take the plank out of your own eye, and then you will see clearly to remove the speck from your brother's eye" (NIV).

I hesitate to cite the last passage because it's too often manipulated to smother legitimate debate ("you judge me when you say I'm wrong"), and I'm also aware of other, more confrontational passages. But these verses bear significance when partisan evangelicals accuse their creation-friendly brothers and sisters of earth-goddess worship, when heretic hunters misunderstand their perceived adversaries and level inaccurate charges, and when thinkers in one theological tribe snub the legitimacy of all others.

Our three beacons have embedded those passages. Timothy Keller unapologetically argues for Calvinism while welcoming others to the table; Vineyard leaders have seen Catholic spirituality through a Protestant lens and offer spiritual direction; and Ed Brown is just an all-round nice guy.

None flees respectful argument; each leaves an imprint of God's love, graciousness, and holiness wherever they go. They understand the difference between disagreement and condemnation.

My guess: Biblically-oriented American Protestants will soon abandon the term, "evangelical" for the same reasons they jettisoned "fundamentalist" in the 1940's. What will be our new brand? I've suggested "Classical Christian," but I really have no idea, nor am I sure it's all that important. Labels aren't as crucial as our calling, which is to humble ourselves, get back to God and his ways, and spread the Gospel through its demonstration and declaration. There *is* hope even in the toxic swamp. After all, swamps eventually transform into into flower-bearing meadows.

I'd love to live long enough to smell the blossoms.

Bibliography

Africa-Ecpo News, "Study: Kenya Loses 5.6 million trees daily," *Capital News*, March 26, 2015, https://www.capitalfm.co.ke/news/2015/03/study-kenya-loses-5-6-million-trees-daily/, accessed, March 23, 2018.

A Group of Clergy Men, "A Letter To Martin Luther King," April 12, 1963, at *Teaching American History*, https://teachingamericanhistory.org/library/document/letter-to-martin-luther-king/ accessed,4/29/2020.

Allen, Bob, "SBC leader denounces papacy," *Baptist News Global*, March 14, 2013, https://baptistnews.com/article/sbc-leader-denounces-papacy/#.WOPGsYjyvIV

Allen, R. Michael, ed., *Karl Barth's Church Dogmatics: An Introduction and Reader* (New York: T&T Clark, 2012, revised edition).

Annan, Kent, "Why We Need to Talk about Trump's Haiti Remarks," *Christianity Today*, 1/12/2018, http://www.christianitytoday.com/ct/2018/january-web-only/trump-remark-immigration-haiti.html, accessed 1/29/2018.

Annual Report, Vineyard Church at Evanston, Illinois, http://evanstonvineyard.org/wp-content/uploads/2018/03/annual_report_41.pdf; accessed, 5/7/2020),

Arakaki, Robert, "Evangelicalism Falling to Pieces?" *Orthodox Reformed Bridge*, October 20, 2016, http://blogs.ancientfaith.com/orthodoxbridge/evangelicalism-falling-pieces/; accessed 5/7/2020

Arnott, John, *The Father's Blessing*, (Orlando, FL: Creation House, 1995).

Baird, Julia, "Is Your Pastor Sexist?" *The New York Times*, April 19, 2017, https://www.nytimes.com/2017/04/19/opinion/is-your-pastor-sexist.html; accessed, 5/7/2020.

Bailey, Sarah Pulliam,"The Trump Effect? A Stunning Number of Evangelicals Will Now Accept Politicians' 'Immoral' Acts," *Washington Post*, October 19, 2016, https://www.washingtonpost.com/news/acts-of-faith/wp/2016/10/19/the-trump-effect-evangelicals-have-become-much-more-accepting-of-politicians-immoral-acts/?noredirect=on&utm_term=.a07d0b88cf6f, recovered, 5/7/2020.

Ball, Jim, *Global Warming and the Risen LORD: Christian Discipleship and Climate Change* (Boise, Idaho: Russell Media, 2010).

———. "Interview with Sir John Houghton on the Mall in Washington, DC, March 11, *Creation Care Magazine*, March 11, 2005.

Banerjee, Neela, "Spreading the Global Warming Gospel," *The Los Angeles Times*, December 7, 2011, http://articles.latimes.com/2011/dec/07/nation/la-na-evangelical-warming-20111207, recovered 5/7/2020.

Banks, Adelle M., "Dobson, Others Seek Ouster of NAE Vice President," *Religion News Service*, March 2, 2007, https://www.christianitytoday.com/ct/2007/marchweb-only/109-53.0.html; accessed, 5/7/2020.

Bauer, Gary, "You Won!," *Newsbeat1, Gary Bauer Today* . . . , November 9, 2016, http://newsbeat1.com/?p=48346.; accessed, 5/7/2020.

Barnes, M. Craig, "Update on the 2017 Kuyper Lecture and Prize: President Barnes addresses concerns raised within the Princeton Seminary community," *Princeton Theological Seminary website*, March 22, 2017, https://www.ptsem.edu/news/update-on-the-kuyper-lecture-and-prize; accessed, 5/7/2020.

———. "What I Learned From Our Seminary's Conflict About Hosting Tim Keller," *The Christian Century*, August 9, 2017, https://www.christiancentury.org/article/what-i-learned-our-seminary-conflict-about-hosting-tim-keller; recovered, 10/13/2017.

Barth, Karl, *Barth's Letters: 1961-1968* (Grand Rapids: Eerdmans, 1981)

Bauer, Gary, "You Won!," *Newsbeat1, Gary Bauer Today* . . . , November 9, 2016, http://newsbeat1.com/?p=48346.; accessed, 5/7/2020.

Bauerlein, Mark, "A Strange Research Project," *First Things*, 5/8/17, https://www.firstthings.com/blogs/firstthoughts/2017/05/a-strange-research-project; accessed, 5/7/2020.

Beaty, Katelyn, "At A Private Meeting In Illinois, A Group of Evangelicals Tried To Save Their Movement From Trumpism," *The New Yorker*, April 26, 2018, https://www.newyorker.com/news-desk/on-religion/at-a-private-meeting-in-illinois-a-group-of-evangelicals-tried-to-save-their-movement-from-trumpism.; accessed, 5/7/2020.

———. "'No more: Evangelical women are done with Donald Trump and his misogyny," *The Washington Post*, October 13, 2016, https://www.washingtonpost.com/news/acts-of-faith/wp/2016/10/13/no-more-evangelical-women-are-done-with-donald-trump-and-his-misogyny/.

Beaty, Katelyn, "I was an evangelical magazine editor, but now I can't defend my evangelical community," *Washington Post*, November 14, 2016, https://www.washingtonpost.com/news/acts-of-faith/wp/2016/11/14/i-was-an-evangelical-magazine-editor-but-now-i-cant-defend-my-evangelical-community/.; accessed, 5.7/2020.

Beisner, Calvin, "Believing in Climate Change is an Insult to God," *Right Wing Watch*, November 19, 2012, nhttp://www.youtube.com/watch?v=r6Q6vkxs3XQ; accessed, 5/7/2020.

Bell, Rob, *Love Wins: A Book About Heaven, Hell, and the Fate of Every Person Who Ever Lived* (San Francisco: Harper One, 2011).

Bender, Bryan, "Chief of US Pacific forces calls climate biggest worry," *Boston Globe*, March 9, 2013, http://www.bostonglobe.com/news/nation/2013/03/09/admiral-samuel-locklear-commander-pacific-forces-warns-that-climate-change-top-threat/BHdPVCLrWEMxRe9IXJZcHL/story.html; accessed, 5/7/2020.

Beverley, James A., *Holy Laughter & The Toronto Blessing*, (Grand Rapids, MI: Zondervan Publishing House, 1995).

———. "Vineyard Severs Ties with 'Toronto Blessing" Church," *Christianity Today*, January 8, 1996, https://www.christianitytoday.com/ct/1996/january8/6t1066.html; accessed, 5/7/2020.

Bielo, David, "A Republican Secretary of State Urges Action on Climate Change," *Scientific American*, July 24, 2013, http://www.scientificamerican.com/article.cfm?id=questions-and-answers-with-george-shultz-on-climate-change-and-energy; accessed, 5/7/2020.

Bird, Michael F., *Bourgeois Babes, Bossy Wives, and Bobby Haircuts: A Case for Gender Equality in Ministry* (Grand Rapids: Zondervan, 2012).

———. "Incorporated Righteousness: A Response to Recent Evangelical Discussion Concerning The Imputation of Christ's Righteousness In Justification," *Journal of the Evangelical Theological Society*, 47/2 (June 2004); 253–275.

———. "What Is There Between Minneapolis And St. Andrews? A Third Way In The Piper-Wright Debate," *Journal of the Evangelical Theological Society*, 54.2 (June 2011); 299–309.

Bliss, Lowell, "What is an Environmental Missionary?," *Flourish Magazine*, Spring, 2010, http://www.flourishonline.org/2010/06/flourish-magazine-global-communitywhat-is-an-environmental-missionary ; accessed, 3/5/2018.

Block, Matthew, "Evangelicals, Heresy, and Scripture Alone," *First Things*, October 4, 2016, https://www.firstthings.com/blogs/firstthoughts/2016/10/evangelicals-heresy-and-scripture-alone; accessed 5/7/2020.

Bloesch, Donald, *Holy Scripture: Revelation, Inspiration, & Interpretation* (Downers Grove, IL: InterVarsity Press, 1994).

Boorse, Dorothy (lead author), *Loving The Least of These: Addressing a Changing Environment*, National Association of Evangelicals, 2011; http://nae.net/wp-content/uploads/2015/06/Loving-the-Least-of-These.pdf; accessed, 5/7/2020.

Bromiley, G.W., "Karl Barth's Doctrine of Inspiration," *Journal of the Transactions of the Victoria Institute* 87 (1955), pp. 66–80.

Brown, Driver, Briggs, and Gesenius (BDBG), *The New Hebrew and English Lexicon* (Peabody, MA: Hendrickson Publishers, 1979).

Brown, Edward R, *Our Father's World: Mobilizing The Church To Care For Creation* (Downers Grove, IL: InterVarsity Press, 2006).

———. *When Heaven and Nature Sing* (South Hadley, MA: Doorlight Publications, 2013).

———. *The Lausanne Global Campaign For Creation Care and the Gospel: A Mid-Campaign Update Report,* (The Lausanne Creation Care Network, February 11, 2016).

Brown, Michael, "Dispelling the Myths About NAR (the New Apostolic Reformation)," *ASKDrBrown*, April 30, 2018, https://askdrbrown.org/library/dispelling-myths-about-nar-new-apostolic-reformation; accessed, 5/7/2020.

———. "Official Statement from the Leadership Panel on Todd Bentley," *ASKDrBrown*, January 2, 2020, https://askdrbrown.org/library/official-statement-leadership-panel-todd-bentley-january-2-2020; accessed, 5/7/2020.

Bruenig, Elizabeth, "Jerry Falwell, Jr., Endorses Donald Trump for President," *New Republic: Minutes, News & Notes*, https://newrepublic.com/minutes/128398/evangelical-jerry-falwell-jr-endorses-donald-trump-president; accessed, 5/7/2020.

Buettel, Cameron, "The Genesis Crisis," February 20. 2015, *The Aquilla Report*, https://www.theaquilareport.com/the-genesis-crisis/; accessed, 5/7/2020.

Burns, Alison, "US Admirals, Generals, Link Climate Change To National Security," *Public News Service*, July 11, 2013, http://www.publicnewsservice.org/index.php?/content/article/33407-1; accessed, 5/7/2020.
Buttry, Daniel, *Christian Peacemaking: From Heritage To Hope* (Valley Forge, PA: Judson Press, 1994).
Calvin, John, *Institutes of the Christian Religion*, Volumes 1 & 2, translated by Henry Beveridge (Grand Rapids: Eerdmans, 1983).
Calvo, Zac, and signatories, "Open Letter to the Abraham Kuyper Center for Public Theology and Dr. Craig Barnes," *ipetitions*, https://www.ipetitions.com/petition/open-letter-to-the-abraham-kuyper-center?utm_source=twitter&utm_medium=social&utm_campaign=pet_share_button; accessed, 5/7/2020.
Cameron, JEM, ed., *The Lausanne Legacy: Landmarks in Global Mission* (Peabody, MA: Hendrickson, 2016).
Carnell, Edward John, *A Philosophy of the Christian Religion* (Grand Rapids: Eerdmans, 1952).
———. *The Case For Orthodox Theology* (Philadelphia: Westminster John Knox Press, 1959).
Carnes, Tony, "Princeton Theological Seminary is 'Unworthy' of its traditions, says Kuyper Conference alumni," *A Journey Through NYC Religions*, April 5, 2017, https://www.nycreligion.info/princeton-theological-seminary-unworthy-traditions-kuyper-conference-alumni/; accessed, 5/7/2020.
Carson, D.A., *The Gagging of God: Christianity Confronts Pluralism* (Grand Rapids: Zondervan, 1996).
———. "The Purpose of Signs and Wonders in the New Testament," *Power Religion*, edited by Michael Scott Horton (Chicago: Moody, 1992), 89–118.
———. *The God Who Is There: Finding Your Place in God's Story* (Grand Rapids: Baker Books, 2010).
Carson, Don; Taylor, Justin, "Why We Have Been Silent about the SGM Lawsuit," May 24, 2013, *The Gospel Coalition*, https://www.thegospelcoalition.org/article/why-we-have-been-silent-about-the-sgm-lawsuit/; accessed, 5/7/2020.
Christian Post Editors, "Donald Trump Is a Scam. Evangelical Voters Should Back Away, CP Editorial," *The Christian Post*, February 20, 2016, http://www.christianpost.com/news/donald-trump-scam-evangelical-voters-back-away-cp-editorial-158813/#FIOzHsB2V3qH0AVE.99/, accessed, 5/7/2020.
Christian Reformed Church News, "Synod Recognizes Climate Change," *Christian Reformed Church*, June 13, 2012, http://www.crcna.org/news-and-views/synod-recognizes-climate-change; accessed, 5/7/2020.
Chu, Jeff, "Soul-searching at Princeton Theological Seminary," *Religion News Service*, April 12, 2017, https://religionnews.com/2017/04/12/soul-searching-at-princeton-theological-seminary/; accessed, 5/7/2020.
CiHizza, Chris, "A fact checker looked into 158 things Donald Trump said. 78 percent were false," *The Washington Post*, July 1, 2016, https://www.washingtonpost.com/news/the-fix/wp/2016/07/01/donald-trump-has-been-wrong-way-more-often-than-all-the-other-2016-candidates-combined/; accessed, 5/7/2020.
City-Data.com, "Lynn, Massachusetts," http://www.city-data.com/city/Lynn-Massachusetts.html; accessed, 5/6/2020.
CNN, "Global Warming Gap Among Evangelicals Widens," March 14, 2007, http://www.cnn.com/2007/POLITICS/03/14/evangelical.rift/index.html; accessed, 5/7/2020.

Compolo, Tony; Claiborne, Shane, "The Evangelicalism of Old White Men Is Dead," *The New York Times*, November 30, 2016, http://www.nytimes.com/2016/11/29/opinion/the-evangelicalism-of-old-white-men-is-dead.html?_r=1.; accessed, 5/7/2020.

Cooperman, Alan, "Evangelical Body Stays Course on Warming," *The Washington Post*, March 11, 2007, http://www.timism.com/GlobalDying/GlobalWarming/Petrophilia/!R-Gen/EvangelicalBodyStaysCourseonWarming070310WashPost.hto ; accessed, 5/7/2020.

Cornwall Alliance, "An Evangelical Declaration on Global Warming," May 1, 2009, https://cornwallalliance.org/2009/05/evangelical-declaration-on-global-warming/; accessed, 5/7/2020.

Cosgrove, Charles H.; Hatfield, Dennis D. *Church Conflict: The Hidden Systems Behind The Fights* (Nashville: Abingdon Press, 1994).

Cottle, Ron, "Definition and Description of an Apostle," *International Coalition of Apostolic Leaders*, 2015, https://www.icaleaders.com/about-ical/definition-of-apostle; accessed, 5/5/2020.

Crouch, Andy, "Speak Truth to Trump: Evangelicals, of all people, should not be silent about Donald Trump's blatant immorality," *Christianity Today*, October 10, 2016, http://www.christianitytoday.com/ct/2016/october-web-only/speak-truth-to-trump.html?visit_source=twitter; accessed, 5/7/2020.

Data, USA, *Bergin, KY*, https://datausa.io/profile/geo/burgin-ky accessed, 5/6/2020.

Davis, John Jefferson, "Ecological 'Blind Spots' In The Structure And Content of Recent Systematic Theologies," *Journal of the Evangelical Theological Society*, 43/2 (June 2000), pp. 273–286.

———. *Evangelical Ethics: Issues Facing The Church Today, Fourth Edition* (Philipsburg, NJ: P&R Publishing, 2004).

———. *Practicing Ministry in the Presence of God* (Eugene, Oregon: Cascade Books, 2015). .

Dayton, Donald, "The Battle for the Bible: Renewing the Inerrancy Debate," *The Christian Century*, November 10, 1976, pp. 976–980, found on-line at http://www.religion-online.org/showarticle.asp?title=1823. ; accessed, 5/6/2020.

———. *Discovering an Evangelical Heritage* (Grand Rapids: Baker Academic, Reprint edition, 1988).

Dayton, Donald; Johnson, Robert K., *The Variety of American Evangelicalism* (Downers Grove, Illinois: InterVarsity Press, 1991)

Dayton, Donald; Strong, Douglas, *Rediscovering an Evangelical Heritage: A Tradition and Trajectory of Integrating Piety and Justice*, Second Edition (Grand Rapids: Baker Academic, 2014),

Deere, Jack. *Surprised by the Power of the Spirit: Discovering How God Speaks and Heals Today* (Grand Rapids: Zondervan, 1993).

———. *Surprised by the Voice of God: How God Speaks Today Through Prophecies, Dreams, and Visions* (Grand Rapids: Zondervan, 1996).

Dobson, James, "Dr. James Dobson endorses Donald J. Trump for President of the United States," *Religion News Service*, July 22, 2016, https://religionnews.com/2016/07/22/dr-james-dobson-endorses-donald-j-trump-for-president-of-the-united-states/ ; accessed, 5/7/2020.

Dongell, Joseph, "10 Things I Wish Everyone Knew About Arminianism: Do Arminians and Calvinists actually disagree as much as they think?," *Remonstrance*, June 4,

2016 , https://remonstrancepodcast.com/2016/06/04/10-things-i-wish-everyone-knew-about-arminianism/; accessed, 5/7/2020.

Doran, Peter; Kendall Zimmerman, Maggie, "Examining the Scientific Consensus on Climate Change," *Eos*, Volume 90, Number 3, January 2009, pages 21–22.

Dorrien, Gary, *The Remaking of Evangelical Theology* (Louisville, KY: Westminster John Knox Press, 1991).

DuBois, Joshua, "Powerful Evangelical Women Split From Male Church Leaders To Slam Trump," *The Daily Beast*, October 10, 2016 http://www.thedailybeast.com/articles/2016/10/10/beth-moore-the-christian-women-speaking-out-about-trump-s-bad-news.html; accessed, 5/7/2020.

Dueck, Lorna, "The Enduring Revival: The 'Toronto Blessing in 1994 was odd and controversial—but its benefits have lasted," *Christianity Today*, March 7, 2014, https://www.christianitytoday.com/ct/2014/march-web-only/enduring-revival.html; accessed, 5/7/2020.

Dunn, James D. G., *Christianity in the Making*, Volume 1, (Grand Rapids: Eerdmans, 2003).

Easterbrook, Greg, "Finally Feeling the Heat," *The New York Times*, June 24, 2006. http://www.nytimes.com/2006/05/24/opinion/24easterbrook.html?; accessed, 5/7/2020.

Eilperin, Juliet, "World on track for nearly 11-degree temperature rise, energy expert says," *Washington Post*, November 28, 2011, https://www.washingtonpost.com/national/health-science/world-on-track-for-nearly-11-degree-temperature-rise-energy-expert-says/2011/11/28/gIQAi0lM6N_story.html; accessed, 5/7/2020.

Eleven Retired Generals and Admirals, "National Security and the Threat of Climate Change," 2007, https://www.npr.org/documents/2007/apr/security_climate.pdf ; accessed, 5/7/2020.

Engle, Lou, "Lou Engle Sounds Urgent Call for 3-Day Esther Fast Over America," *Charisma*, 3/8/2017, https://www.charismamag.com/blogs/prophetic-insight/32093-lou-engle-sounds-urgent-call-for-3-day-esther-fast-over-america?utm_source=Prophetic%20Insight&utm_medium=email&utm_content=subscriber_id:865350&utm_campaign=Prophetic%20Insight%20-%202017-03-06; accessed, 5/7/2020.

Erickson, Douglas R., "The Kingdom of God and the Holy Spirit: Eschatology and Pneumatology in the Vineyard Movement" (2015). Dissertations (2009 -). Paper 552. http://epublications.marquette.edu/dissertations_mu/552.

———. *Living The Future: The Kingdom of God and the Holy Spirit in the Vineyard Movement* (Self-published, 2016).

Eschliman, Bob, "Dr. Richard Land Makes Surprising Announcement About Donald Trump," *Charisma Caucus*, August 24, 2016, http://www.charismanews.com/politics/elections/59481-dr-richard-land-makes-a-surprising-statement-about-donald-trump; accessed 5/7/2020.

Evans, William B., "A Kuyper Prize?," *The Aquilla Report*, March 29, 2017, https://www.theaquilareport.com/a-kuyper-prize/; accessed, 5/7/2020.

Feed The Future, "The US Government's Global Hunger & Food Security Initiative," *Kenya Fact Sheet*, January, 2013, https://feedthefuture.gov/sites/default/files/resource/files/ftf_factsheet_kenya_jan2013.pdf; accessed , 5/1/2020.

Fisher, Bryan; Beisner, Calvin, "Not Using Fossil Fuels is an Insult to God," *Right Wing Watch*, November 30, 2012, https://www.youtube.com/watch?v=MpDd_Kq_vRk;accessed, 5/7/2020.

Fisher, Roger; Ury, William; Patton, Bruce, *Getting to Yes: Negotiating Agreement Without Giving In* (New York: Penguin, 1991).

Foulkes, F., "Peace," *New Bible Dictionary, The New Bible Dictionary, Third Edition* (Downers Grove, Ill: Intervarsity Press, 1996), 891

Frame, John, "Machen's Warrior Children," Frame-Poythress.org, June 6, 2012, https://frame-poythress.org/machens-warrior-children/; accessed, 5/7/2020.

Friederichsen, Donny, "What Hath Amsterdam to do with Princeton?," *The Aquilla Report*, March 20, 2017, https://www.theaquilareport.com/hath-amsterdam-princeton/; recovered, 10/13/18.

Friedman, Thomas, *Hot, Flat, and Crowded*, (New York: Farrar, Straus and Giroux, 2008).

Frizzell, Naomi, "Lausanne Movement Appoints Senior Associate for Creation Care: Appointment Acknowledges Importance of Stewardship of God's Creation," August 6, 2012, https://www.lausanne.org/news-releases/lausanne-movement-appoints-senior-associate-for-creation-care; accessed, 5/1/2020.

Galdamez, Michael Raymond, *Worldview Preaching in the Church: The Preaching Ministries of J. Gresham Machen and Timothy J. Keller*, (unpublished Ph.D. dissertation presented to the faculty of Southern Baptist Theological Seminary, Copyright © 2012 Michael Raymond Galdamez).

Gannett, Amy, "How Evangelicals Are Losing An Entire Generation," *Word & Craft: Lifestyle Theology for the Woman of God*, July 29, 2016, https://amygannett.com/2016/07/29/why-evangelicals-are-losing-an-entire-generation/; accessed, 5/7/2020.

Gehrz, Christopher; Pattie, Mark III, *The Pietist Option: Hope for the Renewal of Christianity* (Downers Grove, Illinois: IVP Academic, 2017).

Geisler, Norman; Farnell, F. David, "The Erosion of Inerrancy Among New Testament Scholars: Craig Blomberg (2012)," *Norman Geisler*, http://normangeisler.com/the-erosion-of-inerrancy-craig-blomberg/; accessed, 5/8/2020.

Geivett, Douglas; Pivec, Holly, *A New Apostolic Reformation* (Wooster, OH: Weaver Book Company, 2014).

General Council of the Assemblies of God, position paper, "Apostles and Prophets," approved by the General Presbytery of the Assemblies of God on August 6, 2001, downloadable as a pdf file, https://ag.org/Beliefs/Topics-Index/Apostles-and-Prophets, accessed, 4/28/2020.

Gerson, Michael, "The Last Temptation: How evangelicals once culturally confident, became an anxious minority seeking political protection from the least traditionally religious president in living memory," *The Atlantic Monthly*, April, 2018, https://www.theatlantic.com/magazine/archive/2018/04/the-last-temptation/554066/; accessed, 5/7/2020.

Gibson, David, "Princeton Seminary Taking Some Heat for Honoring Redeemer's Tim Keller," *Religion News Service*, March 22, 2017, https://religionnews.com/2017/03/21/princeton-seminary-taking-some-heat-for-honoring-redeemers-tim-keller/; accessed, 5/7/2020.

Gillis, Justin, "An Alarm in the Offing on Climate Change," *New York Times Green: A Blog About Energy and the Environment*, January 14, 2015, https://green.blogs.nytimes.com/2013/01/14/an-alarm-in-the-offing-on-climate-change/; accessed, 5/7/2020.

Goodstein, Laurie, "Evangelical Leaders Join Global Warming Initiative," *The New York Times*, February 8, 2006, https://www.nytimes.com/2006/02/08/us/evangelical-leaders-joinglobal-warming-initiative.html; accessed, 5/7/2020.

Gramlich, John,"Five Facts About Crime in the US," *Pew Research Center*, January 30, 2018, http://www.pewresearch.org/fact-tank/2018/01/30/5-facts-about-crime-in-the-u-s/, accessed, 5/7/2020.

Grenz, Stanley, *The Moral Quest: Foundations of Christian Ethics* (Downers Grove, Illinois: IVP Academic, 1998).

———. *Renewing The Center: Evangelical Theology in a Post-Theological Era* (Grand Rapids: Baker, 2000).

———. *Revisioning Evangelical Theology: A Fresh Agenda for the 21st Century* (Downers Grove, IL: InterVarsity Press, 1993).

———. *Welcoming But Not Affirming: An Evangelical Response to Homosexuality* (Louisville, KY: Westminster John Knox Press, 1998).

Griswold, Eliza, "Billy Graham's Striking Gospel of Social Action," *The New Yorker*, February 22, 2018, https://www.newyorker.com/culture/cultural-comment/billy-grahams-striking-gospel-of-social-action; accessed, 5/7/2020.

Gross, Terry, "A Leading Figure in the New Apostolic Reformation," *Fresh Air*, transcript of an interview with Peter Wagner, October 3, 2011, https://www.npr.org/templates/transcript/transcript.php?storyId=140946482, accessed, 5/7/2020.

Grudem,Wayne, "Power & Truth: A Response to the Critiques of Vineyard Teaching and Practice by DA Carson, James Montgomery Boise, and John H. Armstrong in *Power Religion*," Vineyard Position Paper #4, (© March 1993 by The Association of Vineyard Churches)

———. *Systematic Theology: An Introduction To Biblical Doctrine* (Grand Rapids: Zondervan, 1994).

———. "Why Voting For Donald Trump Is A Morally Good Choice," *Townhall*, July 28, 2016, http://townhall.com/columnists/waynegrudem/2016/07/28/why-voting-for-donald-trump-is-a-morally-good-choice-n2199564.; accessed, 5/7/2020.

Gushee, David P., ed., *A New Evangelical Manifesto: A Kingdom Vision for the Common Good* (St. Louis: Chalice Press, 2012).

Hansen, Collin, *Young, Restless, Reformed: A Journalist's Journey With The New Calvinists* (Wheaton, IL.: Crossway, 2008).

Hayboe, Katharine, "Ten Questions for Katharine," The Secret Life of Scientists and Engineers, April 26, 2011, https://video.cptv.org/video/secret-life-scientists-katharine-hayhoe-10-questions-katharine/ ; accessed, 5/7/2020.

Hayhoe, Katharine; Ackerman, Thomas, "Climate Change: Evangelical Scientists Say Limbaugh Wrong, Faith and Science Complement One Another," *The Christian Post, CP Opinion*, August 31, 2013, http://www.christianpost.com/news/climate-change-evangelical-scientists-say-limbaugh-wrong-faith-and-science-compliment-one-another-103470/; accessed, 5/7/2020.

Hayhoe, Katharine; Farley, Andrew, *A Climate for Change: Global Warming Facts for Faith-Based Discussions* (New York, Boston, and Nashville: FaithWords), 2009.

Henig, Jess, "Some 'Climategate' conclusions," *Factcheck.org*, April 15, 2020. http://www.factcheck.org/2010/04/some-climategate-conclusions; accessed, 5/7/2020.

Henry, Carl, *Confessions of a Theologian* (Waco, Texas: Word Books, 1986).

Hodge, Archibald Alexander; Warfield, Benjamin Breckinridge, "Inspiration," *The Presbyterian Review*, No. 6, April, 1881.

Hooper, Joseph, "Tim Keller Wants to Save Your Yuppie Soul," *New York Magazine*, November 29, 2009, http://nymag.com/news/features/62374/; accessed, 5/7/2020.
Horton, Michael Scott, ed., *Power Religion: The Selling Out of the Evangelical Church?* (Chicago: The Moody Bible Institute, 1992).
Horton, Michael, "The Politics of Enthusiasm," *The White Horse Inn*, August 19, 2011, https://www.whitehorseinn.org/2011/08/the-politics-of-enthusiasm/, recovered 10/5/2018.
———, "The Theology of Donald Trump," *Christianity Today*, March 16, 2016, http://www.christianitytoday.com/ct/2016/march-web-only/theology-of-donald-trump.html., accessed 4/28/2020.
Horton, Michael; Olson, Roger, *For Calvinism, Against Calvinism*: Enhanced Edition: 2 books in 1 plus bonus video content (Grand Rapids: Zondervan, 2012).
Houghton, John, "Climate Change: A Christian Challenge and Opportunity," Presentation to the National Association of Evangelicals, Washington DC, March 2005, http://megaslides.com/doc/1472597/climate-change-a-christian-challenge-and-opportunity
Houtz, Wyatt, "Karl Barth's letter in response to Cornelius Van Til's questions," *The Post-Barthian*, https://postbarthian.com/2014/04/29/karl-barths-letter-in-response-to-cornelius-van-tils-questions/; accessed, 5/7/2020.
Hubbard, David Allen. "The Good Ship Fuller: Chapel Message, 1976," *Fuller Theology, News & Notes* (TNN/Issues/Spring 2014/)
Hunter, Todd, "Letter from Todd Hunter on the TAV/AVC Separation, on behalf of the John Wimber and the AVC Board," December 13, 1995, https://groups.google.com/forum/#!topic/bit.listserv.christia/xfHGMmu79-s ; accessed, 5/7/2020.
———. "To the Pentecostal & Charismatic Churches," *Christianity Today*, October 25, 1999, https://www.christianitytoday.com/ct/1999/october25/9tc068.html, accessed, 5/7/2020.
International House of Prayer, Kansas City, "What is IHOPKC's stance on the New Apostolic Reformation?" *International House of Prayer*, https://www.ihopkc.org/press-center/faq/ihopkc-part-new-apostolic-reformation/; accessed, 5/9/2020.
Jackson, Bill, *The Quest for the Radical Middle: A History of the Vineyard* (Cape Town, South Africa; Vineyard International Publishing, 1999).
Jackson, Ruth, "I'm an egalitarian female preacher who believes Tim Keller has been treated horribly," *Premier Christianity*, March 24, 2017, https://www.premierchristianity.com/Blog/I-m-an-egalitarian-female-preacher-who-believes-Tim-Keller-has-been-treated-terribly; accessed, 5/7/2020.
Jaschik, Scott, "OK to Speak, Not to be Honored," March 23, 2017, *Inside Higher Ed*, https://www.insidehighered.com/news/2017/03/23/princeton-theological-seminary-revokes-honor-controversial-speaker-will-let-his-talk; accessed, 5/7/2020.
Johnston, Robert K., *Evangelicals at an Impasse: Biblical Authority in Practice* (Atlanta: John Knox Press, 1979).
Jones, Robert P.; Cox, Daniel, "Clinton maintains double-digit lead (51% vs. 36%) over Trump." *PRRI*. 2016. http://www.prri.org/research/prri-brookings-oct-19-poll-politics-election-clinton-double-digit-lead-trump/; accessed, 5/7/2020.
Jones, Robert "Donald Trump and the Transformation of White Evangelicals," *Time*, November 19. 2016, http://time.com/4577752/donald-trump-transformation-white-evangelicals/?xid=tcoshare; accessed, 5/7/2020.

Joyner, Rick, *The Apostolic Ministry* (Fort Mill, North Carolina: MorningStar Publications, 2004; E-Book Edition, 2010).

Kaiser, Walter; Davids, Peter; Bruce, F.F.; Brauch, Manfred T., *Hard Sayings of the Bible*, (Downers Grove, Illinois, Intervarsity Press, 1996).

Kasprak, Alex, "Abortion Rates Fall During Democratic Administrations and Rise During Republican Ones," *Snopes*, November 11, 2016, https://www.snopes.com/fact-check/abortion-rates-presidencies/ ; accessed, 5/5/2020.

Keller, Kathy, "The Bible, the Church, and Gender Roles," Copyright © Redeemer Presbyterian Church 2006, http://baylyblog.com/files/old/files/timkellerredeemerpca.pdf; accessed, 5/7/2020.

———. *Jesus, Justice, and Gender Roles: A Case for Gender Roles in Ministry* (Grand Rapids: Zondervan, 2012).

Keller, Timothy, "A New Kind of Urban Christian: As a city goes, so goes the culture," *Christianity Today*, May 1, 2006, https://www.christianitytoday.com/ct/2006/may/1.36.html; accessed, 5/7/2020.

———. "The Bible and same sex relationships: A review article," *Redeemer Report*, June 2015, https://www.redeemer.com/redeemer-report/article/the_bible_and_same_sex_relationships_a_review_article; accessed, 10/12/18

———. "Can Evangelicalism Survive Donald Trump and Roy Moore?," *The New Yorker*, December 19, 2017, https://www.newyorker.com/news/news-desk/can-evangelicalism-survive-donald-trump-and-roy-moore; accessed, 5/12/2020.

———. *Center Church: Doing Balanced, Gospel-Centered Ministry in Your City* (Grand Rapids: Zondervan, 2012).

———. "The Case for Commissioning (Not Ordaining) Deaconesses," *byFaith: The Online Magazine of the Presbyterian Church of America*, ISSUE #21, August 25, 2008, http://byfaithonline.com/the-case-for-commissioning-not-ordaining-deaconesses/; accessed,5/7/2020.

———. "Creation, Evolution, and Christian Laypeople," *The Biologos Foundation*, not dated, https://biologos.org/uploads/projects/Keller_white_paper.pdf; accessed, 10/15/18.

———. *Generous Justice: How God's Grace Makes Us Just* (New York: Penguin Books, 2016).

———. "How Do Christians Fit Into the Two-Party System? They Don't," *The New York Times*, September 29, 2018, https://www.nytimes.com/2018/09/29/opinion/sunday/christians-politics-belief.html; recovered, 11/7/18.

———. *Prayer: Experiencing Awe and Intimacy With God*, (New York: Penguin Books, 2014).

———. *The Prodigal God: Recovering the Heart of the Christian Faith* (New York: Penguin Books, 2016).

———. *The Prodigal Prophet: Jonah and the Mystery of God's Mercy* (New York: Viking, 2018).

———. *The Reason For God: Belief in the Age of Skepticism*, (New York: Penguin Books, 2016).

———. "Women In Ministry," *The Gospel Coalition*, August 14, 2008, https://www.thegospelcoalition.org/blogs/scotty-smith/titleitems/; recovered, 10/12/18.

Keller, Tim & Kathy, "Redeemer Church Rejects The 'Hard-Line' Label," *The New York Times*, February 15, 1996, https://www.nytimes.com/1998/02/15/nyregion/l-redeemer-church-rejects-the-hard-line-label-580457.html; accessed, 10/15/18.

———. "Women and Ministry, Redeemer Presbyterian Church," November 2009, http://baylyblog.com/files/old/files/timkellerredeemerpca.pdf; accessed, 10/12/18.

Kerry, John; Graham, Lindsey, "Yes We Can (Pass Climate Change Legislation)," *New York Times,* October 10, 2009, http://www.nytimes.com/2009/10/11/opinion/11kerrygraham.html; accessed, 5/8/2020.

Kim, Jim Yong, "Make Climate Change A Priority," *Washington Post,* January 24, 2013, http://articles.washingtonpost.com/2013-01-24/opinions/36527558_1_global-carbon-dioxide-emissions-climate-change-climate-and-energy, ; accessed,

King, Martin Luther, *A Letter From A Birmingham Jail,* April 16, 1963, African Studies Center, University of Pennsylvania, https://www.africa.upenn.edu/Articles_Gen/Letter_Birmingham.html; accessed, 4/13/2020.

Kuyper, Abraham, *Lectures On Calvinism* (New York: Cosimo Classics, 2007; originally published in 1937).

Labberton, Mark, "Political Dealing: The Crisis of Evangelicalism," a speech given at a private meeting of evangelical leaders on April 16, 2018, *Fuller,* https://www.fuller.edu/posts/political-dealing-the-crisis-of-evangelicalism/; accessed, 5/8/2020.

Ladd, George Eldon, *The Gospel of the Kingdom* (Grand Rapids, MI: Eerdmans, 1959).

———. *The Presence of the Future* (Grand Rapids, MI: Eerdmans, 1974).

Land, Richard, "Donald Trump is a Scam," *Charisma News,* March 3, 2016, http://www.charismanews.com/opinion/55584-richard-land-donald-trump-is-a-scam.; accessed, 5/8/2020.

Lausanne Movement, *Creation Care and the Gospel: Jamaica Call to Action,* November, 20012, https://www.lausanne.org/content/statement/creation-care-call-to-action ; accessed, 5/8/2020.

———. "The Lausanne Movement's Unique Calling," *About The Movement,* https://www.lausanne.org/about-the-movement; accessed, 5/6/2020.

Lederach, John Paul, *The Little Book of Conflict Transformation,* (Intercourse, PA: Good Books, 2003).

Leman, Dianne, "About Dianne," at *Dianne Leman: Author, Speaker, Friend,* https://www.dianneleman.com/; accessed, 5/6/2020.

Le Roy, Michael; Medenblik, Jul, "Joint Statement from Calvin Seminary and College," January 15, 2018, ; accessed, 5/4/18.http://www.calvinseminary.edu/2018/01/15/joint-statement-calvin-seminary-college/.The statement is no longer on the web site.

Lewine, Edward, "Making New Christians," *New York Times,* January 25, 1998, Section 14, p. 1.

Ligonier Ministries & Lifeway Research, *The State of American Theology Study, 2016,* http://lifewayresearch.com/wp-content/uploads/2016/09/Ligonier-State-of-American-Theology-2016-Final-Report.pdf, accessed 5/8/2020.

Lindsell, Harold, *The Battle for the Bible* (Grand Rapids: Zondervan, 1976).

———, *Park Street Prophet: A Life of Harold John Ockenga* (Eugene, Oregon: Wipf & Stock, 2015, previously published by Van Kampen Press, 1951).

Loren, Julia, "The Legacy of a Humble Hero," *Charisma,* October 31, 2007, https://www.charismamag.com/site-archives/508-features/faith-pioneers/2397-the-legacy-of-a-humble-hero; accessed, 5/8/2020.

Lowe, Ben, *Doing Good Without Giving Up: Sustaining Social Action In A World That's Hard To Change* (Downers Grove, IL: InterVarsity Press, 2014)

———. *The Future of Our Faith: An Intergenerational Conversation on Critical Issues Facing the Church* (Ada, Michigan: Brazos Press, 2016).

———. *The Green Revolution* (Downers Grove, Illinois: IVP Books, 2009).

Lucado, Max, "Trump doesn't pass the decency test," *Washington Post*, February 26, 2016, https://www.washingtonpost.com/posteverything/wp/2016/02/26/max-lucado-trump-doesnt-pass-the-decency-test/?utm_term=.42f019ced289; accessed, 5/8/2020.

Macdonald, Jeffrey, "Pawlenty's pastor stays politically neutral," *USATODAY.com*, June 21, 2011, http://usatoday30.usatoday.com/news/religion/2011-06-21-pastor-leith-anderson-tim-pawlenty_n.htm

"Mark Driscoll Says Just Grow Up," *Relevant*, September 9, 2010, https://relevantmagazine.com/god/mark-driscoll-says-just-grow/, accessed, 4/28/2020.

Marsden, George M., *Fundamentalism and American Culture, New Edition* (New York: Oxford University Press, 2006).

———. *Reforming Fundamentalism: Fuller Seminary and the New Evangelicalism* (Grand Rapids: Eerdmans, 1987).

Marshall, I. Howard, *New Testament Interpretation* (Grand Rapids: Eerdmans, 1978).

McCain, John; Liebermann, Joe, "The Turning Point on Global Warming," *The Boston Globe*, February 13, 2007, http://www.boston.com/news/globe/editorial_opinion/oped/articles/2007/02/13/the_turning_point_on_global_warming/; accessed, 5/8/2020.

McDermott, Gerald R., "The Emerging Divide in Evangelical Theology," *Journal of the Evangelical Society*," 56/2, (2013), 355-77.

McGrath, Alister, *The Reenchantment Of Nature; The Denial of Religion and the Ecological Crisis* (New York: Doubleday, a Galilee Edition, 2003).

———. *A Passion For Truth: The Intellectual Coherence of Evangelicalism* (Downers Grove: InterVarsity Press, 1996).

McKibben, Bill, "The Attack on Climate-Change Science: Why It's The O.J. Moment of the Twenty-first Century," *The Huffington Post*, February 5, 2010, http://www.huffingtonpost.com/bill-mckibben/the-attack-on-climate-cha_b_476755.html; accessed, 5/8/2020.

———. *Eaarth: Making a Life on a Tough New Planet* (New York: Henry Holt and Company, 2010).

McKnight, Scott, "Brian McLaren's 'A New Kind of Christianity,' Brian McLaren's 'new' Christianity is not so much revolutionary as evolutionary," *Christianity Today*, 2/26/2010, http://www.christianitytoday.com/ct/2010/march/3.59.html, accessed 1/25/2018.

———. "Five Streams of the Emerging Church," *Christianity, Today*, January 19, 2007, https://www.christianitytoday.com/ct/2007/february/11.35.html ; accessed, 5/8/2020..

———. *Junia Is Not Alone* (Englewood, Colorado: Patheos Press, 2011).

McLaren, Brian, *A Generous Orthodoxy* (Grand Rapids: Zondervan, 2004).

———. *Everything Must Change* (Nashville: Thomas Nelson, 2007).

Mencken, H.L., "Journalist H.L. Mencken's Account of the Scopes Trial," *Digital History*, 1925, http://www.digitalhistory.uh.edu/disp_textbook.cfm?smtID=3&psid=1077 ; accessed, 5/8/2020.

Merrick, J.; Garrett, Stephen M., editors, *Five Views On Biblical Inerrancy* (Grand Rapids: Zondervan, 2013).

Merritt, Carol Howard, "Does teaching submission encourage abuse?," March 17, 2017, https://www.christiancentury.org/blog-post/born-again-again/does-teaching-submission-encourage-abuse; accessed, 5/8/2020.

Merritt, Carol Howard, "More Thoughts on Tim Keller," March 29, 2017, https://www.christiancentury.org/blog-post/born-again-again/more-thoughts-tim-keller; accessed, 5/8/2020.

Merritt, Jonathan. "The Gospel Coalition and how (not) to engage culture," Religion News Service, June 6, 2016, https://religionnews.com/2016/06/06/the-gospel-coalition-and-how-not-to-engage-culture/; accessed 5/8/2020.

———. "The Troubling Trends in America's Calvinist Revival," *On Faith & Culture, Religion News Service*, May 20, 2014, https://religionnews.com/2014/05/20/troubling-trends-americas-calvinist-revival/; accessed, 5/8/2020.

———. "Why Princeton's snub of Tim Keller should outrage progressives," *Religion News Service*, March 22, 2017, https://religionnews.com/2017/03/22/why-princetons-snub-of-tim-keller-should-outrage-progressive-christians/; accessed, 5/8/2020.

Miller, Lisa, "The Smart Shepherd," *Newsweek*, February 9, 2008, https://www.newsweek.com/smart-shepherd-93595; accessed, 5/8/2020.

Miller, Rachel, "Dr. Tim Keller and BioLogos," April 4, 2012, https://www.theaquilareport.com/dr-tim-keller-and-biologos/; accessed, 5/8/2020.

Mohler, Albert, "Character In Leadership: Does It Still Matter?" *Albert Mohler*, June 24, 2016, http://www.albertmohler.com/2016/06/24/character-leadership-still-matter/; accessed, 5/8/2020.

Moore, Russell, "Why This Election Makes Me Hate The Word 'evangelical,'" *The Washington Post*, February 29, 2016, https://www.washingtonpost.com/news/acts-of-faith/wp/2016/02/29/russell-moore-why-this-election-makes-me-hate-the-word-evangelical/; accessed, 4/30/2020.

Morgan, Timothy C., "Franklin Graham's Call to End Muslim Immigration Could Backfire," *Christianity Today*, July 24, 2016, http://www.christianitytoday.com/ct/2015/july-web-only/franklin-grahams-call-to-end-muslim-immigration-could-backf.html/, accessed, 5/8/2020.

Mouw, Richard J., *Abraham Kuyper: A Short and Personal Introduction* (Grand Rapids: Eerdmans, 2011).

———. *Calvinism in the Las Vegas Airport: Making Connections in Today's World* (Grand Rapids: Zondervan, 2004).

———. "From Kuyper to Keller: Why Princeton's Prize Controversy Is So Ironic," *Christianity Today*, March 27, 2017, https://www.christianitytoday.com/ct/2017/march-web-only/kuyper-keller-princeton-seminary-ironic.html; recovered, 10/12/18.

———. *Restless Faith: Holding Evangelical Beliefs in a World of Contested Labels* (Grand Rapids: Brazos Press, 2019).

Myers, Ben, "The Worst Book Ever Written on Karl Barth," Faith and Theology, https://www.faith-theology.com/2005/07/worst-book-ever-written-on-karl-barth.html, accessed, 5/8/2020.

Nader, Laura, "Controlling Processes: Tracing the Dynamic Components of Power, *Current Anthropology*, Volume 38, Number 1, December, 1997, pp. 711–737.

Nathan, Rich,"Women in Leadership: How to Decide What the Bible Teaches?" 2006, http://d397a349e55ce6675f49–800c82752453605a420f881278ef1279.r85.cf2.

rackcdn.com/uploaded/r/0e609953_rich-nathan-women-in-ministry-position-paper.pdf.; accessed, 5/8/2020.

Nathan, Rich; Kim, Insoo, *Both-And: Living The Christ-Centered Life in an Either-Or World* (Downers Grove, IL: InterVarsity Press, 2013).

Nathan, Rich; Wilson, Ken, *Empowered Evangelicals: Bringing Together the Best of the Evangelical and Charismatic Worlds* (Ann Arbor, Michigan: Servant Publications, 1995).

Neaveill, Ryan, "The Insane Theocracy of Conservative Christians," *Smile Politely*, September 10, 2018, http://www.smilepolitely.com/opinion/The_Insane_Theocracy_of_Conservative_Christians/, accessed, 5/5/2020.

Neff, David, "The Accidental Anglican," *Christianity Today*, August 31, 2009, https://www.christianitytoday.com/ct/2009/september/11.66.html, accessed, 5/8/2020.

Newell, Marvin, "Creation Care and Taking Care of the Gospel," *Misso Nexus*, July 14, 2015, https://missionexus.org/creation-care-taking-care-of-the-gospel/; accessed, 5/1/2020.

Nicholson, Steven; Bailey, Jeff, *Coaching Church Planters: A Manual for Church Planters and Those Who Coach Them* (Stafford, Texas: Association of Vineyard Churches, 2001, now out of print).

Nicholson, Steve, "I Said 'Yes' To God,"May 30, 2013, https://vimeo.com/67305624; accessed, 5/1/2020.

———, *Roots of the Vineyard, Part 3*, August 22, 20016, https://vimeo.com/channels/1035872.; accessed, 4/24/2020

———. "Where Do We Go From Here?," *Better Together Diversity Conference Recordings*, November, 2016, http://vineyardjusticenetwork.org/better-together-diversity-conference-recordings/, accessed, 7/6/18.

Nicole, Roger; Michaels, J. Ramsey, eds., *Inerrancy and Common Sense* (Grand Rapids: Baker, 1980).

Niebuhr, H. Richard, *Christ & Culture* (San Francisco: Harper & Row, 1951).

Noll, Mark, *Between Faith and Criticism*, (San Francisco: Harper & Row, 1986).

———. *The Scandal of the Evangelical Mind* (Grand Rapids: Eerdmans, 2010).

———, ed., *The Princeton Theology, 1812–1921: Scripture, Science, and Theological Method from Archibald Alexander to Benjamin Breckinridge Warfield* (Phillipsburg, New Jersey: P&R, 1983).

Oden, Thomas C., *Classical Christianity: A Systematic Theology* (San Francisco: HarperOne, 2009).

———. *The Transforming Power of Grace* (Nashville: Abingdon, 1993).

Oliver Velez, Denise, "Aftermath 2016: Tess Raffrty's hard-hitting statement on the election of Trump," *Daily Kos*, November 17, 2016, http://www.dailykos.com/stories/2016/11/17/1600760/-Aftermath-2016-Tess-Rafferty-s-hard-hitting-statement-on-the-election-of-Trump?; accessed, 5/8/2020.

Olson, Roger E., *Arminian Theology, Myths and Realities* (Downers Grove, IL: IVP Academic, 2006).

———. "Further thoughts on why 'inerrancy' is problematic," *My Evangelical Arminian Musings*, June 11, 2012 http://www.patheos.com/blogs/rogereolson/2012/06/further-thoughts-on-why-inerrancy-is-problematic/; accessed, April 28, 2020.

———. *The Journey of Modern Theology: From Reconstruction To Deconstruction* (Downers Grove, Illinois: IVP Academic, 2013).

———. "Memories of Stanley J. Grenz with Special Attention to Criticisms of His Theology (and Some Hitherto Unrevealed Facts)," *My Evangelical Musings*, December 5, 2014, http://www.patheos.com/blogs/rogereolson/2014/12/memories-of-stanley-j-grenz-with-special-attention-to-criticisms-of-his-theology-and-some-hitherto-unrevealed-facts/; accessed, 10/5/2018.

———. *Reformed and Always Reforming: A Postconservative Approach to Evangelical Theology* (Grand Rapids, MI: Baker Academic, 2007).

———. "When did evangelicalism start to go wrong (right)?," May 11, 2011, https://www.patheos.com/blogs/rogereolson/2011/05/when-did-evangelicalism-start-to-go-wrong-right accessed 4/27/2020.

Olson, Roger; Winn, Christian T Collins, *Reclaiming Pietism: Retrieving An Evangelical Tradition* (Grand Rapids: Eerdmans, 2015).

Paloma, Margaret M., "Gamaliel's Admonition and the Toronto Blessing: A Theo-Sociological Report," *The Hartford Institution for Religion Research*, July 5, 2000, http://hirr.hartsem.edu/research/pentecostalism_polomaart7.html, retrieved, 5/14/18.

———. "Toronto Blessing," *World Religions and Spirituality*, April 3, 2014, https://wrldrels.org/2016/10/08/toronto-blessing/; accessed, 5/8/2020.

———. "New Apostolic Reformation," *World Religions and Spirituality*, August 5, 2016, https://wrldrels.org/2016/10/08/new-apostolic-reformation/; accessed, 58/2020.

Pally, Marcia, *Commonwealth and Covenant: Economics, Politics, and Theologies of Relationality* (Grand Rapids; Eerdmans, 2016).

———. *The New Evangelicals: Expanding the Vision of the Common Good* (Grand Rapids: Eerdmans, 2011).

Parkes, Graham, "The Politics of Global Warming: (2):Two Obstacles to Circumvent," In *Environmental Philosophy: The Art of Life in a World of Limits,*" edited by Liam Leonard (Bingley, UK: Emerald Group, 2013).

Payne, J.B. "Justice," *The New Bible Dictionary, Third Edition* (Downers Grove, Ill: Intervarsity Press, 1996),

Payne, Philip B., *Man and Woman, One in Christ: An Exegetical and Theological Study of Paul's Letters* (Grand Rapids: Zondervan, 2009).

Peters, Gerhard; Woolley, John T., "Press Release—Trump Campaign Announces Evangelical Executive Advisory Board," *The American Presidency Project*, June 21, 2016, http://www.presidency.ucsb.edu/ws/index.php?pid=117958, recovered, April 30, 2016.

Piper, John, *The Future of Justification: A Response to NT Wright* (Wheaton, Illinois: Crossway, 2007).

———. "How Are The Synoptics 'Without Error'?" *desiringGod*, October 7, 1976, https://www.desiringgod.org/articles/how-are-the-synoptics-without-error; accessed, 5/8/2020.

———. "Is There A Place For Female Professors At Seminary?" *desiringGod*. 1/22/2018, https://www.desiringgod.org/interviews/is-there-a-place-for-female-professors-at-seminary; accessed, 5/6/2020.

———. "Should Women Be Police Officers?" *desiringGod*, 8/13/2015, https://www.desiringgod.org/interviews/should-women-be-police-officers; accessed, 5/6/2020.

Potsdam Institute for Climate Impact Research and Climate Analytics, *Turn Down The Heat: Why a 4oC World Must Be Avoided,* Washington DC: The International Bank for Reconstruction and Development/The World Bank, November, 2012, http://documents.worldbank.org/curated/en/865571468149107611/Turn-down-the-heat-why-a-4-C-warmer-world-must-be-avoided; accessed, 5/8/2020.

Pullinger, Jackie, "Chased by the Dragon," in *Power Encounters*, edited by Kevin Springer (San Francisco: Harper & Row, 1988), 198–210.

Pulliam, Sarah, "Interview: NAE President Leith Anderson on Richard Cizik's Resignation," *Christianity Today*, December 11, 2008, http://www.christianitytoday.com/ct/2008/decemberweb-only/150–41.0.html; accessed, 5/8/2020.

Rah, Soong-Chan, *The Next Evangelicalism: Freeing the Church from Western Cultural Captivity* (Downers Grove, IL: InterVarsity Press, 2009).

Ramm, Bernard, *After Fundamentalism: The Future of Evangelical Theology* (San Francisco: Harper & Row, 1983), pp. 11–12.

———. "Misplaced Battle Lines," *The Best of the Reformed Journal*, 105–108; Bratt, James D; Wells, Ronald A. (Grand Rapids: Eerdmans, 2011).

———. *Protestant Biblical Interpretation: A Textbook of He-tics*, Third Revised Edition (Grand Rapids: Baker, 1970).

Redfern, Charles, "Can 'I' Live Apart From 'We'?" *Sojourners*, 12/30/2016, https://sojo.net/articles/can-i-live-apart-we; recovered, 2/25/2019.

———. "Evangelical Moderates Rise Up—Finally," *Huffpost*, 10/17/2017, https://www.huffingtonpost.com/entry/evangelical-moderates-ris_b_12502444; accessed, 5/8/2020.

———. "Is American Evangelical Christianity Sinking On The GOP Ship?" Huffpost, 8/15/2016, https://www.huffingtonpost.com/entry/is-american-evangelical-christianity_b_11459552; accessed, 5/8/2020.

———. "Is It Ever Time to Pound Our Fists On Tables?" *Huffpost*, 7/12/2013, https://www.huffingtonpost.com/entry/is-it-ever-time-to-pound_b_3566710; accessed, 5/8/2020.

———. "Is The National Association of Evangelicals Wandering in the Darkness?" *Christian Ethics Today: A Journal of Christian Ethics*, Volume 22, Number 1, Aggregate Issue 22, (Winter, 2014), 5–8

———. "Moderate Evangelicals Denounce White Supremacy. Will They Stay For The Fight?" *Huffpost*, 8/19/2017, https://www.huffingtonpost.com/entry/moderate-evangelicals-denounce-white-supremacy-will_us_599861c0e4b02eb2fda32061; accessed 5/8/2020.

———. "Moral And Economic Need To Stem Climate Change," *The Day* of New London, CT, 9/07/2014.

———. "Should We Tag Tim Keller With A Trigger Warning?" *Huffpost*, 3/23/2017, https://www.huffingtonpost.com/entry/should-we-tag-tim-keller-with-a-trigger-warning_us_58d446c7e4b0f633072b3601; accessed, 5/8/2020.

———. "We Can Save The Earth and the Economy," *The Day* of New London, CT., December 6, 2016.

———. "Welcome Home: The New Old Evangelicals," *Truthout.org*, January 30, 2013, https://truthout.org/articles/welcome-home-the-new-old-evangelicals/; accessed, 5/8/2020.

———. "When Language Smothers Conversation," *Christian Ethics Today: A Journal of Christian Ethics*, Volume 21, Number 1, Aggregate Issue 89, (Spring 2013) 17–18.

———. "Woot! Leading Evangelical Coalition Catches Up on Climate Change," *Huffpost*, 10/26/2016, https://www.huffingtonpost.com/entry/woot-a-leading-evangelica_b_8387174; accessed, 5/8/2020.

———. "Will The National Association of Evangelicals Sink Into Irrelevance by Dodging Climate Change?" *Huffpost*, 2/18/2014, https://www.huffingtonpost.com/entry/will-the-national-associa_1_b_4803303; accessed, 5/8/2020.

Revkin, Andrew, "Exxon and the Climate Fight," *The New York Times: Dot Earth*, February 8, 2010, http://dotearth.blogs.nytimes.com/2010/02/08/exxon-and-the-climate-fight; accessed, 5/8/2020.

Richter, Greg, "Pat Robertson to Trump: 'You Inspire Us All'" *Newsmax*, February 24, 2016, http://www.newsmax.com/Headline/pat-robertson-trump-inspire-interview/2016/02/24/id/715956/; accessed, 5/8/2020.

Robbins, John W., "An Introduction to Gordon H. Clark," *The Trinity Review*, July-August, (1993),1–10.

Robinson, Tri; Chatraw, Jason, *Saving God's Green Earth: Rediscovering the church's responsibility to environmental stewardship* (Norcross, Georgia: Ampelon Publishing, 2006).

Rogers, Jack B.; McKim, Donald K., *The Authority and Interpretation of the Bible: An Historical Approach* (San Francisco: Harper & Row, 1979).

Romm, Joe, "House of Commons exonerates Phil Jones," *ThinkProgress: Climate Progress*, March 31, 2010, https://thinkprogress.org/house-of-commons-exonerates-phil-jones-10a42f889656/ ; accessed, 5/8/2020

Rosell, Garth, *The Surprising Work of God: Harold John Ockenga, Billy Graham, and the Rebirth of Evangelicalism* (Grand Rapids, MI: Baker Academic, 2008).

Roys, Julie, "Evangelical Trump Defenders Are Destroying The Church's Witness," *The Christian Post*, October 11, 2016, http://www.christianpost.com/news/evangelical-trump-defenders-are-destroying-the-churchs-witness-170657/#2LVlcJjAWs0jV13Z.99.accessed, 4/28/2020

Sande, Ken, *The Peacemaker: A Biblical Guide to Resolving Personal Conflict* (Grand Rapids: Baker, 1991).

Schmittner & all, "Climate Sensitivity Estimated from Temperature Reconstructions of the Last Glacial Maximum," Science, Vol. 334, Issue 6061 (December 9, 2011), 1385–1388.

Schneider, Howard, "World Bank warns of '4-degree' threshold of global temperature increase," *The Washington Post*, November 19, 2012, https://www.washingtonpost.com/business/economy/world-bank-warns-of-4-degree-threshhold/2012/11/19/aa298dd0-3023-11e2-a30e-5ca76eeec857_story.html accessed, 5/8/2020.

Sells, Heather, "Winning Power Was Judas' Goal: These Christian Leaders Pitched Pre-Trump Unity, Now, Not So Much," *CBN News*, 4/18/2018, http://www1.cbn.com/cbnnews/2018/april/winning-power-was-judass-goal-these-christian-leaders-pitched-pre-trump-unity-now-not-so-much, accessed, 5/8/2020.

Sheets, Dutch, "Response to the General Election," November 6, 2008, *Eternal Priesthood Ministries*, https://priest4ever.wordpress.com/2008/12/21/dutch-sheets-response-to-the-2008-presidential-election/S; the authors have deleted this site.

———. "Election 2016: The Christian's Dilemma," *Elijah List*, October 21, 2016, http://elijahlist.com/words/display_word.html?ID=16832; recovered, 8/8/2018.

Shellnutt, Kate, "Global Evangelical Leaders: Trump's Win Will Harm the Church's Witness," *Christianity Today: Gleanings*, November 15, 2016, http://www.christianitytoday.com/gleanings/2016/november/global-evangelical-leaders-trump-win-will-harm-churchs-witn.html.; accessed, 5/8/2020.

———. "Princeton Seminary Reforms Its Views on Honoring Tim Keller," *Christianity Today*, March 22, 2017, https://www.christianitytoday.com/news/2017/march/princeton-rescinds-tim-keller-kuyper-prize-women-ordination.html; accessed, 5/8/2020.

———. "Tim Keller Stepping Down as Redeemer Senior Pastor," *Christianity Today*, February 26, 2017, https://www.christianitytoday.com/news/channel/utilities/print.html?type=article&id=137842; accessed, 5/8/2020.

Sider, Ronald J., "The Most Important Election in My Lifetime," *Christian Ethics Today*, Volume 24, No. 2 (Spring, 2016), 4.

———. *The Scandal of Evangelical Politics* (Grand Rapids, Michigan: Baker Books, 2008).

Sipho, Kings, "Stop Pretending there is a debate over climate change," *Mail & Guardian*, January 8, 2013, http://mg.co.za/article/2013-01-08-stop-pretending-there-is-a-debate-over-climate-change?goback=%252Egde_2792503_member_202344370.; accessed, 5/8/2020.

Smith, Timothy, *Revivalism and Social Reform* (Nashville: Abingdon Press, 1957).

Smith, Traci, "Princeton Theological Seminary, Rev. Dr. Tim Keller, and the Abraham Kuyper Lecture," *Faith & Family & Spirit*, March 10, 2017, http://www.traci-smith.com/pts_timkeller/; accessed, 5/8/2020.

Sorley, Craig, *Christ And Creation: Our Biblical Call to Environmental Stewardship* (Self-published, 2009).

———. "Mobilizing the Church in East Africa Towards a Commitment to Land Care," *Wheaton College*, https://www.youtube.com/watch?v=RQQ0xU7OwVo; accessed, 5/8/2020.

Sprangler, Brad, "Alternative Dispute Resolution (ADR)." *Beyond Intractability*. Eds. Guy Burgess and Heidi Burgess. Conflict Research Consortium, University of Colorado, Boulder. Posted: June 2003, http://www.beyondintractability.org/essay/adr/; accessed, 5/8/2020.

Springer, Kevin, ed., *Power Encounters* (San Francisco: Harper & Row, 1988).

Stafford, Tim, "How Tim Keller Found Manhattan," *Christianity Today*, June 5, 2009, https://www.christianitytoday.com/ct/2009/june/15.20.html; accessed, 5/8/2020.

Stafford, Tim; Beverly, James, "Conversations: God's Wonder Worker: In retirement, John Wimber reflects on what he learned from building the Vineyard," *Christianity Today*, July 14, 1997, https://www.christianitytoday.com/ct/1997/july14/7t8046.html, accessed, 5/8/2020.

Stanley, Tiffany, "The Sex-Abuse Scandal That Devastated a Suburban Megachurch: Inside the rise and fall of Sovereign Grace Ministries," *The Washingtonian*, February 14, 2016, https://www.washingtonian.com/2016/02/14/the-sex-abuse-scandal-that-devastated-a-suburban-megachurch-sovereign-grace-ministries/; accessed, 5/8/2020.

Stassen, Glen H.; Gushee, David P., *Kingdom Ethics: Following Jesus in Contemporary Context* (Downers Grove: InterVarsity, 2003).

Stetzer, Ed; MacDonald, Andrew, "Why Evangelicals Voted Trump: Debunking the 81%," *Christianity Today*, October 18, 2018, https://www.christianitytoday.com/ct/2018/october/why-evangelicals-trump-vote-81-percent-2016-election.html?visit_source=twitter&fbclid=IwAR3eq82l12cjsonBv-PgXuEE_nZP7nNSlraAEOiAhFASHHzjh1IO0Qv4vkc; accessed, 5/8/2020.

Stetzer, Ed, "What Is Going On Inside Trump's Religious Advisory Panel," *Christianity Today, The Exchange*, October 10, 2016, http://www.christianitytoday.com/edstetzer/2016/october/what-is-going-on-inside-trumps-religious-advisory-panel.html; accessed, 5/8/2020.

Stewart, Heather; Elliott, Larry, "Nicholas Stern: I got it wrong on climate change—it's far, far worse," *The Guardian, The Observer* (http://www.guardian.co.uk/environment/2013/jan/27/nicholas-stern-climate-change-davos?goback=%2Egde_2792503_member_208443604); 5/8/2020.

Storms, Sam, "Women In Ministry in the Vineyard USA," *The Journal of Manhood and Womanhood*, JBMW 12/2 (Fall 2007) 20–24..

Strout, Phil, *Better Together: Race, Reconciliation, and the Multi-Ethnic Church*, 2016, https://vimeo.com/ondemand/bettertogether/207703728?autoplay=1, accessed, 5/8/2020..

Sullivan, Amy, "America's New Religion: Fox Evangelicalism," *New York Times*, December 15, 2017, https://www.nytimes.com/2017/12/15/opinion/sunday/war-christmas-evangelicals.html ;accessed, 5/8/2020..

———. *The Party Faithful: How and Why The Democrats Are Closing The God Gap*, (New York: Charles Scribner's & Sons, 2008).

Swartz, David A., *Moral Minority: The Evangelical Left in an Age of Conservatism* (Philadelphia: University of Pennsylvania Press, 2012).

Synan, Vincent, *The Holiness-Pentecostal Tradition: Charismatic Movements in the Twentieth Century* (Grand Rapids: Eerdmans, 1997).

Teague, Jim, *Eloise McDowell Retirement Celebration*, https://www.youtube.com/watch?v=GmBYAGp2IWA/ ; accessed, 5/6/2020.

Thompson, Mark, "Women on a Theological Faculty?," The Gospel Coalition Australia Edition, 7/02/2018, https://au.thegospelcoalition.org/article/place-women-theological-faculties/; accessed, 5/8/2020.

Tooley, Mark, "The Heresy of Doubting Apocalyptic Global Warming," *Juicy Ecumenism: The Institute on Religion and Democracy's Blog*, http://juicyecumenism.com/2013/11/13/the-heresy-of-doubting-apocalyptic-global-warming/; accessed, 5/8/2020.

———. "Opposing Tim Keller at Princeton Seminary," *Juicy Ecumenism*, March 18, 2017, https://juicyecumenism.com/2017/03/18/opposing-tim-keller-at-princeton-seminary/; accessed, 5/8/2020.

Torrance, Thomas F., "Review of C. van Til, *The New Modernism: An Appraisal of the Theology of Barth and Brunner*, *The Evangelical Quarterly* 19 (1947): 144–149.

Truesdale, Al, ed., *Square Peg: Why Wesleyans Aren't Fundamentalists* (Kansas City: Beacon Hill Press, 2012).

———. *Whatever Happened to Evangelicalism?* (Kansas City: Beacon Hill Press, 2017).

UN News Center, "New UN report cites 'unprecedented climate extremes' over past decade," http://www.un.org/apps/news/story.asp?NewsID=45330#.Ud1eNvmkq9Z; accessed, 5/8/2020.

Van Til, Cornelius,"Karl Barth on Creation," *The Presbyterian Guardian*, Volume 3, Number 10 (February 17, 1937), p. 205.

———. "The Text of a Complaint," *Notes on Gordon H. Clark*, http://notes-on-gordon-h-clark.blogspot.ca/2014/07/document-1944-text-of-complaint.html, accessed 5/5/2020.

Van Til, Kent, "Subsidiarity And Sphere-Sovereignty: A Match Made In...?" *Theological Studies*, 69, (2008), 610–636.

Velez, Denise Oliver, "Aftermath 2016: Tess Raffrty's hard-hitting statement on the election of Trump," *Daily Kos*, November 17, 2016, https://www.dailykos.com/stories/2016/11/17/1600760/-Aftermath-2016-Tess-Rafferty-s-hard-hitting-statement-on-the-election-of-Trump; accessed, 5/8/2020.

Wagner, C. Peter, *Apostles and Prophets: The Foundation of the Church* (Bloomington, Minnesota: Chosen Books, 2000).

———. *The New Apostolic Churches; Rediscovering the New Testament model of Leadership and why it is God's desire for the Church today* (Grand Rapids: Baker, 2000)

———. "The New Apostolic Reformation Is Not a Cult," *Charisma*, 8/24/11, https://www.charismanews.com/opinion/31851-the-new-apostolic-reformation-is-not-a-cult, recovered, 6/7/18.

Wallace, Daniel B. "My Take on Inerrancy," August 10. 2006, https://bible.org/article/my-take-inerrancy; accessed, 5/8/2020.

Walsh, Bryan, "Has 'Climategate' Been Overblown?" *Time Magazine*, December 7, 2009.

Warfield, Benjamin B., *Inspiration and Authority of the Bible*, Second Edition (Philipsburg, New Jersey: P&R Publishing, 1980).

Wassink, Adey; Wilson, Michelle, *One In Christ: Men And Women Together In Ministry*, Vineyard USA, not dated, https://docs.google.com/viewerng/viewer?url=https://d1h8uvf6sd4tvp.cloudfront.net/wp-content/uploads/20160520115159/WomenInLeadership1.pdf&hl=en; accessed, 5/2/2020.

Wax, Trevin,"The Justification Debate: A Primer," *Christianity Today*, June 26, 2009, http://www.christianitytoday.com/ct/2009/june/29.34.html?start=2;, accessed, 5/8/2020.

Wehner, Peter, "What Wouldn't Jesus Do?," *The New York Times*, March 1, 2016, http://www.nytimes.com/2016/03/01/opinion/campaign-stops/what-wouldnt-jesus-do.html?rref=collection%2Fcolumn%2Fpeter-wehner&action=click&contentCollection=opinion&region=stream&module=stream_unit&version=latest&contentPlacement=9&pgtype=collection&_r=0/.; 5/8/2020.

Wells, David, *No Place For Truth: or Whatever Happened To Evangelical Theology* (Grand Rapids: Eerdmans, 1994).

White, John, *When The Spirit Comes With Power: Signs and Wonders Among God's People* (Downers Grove: InterVarsity Press, 1988).

Williams, Layton E., "Princeton Seminary President Talks Tim Keller, Women's Ordination, and How One Award Ignited Christian Twitter," *Sojourners*, 4/12/2017, https://sojo.net/articles/princeton-seminary-president-talks-tim-keller-women-s-ordination-and-how-one-award-ignited; accessed, 5/8/2018.

Wilson, Andrew J., "Where Did We Come From? How Milton, Paley, and Darwin help us answer the question," *Christianity Today*, October 1, 2013, https://www.christianitytoday.com/ct/2013/october/where-did-we-come-from.html?share=7ZtKUxgDLLUpPMUBsS8%2b3B8N2qukGspQ.; accessed, 5/8/2020.

Wimber, Carol, "A Hunger For God," *Power Encounters* (San Francisco: Harper & Row, 1988) edited by Kevin Springer, 1–14..

———, *John Wimber: The Way It Was* (London: Hodder & Stoughton, 1999).

Wimber, John; Springer, Kevin, *Power Evangelism* (San Francisco: HarperCollins, 1986).
———. *Power Healing* (San Francisco: HarperCollins, 1987).
———. *Power Points* (San Francisco: HarperCollins, 1991).
Wimber, John; Wimber, Christy, ed., *Everybody Gets To Play: John Wmber's Writings and Teachings on Life Together in Christ* (Boise, Idaho: Ampelon, 2008).
Witherington, Ben III, *The Problem with Evangelical Theology: Testing the Exegetical Foundations of Calvinism, Dispensationalism, Wesleyanism, and Pentecostalism*, revised edition (Waco, Texas: Baylor University Press, 2016).
Worthen, Molly, *Apostles of Reason: The Crisis of Authority in American Evangelicalism* (New York: Oxford University Press, 2014).
Wright, NT, *Justification: God's Plan & Paul's Vision* (Downers Grove: InterVarsity Press, 2009).
Wright, Richard T.; Boorse, Dorothy F., *Environmental Science: Toward A Sustainable Future, 13th Edition* (Boston: Pearson, 2017).
Wunderink, Susan, "Tim Keller Reasons with America: The New York pastor explains why he's taking his ministry model on the road," *Christianity Today*, June 20, 2008, https://www.christianitytoday.com/ct/2008/june/23.38.html; accessed, 5/8/2020.
Zylstra, Sarah Eehoff, "The Life and Times of Redeemer Presbyterian Church," *The Gospel Coalition, US Edition*, May 22, 2017, https://www.thegospelcoalition.org/article/life-and-times-of-redeemer-presbyterian-church/; accessed, 5/8/2020.